Transition to Higher Education: Challenges and Opportunities

Transition to Higher Education: Challenges and Opportunities

Editor

Diana Dias

 Basel • Beijing • Wuhan • Barcelona • Belgrade • Novi Sad • Cluj • Manchester

Editor
Diana Dias
Universidade Lusófona
Porto
Portugal

Editorial Office
MDPI
St. Alban-Anlage 66
4052 Basel, Switzerland

This is a reprint of articles from the Special Issue published online in the open access journal *Education Sciences* (ISSN 2227-7102) (available at: https://www.mdpi.com/journal/education/special_issues/transition_higher_education).

For citation purposes, cite each article independently as indicated on the article page online and as indicated below:

Lastname, A.A.; Lastname, B.B. Article Title. *Journal Name* **Year**, *Volume Number*, Page Range.

ISBN 978-3-0365-9010-3 (Hbk)
ISBN 978-3-0365-9011-0 (PDF)
doi.org/10.3390/books978-3-0365-9011-0

Cover image courtesy of Diana Dias

Contents

About the Editor

Diana Dias

Diana Dias is a psychologist with master's degrees in psychology. She holds a PhD in Educational Sciences and completed public aggregation exams in psychology and management in 2017 and 2022, respectively. She chaired the Executive Committee of two PhDs, one in management and another in psychology. She was vice-rector for research, quality, and academic innovation. A full professor, Dr. Dias is currently pro-rector for research and innovation. She is also the dean of two faculties of Economic, Social, and Business Sciences (Lusófona University Porto and Lusófona University Lisbon). She is a senior researcher at the Center for Research on Higher Education Policies (CIPES). She has published an extensive amount of material in indexed scientific journals and is the author of several books on management, psychology, and education. She is also a consultant on higher education policies at the European University Association (EUA); United Nations Educational, Scientific, and Cultural Organization (UNESCO); and the Organisation for Economic Co-operation and Development (OECD).

Article

Study to Live or Live to Study: The Link between Social Role Investment and Academic Success in First-Year Higher Education Students

Diana Dias [1,*] and Gina Santos [2]

[1] Lusófona University, School of Economic and Organizational Sciences, 1749-024 Lisboa, Portugal & CIPES Research Centre

[2] Lusófona University, Faculty of Economic, Social and Business Sciences, 4000-098 Porto, Portugal & CETRAD Research Centre; gina.santos@ulusofona.pt

* Correspondence: diana.dias@ulusofona.pt

Abstract: Becoming a student, i.e., learning a set of new skills and lifestyles is an inevitable task for young people joining higher education (HE). Using Perrenoud's (1995) conceptualization of the student's role as a theoretical framework, this paper intends to reflect on the construction of students' identities and its repercussions on their academic success through analysis of the discourse between HE students. How students try to intertwine their personal lives with the demands of their new roles as higher education students is also discussed. Qualitative data analysis was conducted using semi-structured, in-depth interviews with 30 engineering students. Our analysis of the results confirmed that attending HE can indeed be conceptualized as the exercise of a "craft". This craft could be taught in different ways, with more or less success, in the light of the construction of one's own social identity with more focus on either their role as student or their role as a young person. The results allow for the emergence of a conceptual framework which, crossing the investment in their social role as students with academic success, brings out distinctive dimensions: "Live to Study", "Study to Live", "Study without living" and "Live without study". These dimensions provide four major student profiles that can advise the management of higher education institutions to strategically take actions to promote not only student success, but also the pedagogic efficiency of their educational programs.

Keywords: higher education students; students' profiles; students' identities; social role investment; academic success

Citation: Dias, D.; Santos, G. Study to Live or Live to Study: The Link between Social Role Investment and Academic Success in First-Year Higher Education Students. *Educ. Sci.* 2023, 13, 758. https://doi.org/10.3390/educsci13070758

Academic Editor: Han Reichgelt

Received: 30 May 2023
Revised: 12 July 2023
Accepted: 18 July 2023
Published: 24 July 2023

1. Introduction

Education is a long and sometimes painful journey. To be a student is to take on a long-term individual and social identity, assumed by children, adolescents, and young adults, which has been embedded in them by an external order that is mandatory and non-negotiable. Being a student is inevitable in the development process of any member of society, and this inevitability becomes so ingrained in the processes of our lives that it happens so naturally that it is not questioned nor challenged.

In Portugal, at the age of six, all children join school, which is not necessarily the same as being integrated into school. In fact, all initial education leads to this transition by which the pre-school stage, as the name suggests, consists of the anticipation of school integration: it prepares children for (real) school. With this study, we intend to deepen the existing knowledge on identity construction in young people who are in the transition from adolescence to adulthood and who are also higher education students. With this exploration, we anticipate that we will contribute to a better clarification of the identity formation process of higher education students, which, by itself, is a complex process affected by changes in higher education structures as well as external environments.

Although there is no deficit of research interest in identity construction, studies explicitly focusing on the interface of identity and education is still scarce [1]. By using

Perrenoud's [2] conceptualization of the student's craft as a theoretical framework, this paper intends, through the analysis of higher education (HE) students' discourse, to reflect on the construction of students' identities. As such, a qualitative data analysis was carried out using semi-structured, in-depth interviews with 30 first-year engineering students who enrolled in one of the better-known Portuguese universities. The aim of this study was to determine whether attending HE may be conceptualized as the exercise of a craft: the student craft. The ways in which students attempt to harmonize their personal lives with the requirements of their new roles as higher education students are also discussed.

After this introduction presenting the work to be carried out, the second section provides the theoretical background, composed of subsections titled "Student's Identity under Construction" and "The Imbalance between Youth and Student Life".- The third section describes the methodology, including the methods and tools used. The fourth section presents an analysis and discussion of the results, while the final section offers final remarks on the research.

2. Theoretical Background

2.1. Student's Identity under Construction

Marcia's [3] and Erikson's [4] research on identity development suggests that relationships with same-sex students, university staff, and parents can act as either facilitators or constraints on university students' development of identity as they progress into adulthood (e.g., [5]). According to Erikson [4], university can be seen as a place that provides students with opportunities to experience different roles and values, acting, throughout their identity construction processes, as a basis for their academic and professional identities. From a global point of view, the construction of the student's identity becomes slow over time (according to the Identity Status Theory of Marcia) [3], especially during the period of compulsory schooling. In fact, the child and/or his/her carers are never given any chance to choose either the path or conditions offered by the school, or even alternatives to the school itself.

Hence, in the words of Claude Dubar [6], there is an objective transaction between the assigned/proposed identity (you will be a student) and the assumed/incorporated identity (I am a student); furthermore, there is also the assumption of a social identity assigned by the school system and legitimized by the societal structure. Indeed, as Brunton and Buckley [7] (p. 2698) noted, "the new identity must be worked into the individual's overall story to themselves and others of 'who they are', and day-to-day changes between identities must become relatively straightforward if identity struggle is to be minimized"

From the first day of school onward, students are confronted with their own representations of being a student (built by the child through the integration of a set of external experiential fragments collected through their family, stories, media...) and the reality of the institution with which they have just been integrated [8]. These representations are shaped and reshaped throughout the student's school pathway as they learn specifically what characterizes each school year [8–10]. In fact, the subsequent transitions between levels of education bring a constant process of adaptation to the school universe that accepts the student into its previous existing mechanism.

Becoming a student works, thus, as an identity process from which no child or adolescent (and even young adult) can escape, although the effects of that experience may be extremely varied in terms of how their personal and social identities are built. As Perrenoud [2] states, the student is at the confluence of three types of influences: (1) those from family and social group they belong to; (2) those from the different classes and successive teachers which a student has throughout their school pathway; and (3) those from their peer groups, i.e., the other students.

However, if the reason for the inevitability of school is questioned, the answer assumes a binding and finished nature, linking the education system with its fundamental function of preparing for the future. According to Pais [11] (p. 50), "the future is the time that seems to legitimize the rationale of the educational system, by preaching that it allows the 'education of the men of tomorrow'." From this perspective, the same author ascribed to young students the label of "beings in transit", as "potential adults of the future" [11], a concept in which the present is devalued regarding the future. They exist not according to what they are, but to what they will become. There is an intrinsic depreciation of young people's experiences of the present, only valued for their reflections on the future. Moreover, education is seen as a "waiting room" upstream of professional inclusion. That is, the development of identity is a long-term process that is shaped by all the daily experiences that happen not only in school, but also within the wider sociocultural and familiar contexts [7].

2.2. The Imbalance between Youth and Student Life

Nevertheless, the role of the student is not (nor should it be) unique: students are part of many other systems from which they cannot be disconnected: family, friends, hobbies, sports, inhabitants of a region, city, or neighborhoods. Adopting systemic terms, if an individual cannot be detached from his/her context, neither can context be conceived without links between them. Thus, if an individual does not make a school, the school, as an individual and social construction, owes its existence to the individuals who are part of it, that is, it emerges from all the elements that compose it. Hence, if all schools are equal, because they are schools, they all are different, because they are formed by different people. From this perspective, both the individual and the school are considered as systems that, as such, are only likely to be perceived in terms of the interactions between the parts that compose and form them. However, as Edgar Morin [12] (p. 53) states, "we cannot reduce ourselves to the system, we must enrich the system". Referring precisely to school, Morin [12] further proposes the holographic principle, which states that if it is true that the whole is greater than the sum of its parts, it is no less true that each part contains the whole. To fully grasp systemic complexity one must approach it by thinking both from the parts to the whole and from the whole to the parts, reclaiming the place and the importance of the individual within the system.

The adolescent and young adult are actors in school. While exercising their student crafts [2], they are confronted with opportunities to exercise diverse roles, such as the role of the good student, of the future adult, of the element of the class, etc. Therefore, for the student to be able to select the role which they feel best meets not only their personal needs, but also the objectives of the system to which they belong, it is necessary to broaden the choices of roles. In this regard, it is worth quoting Ausloos [13] (p. 37): "It is also necessary that the adolescent holds the required information to make those choices and that the system in which he/she evolves authorizes him/her to represent the roles he/she chooses, which means allow him/her empower, since following his/her own rules is also making his/her own choices".

Using Perrenoud's [2] conceptualization of the student's role as a theoretical framework, this paper intends, through the analysis of the discourse of HE students, to reflect on the construction of students' identities and the repercussions on their academic success. How students try to integrate their personal lives with the demands of their new role as higher education students is also discussed.

3. Methodology

The methods of construction of the student craft were analyzed by applying a qualitative analysis methodology to our empirical data. In this research, interviews were considered to be the best approach with which to capture the richness and complexity of the reality under analysis and to grasp its meanings. Thus, in-depth, semi-structured interviews were the procedures chosen for data collection. These interviews are part of a broader project which aims to analyze the integration of first-year students into higher education. However, the data analyzed for this paper represent only a part of all the data dealing with the construction of the student craft. Thus, the students in our sample were questioned about their daily academic, family, and social lives. The demographic data of the involved students were collected, namely, their family backgrounds and their socio-economic origins. Within this context, the focus was on study methods, time management, strategies to cope with assessment, and the appropriation of spaces. Furthermore, the interviews highlighted the students' attitudes and feelings towards the formal school curriculum, as well as the pattern of the relationships established not only with peers, but also with individuals of the whole institution, especially their teachers. The ways in which students try to balance their personal lives with the requirements of their new role as higher education students was also questioned.

Therefore, the interviews were performed with first-year students who had been attending university for six months. The sample was composed of 30 students (from a total of 43) who enrolled in electrical and computer engineering (ECE) in one of the better-known Portuguese universities. In Portugal, engineering studies (especially electrical and mechanical engineering) remain a very prestigious and popular scientific field for higher education candidates [14].

The strategy used for selecting the target population was the probability sampling method with a stratified random sample, ensuring that the sample would be able to represent not only the overall population, but also a fair distribution of access grades. There were 25 male and 5 female participants, a gender distribution identical to the population, which contains 22% women. With a median age of 19 years in a range of 18 to 20 years, the ethnic composition of the sample was 100% Caucasian. The analysis of socio-educational indicators made the prevalence of students coming from families with higher levels of education evident.

Data analysis was performed through content analysis using the QSR N6 software. This statistical tool allows documents to be codified and for that codification to be analyzed and explored. The choice of this software was based on its versatility and flexibility, which allowed it to encompass the methodological orientation adopted in this research. Moreover, this software tool assumed a critical role in the efficiency of data treatment, favoring the management and comparison of a considerable amount of non-structured data. This methodological option arose from considering language as a carrier of meanings and as a representation of reality. Therefore, the content analysis prioritized the semantic approach over the syntactic one. Key to implementing this methodological approach were the works of Weber [15] and Krippendorff [16].

It should be noted that all the names of the students used in this manuscript are fictitious, and that their anonymity has been preserved. The methodological procedure was approved by the institutional research ethics committee.

4. Analysis and Discussion of Results: The Student Craft

Being a student is more than a transitory social status; it is a learning process of the *modus faciendi* of the student craft [2]. In fact, to perform a craft, i.e., "to have a job", is a form of social recognition, a way to exist as a member of a society. But the student craft assumes several features that clearly distinguish it from other crafts. It is heavily dependent on external and "distant" entities (e.g., ministries and governmental agencies) for which control is not only difficult, but also, in most cases, unfeasible. Both the purposes and global conditions for exercising student craft and its specific regulation in each school year and for each school level are dependent on those entities. Furthermore, this is a craft for which choice was made less freely: entering school comes as a transition that is not only expected, but explicitly compulsory. It is not only the educational system that compels children and adolescents to become students; the social pressure towards schooling also plays a critical role.

One's family and social group are good examples of influences on a student's set of extra-school means, put forward by Perrenoud [2] as the first level of influence. Mathew coming from a family of a high socio-cultural and socioeconomic level, told us: "The only degree I would ever consider changing to was Sports. But when I made the choice, I didn't even think about it. My dad would kill me! He says it's not occupation. . ." Greg, middle class, confirmed this family influence: "In the 9th grade, I was going to choose Accounting or Economics, but my dad said he didn't want his three children with the same degree, and I then went to the Technology of Electronics. [...] But if it wasn't for my father, I would probably also be in School of Accounting, like my brothers."

The second level of influence pointed out by Perrenoud [2], which comprises different teachers, classes, or even the school attended, were also confirmed by the students' discourse. For example, Nicholas, coming from a low socio-cultural and economic family, stated: "I decided at the 12th grade, because I even considered start working, but one of my teachers advised me to join higher education... He wanted me to go on studying and to come here."

Regarding the influence of peers, which was referenced by the same author [2], Greg also stated: "At the end of the 12th grade, I and my colleagues made a deal to all try to go to the School of Engineering. Almost all of us came." In turn, Sophia, when referring to her career choice, stated that "I had no support, only from my colleagues."

James, referring to the various influences he experienced when making decisions about school, provided an overall picture of the three types of influences mentioned above: "Everyone helped me: teachers, my parents and my friends. They all gave their opinion."

These influences may, however, follow more than one path, since the child, the adolescent, or the young adult learns the duties inherent to his/her status as a student through three different processes [2] (p. 95):

- By appropriation of social representations of what one is meant to be and to do as a student, these representations flow both among their peers and among adults (parents, teachers, etc.): Andrew says: "Teachers warn us all the time: 'You study, because this is really difficult, it requires too much work'", and Mark adds: "There are older students who say that it's not worth attending certain classes and the freshmen believe them."
- By conscious imitation of the ways of living and acting that are seen in the classroom and that are the reality of school—George shares his insight on some colleagues regarding their study habits: "I sometimes think that some say they don't study and after all they do, but don't want to be called nerds. To become part of the group, to integrate better. I don't know. I think that's it..."
- By the internalization of objective imitations that lead to responses that are appropriate for everyday school situations—Daniel states: "I usually attend almost all the lectures. I just miss when I think the subject is easy."

Despite its transient status and despite being subject to a multitude of influences, this is a real craft, as it is expected to precede the rise of a new and improved craft. Brian described to us his expectations regarding his future after graduation: "[...] I hope to get a good job, where I have a good wage and I do what I like." However, the duration of this provisional craft may be planned, but not thoroughly, as it entirely depends on the success and strategy of each student, that is, on his/her mastery in terms of performing his/her craft. As Nicholas noted, "I have to do this in five years. My parents cannot afford to have me here failing or fooling around." Paradigmatic examples of the unpredictability of the duration of schooling are undoubtedly the current failure and dropout rates of Portuguese higher education. Data referring to 2021, transmitted by the University Rector's Office, provide information about the success rates of the Integrated Masters of the School of Engineering of this academy, pointing out an average success rate of 27%.

Daniel reflected on this issue by referring to the consequences of academic failure that he perceives in his school: "I think that this failure somehow affects the image of students from the School of Engineering, people think they don't want to do anything. I think that it affects even the School of Engineering itself. People know that this is a very demanding School, but you know: the evidence..."

Another specific feature of the uniqueness of the student craft within the overall framework of crafts is the fact that it is constantly developed under the control of others. Not only are the results controlled, but the way in which the whole process is carried out is regimented as well. This control leads to a constant subjection to evaluation criteria that emphasize not only the student's cognitive skills and general knowledge, but also the student as an individual with a unique personality. Anne complained explicitly of the uncontrollability to which she is subjected by the evaluation forms: "Sometimes the teacher plays tricks: the test has nothing to do with anything... There are teachers with lots of imagination!".

Although students spend most of their week at school, adult society does not regard it as a job in the real assertion of the word and does not include it in the so-called working world. This approach (which might be called work-centered, as opposed to school-centered) by stating that the purpose of school is to prepare for life, resigns those who attend in order to live inside the school, leaving them with the only option of living for the school. From this perspective, school does not imply action, but simply prepares students for action in the future. As Perrenoud [2] (p. 21) argues, "on one side there is school, where there is no real living yet, where we prepare to enter life, the life that matters, the one in which we will have a craft and a salary. Then, we enter the workforce. And then, of course, we are no longer in school, we earn a living, we spend it, we waste it." The student craft is thus, embodied mainly by the future for which it supposedly prepares the students, while the school makes them believe that the prospect of that future should be sufficient to give meaning to the daily work of learning. The same author [2] draws attention to the fact that one often "ignores that the student's functioning in school prepares him/her for an essential facet of his/her craft as an adult: to become a native of big organizations to which he/she owes his/her employment and his/her identity".

The uniqueness of the student craft is closely related to the cyclical factors that contribute to its specificity, inducing a "system of pedagogical work" which Perrenoud [2] (p. 16) operationalizes in terms of several general features, which will be analyzed through interviews with the protagonists of this study (students in the 1st year of ECE).

In this context, the first indicator for Perrenoud [2] was a permanent lack of time and flexibility to take shortcuts and to seize opportunities. Fred talked about his strategies for studying for exams: "For example, for maths, I only study by the exercises, because there's no time". Later, he justified his failure in a very pragmatic way: "Lack of study. To study more, I had to give up some things that are much too important for me". The studying strategy appears to be undisputed: first, the theoretical approach, and exercises only afterwards. But in face of a lack of time, a step is skipped (the study of theory), despite its importance being recognized, and priorities are established. Josh even suggested a strategy aiming to mathematically verify the lack of time that overwhelms the students in their academic lives: "I would create a syllabus where all the teachers would indicate the hours they think students should study for their course and then I would cross it with the 24 h of the day, and then I would come to the conclusion that the 24 h wouldn't be enough" It should be noted that Josh's suggestion meets one of the basic statements of Bologna.

Another perspective of the pedagogical work induced by the assumption of the student work as a craft lies in the strong reluctance of the teachers to negotiate with their students. Nicholas complained that "Most teachers just pour the contents". Mathew corroborated this statement explaining the inflexibility of which he accuses some teachers: "Some are harsh but I think it is because they are outdated. So, nobody has the nerve to question them".

In pedagogical work, the constant use of external rewards or sanctions (such as grades to promote the students' levels of work is also perceptible. This strategy may lead, according to Perrenoud [2], to a utilitarian view of student work depending on the grade, rather than on the knowledge or the know-how. Daniel mentioned his study plans, and the importance of the grade as a reward for his work is clear: "When I work more, my grades turn out to be better". However, grades (or at least good grades) do not seem to be critical for all students. Some consider that a good student is the one that "knows what he wants and has goals. He is more concerned about knowing than about having good grades. I think these are the good students and not those who just study and study, but who then know nothing besides what they have studied." (Peter). Others even doubt the practical usefulness of obtaining high grades: "It's cool to get good grades, but I do not know if it pays off: they only live to study. What a stupid life!" (Mathew). Other students reflect on how their colleagues' study, questioning the importance ascribed to evaluation: "It's not what matters: what matters is to know, not to study. It would be cool if there were a way of knowing without studying..." (David).

It should be noted that all these students that question the added value of grades tend to attempt to manage their study tasks according to issues carefully selected as being the most important, or at least the most likely to be assessed. Thus, there is an effort to recognize teachers' strategies, aiming at monetizing time and resources, to achieve a balance between what is expected from them and what they are willing to invest. This scheme, although it is effective for course completion, prevents them from striving for very high grades, but this does not seem to be their ambition. Thus, striving for high grades would require extra effort, hindering other investments which they consider to be essential to their well-being (for instance, social life—Alexis stressed the difficulty of this task: "Studying takes a lot of time from friends. Sometimes it's hard to choose..."). However, this strategy of seeking efficiency should not be mistaken for a certain carelessness or a lack of investment in academic activities. For these students, their roles as HE students are important in their lives, albeit not unique. The motivation to succeed in higher education is real and energizing, unlike for others, who invest all personal resources into their roles as students. The latter type turns the student's role into the axis around which their existence revolves. Sophia stated: "Here, it's all about studying. That's what I'm here for". And Mathew criticized this statement: "If you live for this, you are unbalanced. I do not mean psychologically unbalanced but having an unbalanced life." James went further, stating that "there's always the black sheep, those who live for studying and do not look to anything else". Besides these perspectives, there are also students who do not invest in studying tasks due to a lack of motivation to achieve their objectives. According to Michael, these colleagues are "lost and lead a dissolute life". Sophia added: "Sometimes I even get sick when I see so many people wasting their lives like this..." And Mathew continued: "Some are here by mistake; they don't know what they want".

While the first type of student lives while studying what is necessary, the second type lives to study, and the third goes on living without studying.

Moreover, Perrenoud [2] also noted the high homogenization that characterizes the educational system, particularly regarding:

- Schedules (Andrew proposed changes in the time management of teaching periods: "I think that one hour and half lectures are exaggerated, because ultimately there is no efficiency. I think that it could be changed, as in high school.");
- Spaces (the same student also criticized the teaching spaces: "The amphitheatre is not the best option for a classroom. They should be smaller and more comfortable...");
- Syllabus (Lloyd mentioned his perception of the low differentiation between the syllabi of two different courses: "I chose ECE, just in case. I preferred Computing Engineering, but the access was much more difficult, and I did not want to take a chance. It was all the same to me. It's almost the same thing...");
- Teaching methods (Fred says that he selected lectures depending on the method used by the teacher, stating that "some are not worth going. I don't go, because it is so boring: they are reading the slides, which does not captivate me at all".);
- Teacher training (Anne stated that: "Teachers should have a pedagogical training for not using only slides").

Although the aims of higher education emphasize active learning, the fact remains that students continue to refer to a great weight of closed tasks, exercises, and routines. Earlier, Fred mentioned the importance of exercises as a form of study, which appears to be common for most of his peers, not only when they study regularly, but also when they prepare for an exam. Moreover, students strongly criticize content-based lectures ("Most of the teachers just pour the contents" (Nicholas)) and the massive use of slides ("So could I teach too: I would have to get some slides, read them and earn my money", Fred). John defined the types of teachers in his program as follows: "He does not need to prepare, as he has everything done already from the previous year. He just goes there and pours."

Perrenoud [2] also found that students are subject to a certain degree of coercion and even control to attend classes, even without any desire or interest. George confirmed this: "I don't attend all classes: only the practical ones; they are compulsory". The great majority of respondents spontaneously agreed that the attendance of practical classes has a mandatory nature, contrary to the lectures, for which attendance is not mandatory and which are subject to the assessment of "utility" according to the most diverse criteria:

- Teaching methodology: "I only attend the lectures which force me to think, to do things. I hate to be only a bystander" (Simon);
- Interest raised: "In the beginning of the semester I usually go to see, to assess whether it is worth keeping going or not, but some are not really worth going" (James);
- Level of difficulty: "I usually attend almost all lectures. I just miss when I think the subject is easy and I don't need to go there and listen to the teacher" (Daniel);
- Teacher: "I attend only the ones which teachers are less boring" (Sean);
- Schedule: "I attend almost all lectures. I only miss when I have many in a row and I can't make it. I do not want to go there to sleep!" (Charles);
- Method of study: "I attend almost every class because I prefer to study by my own notes. Some are very boring, but I must. . ." (Susan).

The time taken up by formal assessment at the expense of teaching time is another basic assumption, proposed by Perrenoud [2], that influences the construction of the student craft. Indeed, and especially in higher education, the assessment periods exert enormous pressure upon students to invest in study and are associated with intensive, and often circumstantial, preparation for an extensive set of exams. Diana explained pragmatically how to face the exam period: "I must do exams to finish the degree, right? But it's boring, that's the truth. They really must be mandatory, otherwise nobody would take them. I study because I must: I take no pleasure in it". Fred also reflected on the inevitability of evaluation and indicated his anxiety: "It must be done. I study till the end. But after all it's the only way to be evaluated, but it's painful".

Finally, the aforementioned author focused on the bureaucratized relationships established between teachers and students, each considering their role, their craft, and their territory. Lawrence appeared to be resigned to this power structure: "The relationship is normal. Each has his duties. They have power and I don't: I just must turn around and follow the pathway they suggest". Greg expressed the same sentiment: "Distant: to each his own". Lloyd was more radical: "What relationship? A relationship involves at least two people, right? There, there are more than two, but there is no connection, there is nothing bonding us, not even the syllabus".

In terms of the student craft, success is never complete; there is always the feeling (or induction) that one could do more or better. In fact, during the (at least) twelve years spent in school, the student is exposed to the omnipresent threat of failure (in school and, thus, in life) if they do not work hard or if they do not meet all the requirements they face throughout their school pathway. Lloyd reflected on the pressure for success with which he is confronted: "The guys are not used to this crazy pace. They don't study what they should: night and day, right? Sometimes, I think that even if I studied night and day, I wouldn't get the highest grade".

Thus, integrating the investment that students make in their social identities, which is more focused either on their role as a student or their role as a young person, with their academic success, we arrive at a matrix (Figure 1) that identifies four quadrants—"Live to study", "Study to live", "Study without living", and "Live without studying"—based on their familial, social, and structural backgrounds as well as their study methods, time management, and strategies to cope with assessments. On the horizontal axis, academic investment is considered, and on the vertical axis is academic success.

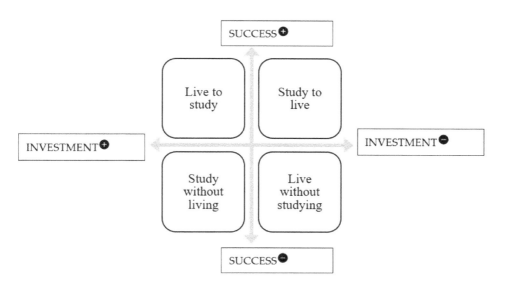

Figure 1. Academic Investment/Academic Success Matrix Identity Construction Framework.

Students who center their lives on study-related goals and who succeed academically fall into the first quadrant: "Live to Study". Those who are academically successful but manage to balance their academic investment with their lives as young people can be placed into the second quadrant: "Study to live". On the other hand, students who fail academically may take different positions in terms of investing in their role as students. Some invest academically, but failed; these students fall into the third group: "Study without living". Finally, others do not even try, and these are categorized in the fourth quadrant: "Live without studying".

It is within this framework that students shape their identities. Each of them is in a transition between adolescence and adulthood, which implies a rapid adaptation to the roles expected of them. Moreover, in a sense, the development of their activities takes place according to pledges of investment from different authority figures.

In this matrix, we present a proposal of prototypes for the categorization of young students in higher education that may greatly aid in the identification, adaptation, and application of more efficient pedagogical support. It is in this sense that it is fundamental to support young adults' routes of entry into higher education. Thus, it is at this moment, upon admission to HE, that the student's identity begin to be forged. This occurs through learning the rules of the game, which enhances the acquisition of knowledge and encourages young adults to abandon conformism and to seek to improve their levels of competence, both as people and as students. In this way, we look at the process of identity formation of these young students as a product of interrelation between the individual person, who integrates the different levels of influences (family, social, school, and peer group factors) and the context, highlighting the interaction between the processes of development and learning.

5. Final Remarks

Adopting the student craft conceptualization proposed by Perrenoud [2] as a theoretical reference for the data analysis of students' discourse, this paper sought to reflect on the identity construction of students attending HE. In fact, the presented results confirm that attending HE may indeed be conceptualized as the exercise of a craft: the student craft. Thus, all the assumptions of the student craft which were advocated for by Perrenoud [2] for the initial school levels were also verified by the present research for HE.

As with all crafts, this craft reflects a tension between its ideal aim and its effective implementation. Ideally, it is up to students to learn; that is the very purpose of their craft.

But is it lawful (or wise) to take for granted that students hold, in themselves, an intrinsic motivation that drives them to manage and to overcome a set of obstacles imposed by the unique characteristics of their craft?

Several authors [2,17] have reflected on the difficulty of requiring, or at least expecting, motivated students when their work seems so segmented and discontinuous (classes with limited time and without a logical sequence in the time schedule). The work structured according to different courses in one segment of the day and, consequently, different subjects, different teachers, and different teaching approaches. In particular, the systematic changing teachers, with all that it entails in terms of the need to adapt to different structures and diverse rhythms (image, space, methods, techniques, level, and requirements' quality is varied.

Goffman [18] sees school as a totalitarian institution which is necessary in order to survive. Power and authority are long-accepted aspects of it, and are considered, even today, to be fundamental for meeting the ultimate objective of the educational system preparing for the future. Otherwise, how can it be explained that children who are not yet educated assume, in play situations, the roles of teachers, adopting positions of totalitarian and unquestioned power?

The students have no alternative, then, but to find more or less effective strategies to perform their craft. One of these strategies may consist of the intensive exercise of the student craft, in which success constitutes a fundamental value and ultimately creates a utilitarian relationship with knowledge, with work, and with the other. But it may also involve survival, and the student may use their cunning, pretension, or even strategic subservience, using alternative schemes such as cheating, preparing just the day before "pretending" to go unnoticed, missing classes as much as possible, etc. Perrenoud [2] advocates for those students in their endeavors to survive in HE, as they tend to devalue knowledge and learning as ways to satisfy their own pleasure and curiosity. It is about looking good in the competition to attain good grades, using all means, including the less desirable, from pedagogical or ethical standpoints.

In short, the results from the present study allow for a conclusion to be made that the construction of student craft can be achieved through different weights of investment: the individuals who live to study and the individuals who study to live (see Figure 2).

While in the former group of students, the student's craft is assumed as the capital identity role in their lives, in the latter group, the student's craft is a systematic exercise of balance between all the roles concurring in their lives. It should be noted that students from both groups may attain success in their academic pathways, achieving mastery in their craft despite making different choices and using different strategies to do so. However, there are those students, the fact of exercising their craft notwithstanding, who do not achieve success because they exercise it inadequately with only the basic skills required for the student craft. Moreover, there is still a fourth official group of students in the system but they do not carry out their craft, only bearing the title. These are not real students but sheer figurants in a movie produced and directed by external entities that manage the educational system as an unavoidable experience.

As for theoretical implications, we emphasize that with greater knowledge of the profiles of students entering HEIs, we will be able to establish policies that meet the real needs of these "young/adult students" in order to improve their academic success, which holds value for all those who interact with them. It also allows for different roles to be generated in the lives of these "young/adult students", stimulating the taste for knowledge and for personal, social, and academic success, that is, being wise in their choices and efficient in managing their roles in life.

Figure 2. Results of the application of the framework.

Regarding practical implications, we believe that we have contributed to developing support systems for students enrolling in higher education institutions such that the goals of each young adult who is expected to be an "engineer" can be established and achieved Furthermore, according to students' admission profiles to higher education, teachers can design classes which are more interactive, where students can be creative and learning is student-centered. With this tool, we can outline strategies that motivate students to make time to manage their lives in various aspects.

As for the limitations of our study, we emphasize that our sample was focused on engineering students, and it would be interesting to assess the profiles and the approaches of students in other scientific areas, such as business students. It would be relevant to conceptualize and test a scale for quantitative studies.

Thus, the limitations which we present are also opportunities for future research. We would also like to emphasize the relevance of applying the proposed model to HEIs in other national and international territories, with students from different backgrounds and experiences, so that policies and pedagogies can be determined by which "young/adult students" can review themselves and feel that they are an integral part of the academy that welcomes them.

Author Contributions: Conceptualization, D.D.; methodology, D.D.; software, D.D.; validation D.D. and G.S.; formal analysis, D.D. and G.S.; investigation, D.D. and G.S.; resources, D.D.; data curation, D.D.; writing—original draft preparation, D.D.; writing—review and editing, D.D. and G.S. visualization, D.D. and G.S.; supervision, D.D.; project administration, D.D. All authors have read and agreed to the published version of the manuscript.

Funding: This research received no external funding.

Institutional Review Board Statement: Not applicable.

Informed Consent Statement: Informed consent was obtained from all subjects involved in the study

Data Availability Statement: Not applicable.

Conflicts of Interest: The authors declare no conflict of interest.

References

1. Flum, H.; Kaplan, A. Identity Formation in Educational Settings: A Contextualized View of Theory and Research in Practice *Contemp. Educ. Psychol.* **2012**, *37*, 240–245. [CrossRef]
2. Perrenoud, P. *Ofício de Aluno e Sentido do Trabalho Escolar*; Colecção Ciências da Educação, Porto Editora: Porto, Portugal, 1995.
3. Marcia, J. Identity in adolescence. In *Handbook of Adolescent Psychology*; Adelson, J., Ed.; Wiley & Sons: New York, NY, USA, 1980
4. Erikson, E. *Identity: Youth and Crisis*; Norton: New York, NY, USA, 1968.
5. Adams, G.R.; Berzonsky, M.D.; Keating, L. Psychosocial Resources in First-Year University Students: The Role of Identity Processes and Social Relationships. *J. Youth Adolesc.* **2006**, *35*, 78–88. [CrossRef]
6. Dubar, C. *A Socialização: Construção de Identidades Sociais e de Identidades Profissionais*; Porto Editora: Porto, Portugal, 1997.
7. Brunton, J.; Buckley, F. "You're Thrown in the Deep End": Adult Learner Identity Formation in Higher Education. *Stud. High Educ.* **2020**, *46*, 2696–2709. [CrossRef]
8. Dias, D. Engineering Learning Outcomes: The Possible Balance between the Passion and the Profession. *Soc. Sci.* **2023**, *12*, 37 [CrossRef]
9. Dias, D. Students strategies to survive the academic transition: Recycling skills, reshaping minds. *Eur. J. Eng. Educ.* **2022**, *47*, 1050–1060. [CrossRef]
10. Dias, D. The Higher Education Commitment Challenge: Impacts of Physical and Cultural Dimensions in the First-Year Students Sense of Belonging. *Educ. Sci.* **2022**, *12*, 231. [CrossRef]
11. Pais, J.M. *Ganchos, Tachos e Biscates: Jovens, Trabalho e Futuro*; Ambar: Porto, Portugal, 2001.
12. Morin, E. Éduquer c'est toujours un peu vouloir briser les differences. *Cah. Pédagogiques* **1988**, *268*, 45–46.
13. Ausloos, G. As Competências das Famílias. In *Tempo, Caos, Processo*; Climepsi Editores: Lisboa, Portugal, 1996.
14. Amado-Tavares, D. *O Superior Ofício de Ser Aluno: Manual de Sobrevivência do Caloiro [The Superior Craft of Being a Student: Freshman's Survival Manual]*; Edições Sílabo: Lisboa, Portugal, 2008.
15. Weber, R. *Basic Content Analysis*; Sage: Newbury Park, CA, USA, 1990.
16. Krippendorff, K. *Content Analysis: An Introduction to Its Methodology*; Sage: Newbury Park, CA, USA, 1980.

7.   Coulon, A. *Le Métier D' Étudiant: L'entrée dans la Vie Universitaire*; Presses Universitaires de France: Paris, France, 1997.
8.   Goffman, E. *Estigma: Notas sobre a Manipulação da Identidade Deteriorada*; Guanabara Koogan: Rio de Janeiro, Brazil, 2004.

Article

Understanding Influencers of College Major Decision: The UAE Case

Mohammad Amin Kuhail [1,*], Joao Negreiros [2], Haseena Al Katheeri [2], Sana Khan [2] and Shurooq Almutairi [3]

[1] College of Interdisciplinary Studies, Zayed University, Abu Dhabi P.O. Box 144534, United Arab Emirates
[2] College of Technological Innovation, Zayed University, Abu Dhabi P.O. Box 144534, United Arab Emirates
[3] College of Computer and Information Sciences, Princess Nourah bint Abdulrahman University,
    Riyadh 11671, Saudi Arabia
* Correspondence: mohammad.kuhail@zu.ac.ae

Abstract: This study aims to understand and analyze what influences female students to choose a college major in the United Arab Emirates (UAE). To accomplish our target, we conducted a survey with mostly female first-year undergraduate students (N = 496) at Zayed University to understand the personal, social, and financial factors influencing students' major choices. Further, this study also asked students to specify their actions before deciding on their major and assessed the information that could be helpful for future students to decide on their majors. Last, the study investigated how Science, Technology, Engineering, and Mathematics (STEM) students differ from other students in their major decision. The results show that financial factors such as income and business opportunities related to the major are crucial. Further, gender suitability for the job and passion are influential. Students conduct internet searches, use social media, and read brochures in the process of major decisions. Moreover, students think job alignment with the UAE vision and information related to job availability, income, and skills are critical for future students to decide on their major. Finally, STEM students are more influenced by business opportunities, prestige, and career advancement than others.

Keywords: major selection; college major decision; STEM; career choices; university education; female students

Citation: Kuhail, M.A.; Negreiros, J.; Al Katheeri, H.; Khan, S.; Almutairi, S. Understanding Influencers of College Major Decision: The UAE Case. *Educ. Sci.* **2023**, *13*, 39. https://doi.org/10.3390/educsci13010039

Academic Editor: James Albright

Received: 20 October 2022
Revised: 17 December 2022
Accepted: 26 December 2022
Published: 30 December 2022

1. Introduction

Higher education (HE) continues to grow globally. Indeed, a recent study projects the global demand for HE to grow through 2040. Further, the study predicts that nearly 600 million students will be enrolled in universities worldwide by 2040 [1]. The demand for HE comes as no surprise since it contributes to economic growth by enhancing individuals' productivity, thereby increasing their human capital stock [2,3]. In the United Arab Emirates (UAE), HE has tremendously grown since founding its first university in 1976 [4], as the country has actively supported and invested in HE [5]. Further, the UAE has attracted several well-reputed foreign universities to establish campuses [6]. The UAE's investment in HE aligns with its commitment to a knowledge-based society [7].

Despite the growing demand for HE globally and in the UAE, some students find selecting a college major stressful [8]. Research suggests that many students base their decision on college majors on assumptions rather than facts [9,10]. Students' inability to successfully select what and where to study may greatly impact returns of higher education [10], and the labor market [11]. Thus, understanding how students choose their majors and what influences them will allow policymakers to define appropriate measures and incentives for labor supply adjustments based on market needs and other strategic goals [12].

Several studies have investigated what influences students' decisions of major and university. For instance, a study in Poland has found that social factors are influential [13]

while a study conducted in Canada identified earnings as an essential factor [14]. Other studies determined that gender, personal interest [15], and enrollment criteria [16], are crucial in the major selection process. In general, there is an agreement on the impact of gender and earnings on major selection. However, varied findings are available on the effect of social factors and students' abilities [12].

Despite abundant global studies on major choice determinants, only a few studies approached the topic in the UAE context. The UAE context is unique as the country has rapidly developed over the last few decades and is now transitioning into a knowledge-based economy. Thus, the UAE seeks to provide an educated and qualified workforce, which will resume the economic development of the country [17]. Amongst the few relevant studies conducted in the UAE is a study completed by Davies et al. [18], who assessed the motives behind students' choices of business majors in multiple countries, including the UAE. The findings point to parental pressure and reputation, among other motives. Another study by Makhmasi et al. [19] discussed factors influencing students' choice of Science, Technology, Engineering, and Mathematics (STEM) fields. The study cites passion and expected earnings as influential motives. Hammour studied the correlation between UAE students' intentions to major in accounting and their attitudes towards and perceived behavioral control [20]. While these studies have contributed to the body of literature, they concentrated on specific majors [18–20]. Further, rather than analyzing the factors influencing the students' major decisions, the studies had a specific objective in mind, such as comparing students from different countries [18] or correlating students' attitudes with intentions of majoring [20].

This study analyzes, explains, and evaluates the major choice of mostly female students at Zayed University. This study uses descriptive and inferential statistics to assess the personal, social, and financial influences on students' major choices. Further, the study explores the actions and data required by students to make well-informed major decisions. Moreover, the study uncovers information helpful for future students to decide their majors. Last, the study assesses how STEM students differ in what influences their major selection decision.

2. Literature Review

Several researchers discussed how students select their college major. The literature sheds light on the various factors influencing students' major decisions.

2.1. Social Pressure and Self-Motivation

We define social pressure as the influence of family members, friends, or teachers' opinions on students' major decisions. Research regarding family and peer pressure shows different trends. For instance, according to a survey conducted in Saudi Arabia [21], peer and family pressure has little influence on students in selecting their majors. Interestingly, two studies conducted in the U.S. [22] and Sri Lanka [23] also found that parents and guardians are less influential than other factors. However, a study conducted in Poland [13] highlighted that the opinion of family members influences students.

In addition to social pressure, motivation plays a significant role in students' major choices. For instance, a study by [24] reported that self-motivation to choose a college major significantly predicts academic decisions and well-being outcomes. Teachers and parents may encourage such motivation, which affects students' interest and enrollment in certain majors such as STEM [25] and accounting [26].

2.2. Expected Earnings

Research shows that students consider the salary [21] and job market before selecting their college major [26]. Some students may not have realistic income expectations despite the importance of expected earnings in major selection decisions. For instance, community college students in California believe that salaries are 13% higher than they actually are, and students underestimate the probability of being employed by almost 25% [27]. As another example, a large-scale survey of Chilean college applicants found that students overestimate the earnings of the alums of their preferred college major by 39.3% [10].

2.3. Socio-Economic Status (SES)

The choice of college major and its related knowledge varies with students' backgrounds. Students from low socioeconomic backgrounds tend to be influenced by the program's cost and finances. In terms of program-related knowledge, low-SES background students are more inclined to gather information from advertisements and less inclined to find program-related information on government websites or in their schools [10]. Low SES students are more likely to have large errors in estimating the probability of employment than their high SES peers [27].

2.4. Demographics

Research shows that demographics such as gender and race can play a crucial role in students' major decisions. For example, a study conducted in Chile [28] found that fathers influence the decisions of male students, while both parents influence female students. Further, female students are more likely to be influenced to change their major decision than their male counterparts [22]. Gender also plays a role concerning earnings. For instance, a study [14] found that male students, in particular, are more sensitive than their female counterparts about the initial income of a prospective profession, while women are more sensitive than men to the earnings' rate of growth variations. Female students are generally less influenced by expected earnings compared to men [29].

Research shows that female students are still reluctant to choose STEM majors. For instance, female, first-generation college students were less likely to be certain about choosing an engineering major than their male counterparts [30]. In contrast, male, Asian, and high-SAT Math students dislike humanities [31] and prefer STEM-related majors [32]. Male students generally opt for math, science, and business-related fields, while female students are in the majority in humanities, social science, and education fields [33], and are more likely to apply to health majors and less likely to apply to civil engineering and technology. The tendencies of male and female students to gravitate around certain majors could be explained by the phenomenon that higher interaction with students of a certain gender increases the probability of following the application pattern of that gender [28].

Choosing a major affects the career path differently for females and males. For instance, a study by [34] found that 43% of women leave full-time STEM employment after their first child compared to 23% of new fathers. Indeed, recent research also shows that women who succeed in pursuing STEM careers frequently abandon the industry for various reasons, including hostile or unpleasant working conditions, unequal pay, a lack of mentoring and coaching, and rigid work schedules that conflict with family duties [35]. Similar concerns have been reported in [36].

2.5. Interest and Self Efficacy

Research shows that for students to function optimally in college, the choice of major must be based on personal interest or identification [24]. Several studies show that personal interest in the major is very influential in students' major decisions [22,25,37,38]. For example, in a study in Chile, students reported that they found the jobs associated with their prospective majors enjoyable [10]. Similar results can be found in a study conducted at King Fahad University, where newly admitted students made their major choices based on interest in the major [21].

Interest alone does not explain students' major choices. Indeed, students' perceptions of their abilities play a role in their major choice. For example, a study explains how male and female students in Chile select their college major based on their academic performance [28]. Additionally, a study investigated the relationship of mathematics self-efficacy expectations to the selection of science-based majors. Results indicated that mathematics self-efficacy expectations were significantly related to the extent to which students selected science-based college majors [39]. However, research shows that students need guidance to help them align their self-perceived abilities with their goals when selecting their majors [8,21,23,37].

2.6. Major Selection Surveys

Table 1 shows an overview of various surveys conducted to investigate students' major decisions. A study conducted in Saudi Arabia analyzed the factors that affected newly admitted students' college decisions. The study concluded that several factors influence students' decisions, including job opportunities, prospective salary, and social status. Likewise, job opportunities are crucial for students in Chile [37] and the U.S. [21], where business students also listed job opportunities and expected earnings. Still, students' interest in the subject was the most crucial factor. Further, subject interest has been identified as a crucial deciding factor in a study conducted in the U.S. [40] and another in Qatar [37]. On the other hand, two studies conducted in Pakistan [41,42] revealed the societal influence on students' major decisions, while a study in Estonia [43] identified prior experience with the field influences students' major decisions. At last, a study in the UAE [20] identified a correlation between students' attitudes and their intentions to major in accounting.

Table 1. An overview of the major selection surveys.

Study	Location	Year	Aim	Participants	Data Analysis (Statistical Tool)	Main Findings
[10]	Chile	2016	Explore how students form beliefs about earnings and cost outcomes at different institutions and majors and how these beliefs relate to degree choice and persistence.	7382 students	Significance tests (for the difference between values for high-SES relative to low-SES); linear probability models	Interest in jobs associated with the major is a highly influential factor.
[20]	UAE	2018	Assess the association between students' attitudes and their intentions to major in accounting	442 undergraduate students	Multivariate analysis	A strong correlation between students' attitudes and their intentions to major in accounting.
[21]	Saudi Arabia	1996	Analyze the factors influencing the selection of college majors by newly admitted students.	412 new orientation year students	Importance index	Important factors: Job opportunities, expected earnings, social status, and prestige of the major.
[22]	The U.S.	2005	Examine why students initially select majors and which positive and negative factors relate to later changes in those choices.	788 business students	ANOVA	Students' interest in the subject is highly important, followed by job opportunities, and expected earnings.
[37]	Qatar	2016	Investigate the selection of an engineering major in the gulf region	440 university students	Manual and Thematic Analysis.	Passion for the subjects in the major was the main reason for choosing a major (30.9%), followed by family influence and business opportunities.
[40]	The U.S.	2008	Examine factors influencing students' selection of a college major and students' perceptions of the Information Systems major	429 responses from students who enrolled in on-campus and high school concurrent enrollment college	Independent T-test between college-aged respondents and high school-age respondents.	Students' genuine interest in the subject, long-term earning potential, and job market stability were highly influential.

Table 1. *Cont.*

Study	Location	Year	Aim	Participants	Data Analysis (Statistical Tool)	Main Findings
[41]	Spain	2022	Explore the main factors influencing students to choose engineering studies in Spain, analyzing gender differences.	624 UG engineering students from eight different universities	Independent sample T-tests were used to determine significant differences between the answers of male and female students.	Four factors influence students' major choices such as: "Interest and development", "Career advice and previous contact", "Outcome expectations", and "Social influences".
[42]	Pakistan	2014	Assess major factors which influence Pakistani graduates to make career choices.	370 students from eight different universities	T-test/ANOVA to determine significant differences between gender and the career-choices.	Graduates consider factors such as growth opportunities, occupational charm, societal inspiration, and self-esteem.
[43]	Pakistan	2019	Explore the roles of mothers, fathers, tutors, future income, future status, and societal in the career choice of young students	167 University of Karachi students	One sample t-test and one-way repeated Measure ANOVA by employing SPSS statistical package.	Students consider future status, future income, and societal and family influence.
[44]	Estonia	2014	This study explores what has influenced first-year students to study ICT (Information and communication technology)	517 first-year students from three different universities	A chi-square test	Several factors affected students' choices: owning a computer, computer lessons, family pressure, and earning expectations.
[45]	The U.S.	2014	Understanding pre-college factors that influence students to pursue STEM disciplines	335,842 students from 617 institutions	Logistic Regression	The authors confirmed the effects of academic self-confidence and mathematics self-confidence on engineering major choice.

All these studies in Table 1 have shed light on understanding how students select their majors. However, there remain some gaps to be bridged. First, the existing studies mainly assess what influences the students' decisions, but they do not examine the major decision process itself. For example, students may collect information or conduct an internet search to help them decide on their major. Second, the existing studies have not attempted to answer how future students could be helped to decide their major better. Third, the existing studies were conducted in various countries. However, in the context of the UAE, there is a lack of studies conducted to investigate the personal, social, and financial factors influencing students in deciding their decision.

This study identifies the factors influencing mostly the intentions of mostly female students at Zayed University to choose college majors. Further, the study examines students actions while deciding on their college majors. Finally, the study identifies the information that could be useful for future students desiring to select their majors.

3. The Development of Research Hypotheses

To arrive at a deep analysis of how female students at Zayed University choose their college majors, we developed various hypotheses grounded in the related existing literature. Since STEM fields have been considered a high priority [46] and are the main drivers of the economy, some hypotheses focused on students choosing STEM majors. Other hypotheses were formulated simply due to several parameters that could potentially influence the major decision, such as students' gender, the influence of social factors, and skills.

According to the extant literature, students declaring a STEM major had a higher school Grade Point Average (GPA) and American College Testing (ACT) score and earned more credit hours than those who declared a non-STEM major [47]. Similarly, another study found that the intent to major in STEM is directly affected by 12th-grade math achievement, exposure to math and science, and math self-efficacy beliefs [48]. Similar findings were reported by a study where students with disabilities who enrolled in STEM majors showed higher high school GPAs in math compared to non-STEM students with disabilities [49]. Based on this discussion, we hypothesize:

H1. *The 12-Year GPA affects students' decision to choose STEM majors.*

Students will likely select majors offering high future earnings streams [50]. Research shows that students exposed to higher unemployment rates during typical schooling years select majors that earn higher wages, have better employment prospects, and more often work in a related field [51]. Further, STEM fields such as computer science and engineering fields are chosen by some students as they believe their expected earnings will be higher than job prospects related to humanities and arts [31]. Thus, we hypothesize:

H2. *Expected earnings affect students' decision to choose STEM majors.*

A study calls for more research to understand what drives students to become entrepreneurs [52]. Research shows that STEM university students will likely become entrepreneurs if they select a more specialized study plan [53]. Similar findings are reported in [54]. Interestingly, a recent study conducted in Canada has found that international students, especially those specializing in STEM-related degrees, are more likely to become entrepreneurs [55]. Based on the discussion, we hypothesize:

H3. *Business Opportunities affect students' decision to choose STEM majors.*

According to a recent study, undergraduate students consider STEM fields such as engineering and natural sciences highly prestigious and well-respected fields in society. Further, the students associate STEM majors with high-income and status jobs [56]. Indeed, the prestige attached to the profession is among several factors that affect students' career choices [38]. Accordingly, we hypothesize:

H4. *Prestige affects students' decision to choose STEM majors.*

Research shows that engineering students, in particular, indicate that career upgrading is among the reasons for selecting their majors [57]. Another study shows that career advancement, particularly for male students, is among the influential factors in major selection [22]. Based on this discussion, we hypothesize:

H5. *Career advancement affects students' decision to choose STEM majors.*

Research shows that women are likely to leave jobs where long hours leave less time for family considerations [58]. Similar findings can be found in [59]. Similarly, another study found that women with college degrees value flexible jobs [60]. As such, we hypothesize:

H6. *Career flexibility affects female students' major decisions.*

Research shows that students' beliefs about their skills overlap with their major choices [61]. For instance, students who considered themselves engineers had perceptions of themselves as capable mathematics learners [30]. Belief in one's skills and academic performance predicted students' major choices, particularly in STEM [62]. Thus, we hypothesize:

H7. *Students who are passionate about a certain major also tend to have the right skills for it.*

4. Methodology

This section gives a brief background about the institution where the survey was conducted. After that, the section presents the objective of the survey and tersely presents its questions.

4.1. Study Background

The study was conducted at Zayed University, a public UAE-based university. The university was founded in 1998, features campuses in Dubai and Abu Dhabi, and welcomes national and international students. The university offers graduate and undergraduate programs across different colleges, including interdisciplinary studies, humanities and social sciences, business, communication and media sciences, natural and health sciences, technological innovation, and art and creative sciences.

This study aims to identify what motivates UAE students to choose college majors. A total of 497 students (22 males and 475 females) in the UAE participated in this study. The gender ratio of 95.6% female versus 4.4% male. As such, the sample represents UAE female students more than male students. The students were 481 first-year students and four second-year undergraduate students. Further, there were 4% international students and 96% local students.

We distributed online questionnaires to students so they could respond electronically using an online survey platform. Before conducting the study, we obtained ethical clearance for conducting the study from the University research ethics committee. The questionnaire was administered from August 2021 to November 2021. The questionnaire included a cover letter explaining the purpose of the survey at the beginning. Informed consent was obtained from the students before participating in the study. Further, participation was voluntary, and the questionnaire was anonymous and confidential. The researchers conducting this study are diverse in terms of countries of origin, cultures, and genders. When the team analyzed the data, they had internal discussions amongst themselves to maintain objectivity.

4.2. Questionnaire Design

The questionnaire used in this study collected students' demographic information such as gender, high school average score, the language of instruction in school, type of school (private/government), and emirate of residence. Figure 1 shows the influential factors, actions, and decision-support information asked in the questionnaire. The influential factors included personal, social, and financial factors. The students were asked to rate each of the factors using a Five-point Likert scale where 4 is very influential and 0 is not at all influential. Further, the questionnaire asked the students to specify whether they performed certain actions during the major selection process. Students rated each item using a Six-point scale as follows: 5: I did this, and it highly influenced my major choice, 4: I did this, and it influenced my major choice to a certain degree, 3: I did this, and it moderately influenced my major choice, 2: I did this, but it barely influenced my major choice, 1: I did this, but it did not influence my major choice, 0: I did not do this.

Moreover, students were required to rate on a 5-Likert scale several decision-support information that could help future students decide on their college major, where 4 is very helpful, and 0 is not helpful. At last, the questionnaire allowed students in free-text fields to add factors, actions, and decision-support information that might not have been included in the questionnaire. The questionnaire can be found online [63]. We used Cronbach's Alpha value to measure the reliability of the scales used in the questionnaire. The result indicates that the coefficient value is 0.904 (no. of items: 31 and acceptance of the Normality distribution assumption by the Kolmogorov–Smirnov test whose SPSS p-value equaled 0.26), indicating the high inner reliability of the scales used.

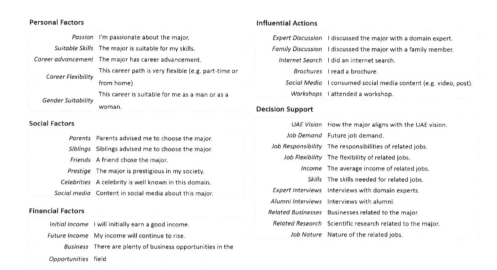

Figure 1. Questionnaire Influential Factors, Actions, and Decision Support Information.

5. Results

5.1. Descriptive Results

5.1.1. Population Analysis

As stated previously, a major survey was given to 497 first and second-year students at Zayed University in Abu Dhabi and Dubai, UAE. Regarding gender, it is a high skewness distribution of 4.445 since 475 were females. A total of 75% of the students are bilingual (Arabic and English) according to the primary language of education (Figure 2). Just over a third (38%) of the students studied in private schools, while the remaining attended governmental ones. Interestingly, the Kurtosis (peakedness) regarding "Have you decided your major when in high school? [1—not sure ... 5—very sure]" was −0.895 (a flat distribution with thin tails).

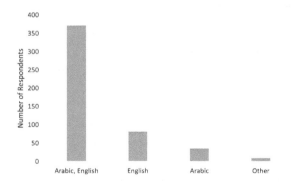

Figure 2. Students' primary languages of education.

Figure 3 shows the distribution of the students' 12-year GPA in school. The GPAs vary between 75% and 99%. Further, we conducted an OLS (Ordinary least squares) regression analysis to understand the population (Figure 4). The year-12 GPA (dependent variable) estimation based on the independent variables of Gender, Main Language of Education, and School Type (public or private) holds a fair R^2 of 33.9%: Year-12 GPA = 93.5 − 5.22

$\times$ Gender $- 2.19 \times$ MainLanguage $- 9.24 \times$ SchoolType. No multicollinearity (VIF) was found among these independent variables; thus, globally, this is an acceptable model as the F statistics is high (85.438). All T-independent tests for each beta were also significant for a 95% confidence level.

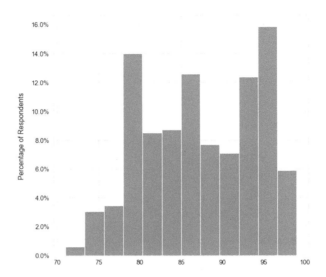

Figure 3. Distribution of Students' Year-12 GPA.

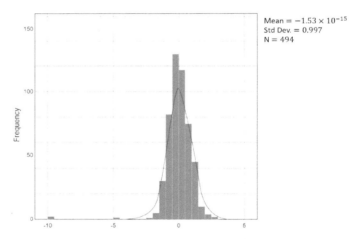

Figure 4. The residuals follow a Gaussian distribution confirmed by the Durbin-Watson test of 2.117

Moreover, as we move along in the main language of education set (Arabic-English-0 English-1, Arabic-2, Others-4), the average 12-year GPA worsens by 2.199 points. At last students studying in private schools achieved higher scores than their counterparts in government schools by 9.249 points, on average.

5.1.2. Influential Factors

Figure 5 shows how the students rated the personal, social, and financial factors on how influential they are to their college major decision. Additionally, Table 2 depicts statistica data about the influential factors. Concerning personal factors, 74.2% of the students cited that gender suitability is highly influential or moderately influential in their college major decision. In comparison, 71.6% of the students considered career advancement highly or moderately influential. The remaining factors, passion, skill suitability, and career flexibility, were less influential in major selection decisions.

Figure 5. Students' ratings of the influential factors of major choice.

Table 2. Influential Factors Statistical Data.

	Personal Factors					Social Factors						Financial Factors		
	Passion	Suitable Skills	Career Advancement	Career Flexibility	Gender Suitability	Parents	Siblings	Friends	Prestige	Celebrities	Social Media	Initial Income	Future Income	Business Opportunities
Mean	2.93	2.85	3.06	2.46	3.10	1.90	0.77	0.78	2.28	1.13	1.69	2.57	2.55	2.67
Median	3.00	3.00	3.00	2.00	4.00	2.00	0.00	0.00	2.00	0.00	2.00	3.00	3.00	3.00
Mode	4	3	4	2	4	2	0	0	2	0	0	2	3	4
StdDev	1.060	1.044	1.040	1.23	1.164	1.41	1.25	1.22	1.316	1.41	1.498	1.158	1.156	1.229
Skew	−0.834	−0.846	−0.923	−0.319	−1.232	0.055	1.47	1.37	−0.247	0.901	0.243	−0.437	−0.479	−0.524
Kurtosis	0.111	0.321	0.177	−0.872	0.658	−1.26	0.879	0.621	−0.991	−0.600	−1.350	−0.593	−0.517	−0.739

Socially, 44.4%, 35.9%, and 31.5% of the students considered prestige, parents, and social media, respectively, highly or moderately influential. In contrast, celebrities, siblings, and friends are much less influential in college major decisions.

Financially, 56.5%, 54.43%, and 53.62% of the students considered business opportunities, future income, and initial income, respectively, highly or moderately influential.

When asked if there were factors influencing students' major choices other than the ones suggested by the questionnaire, only a few students (N = 16) indicated that they chose a certain major because they were restricted by what is offered, and a few others (N = 5) cited that they chose a major close to what they desired.

5.1.3. Influential Actions

Figure 6 shows the actions that students performed before deciding on their major. Most students (85%) performed an internet search, with 32.8% and 19.8% finding it highly and moderately influential, respectively. Similarly, 90.1% of students discussed their prospective major with their families, but only 23.4% and 18.9% found the discussions highly and moderately influential, respectively. In comparison, 81.9% of the students consumed social media content related to their major, with 24% and 15.5% finding social media highly and moderately influential, respectively. Other actions such as reading brochures, discussing the major with an expert, or attending workshops were performed by fewer students. These actions were less influential in deciding the major.

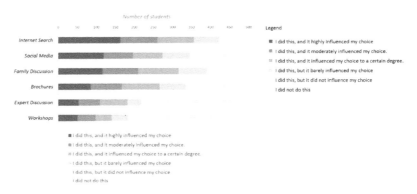

Figure 6. Actions students performed before deciding on their major.

When asked if there were actions other than the ones suggested by the questionnaire, only a few students (N = 3) pointed out that they read the major requirements.

5.1.4. Decision Support

Figure 7 shows the students' ratings of the information that could help future students decide on their major. Most students found all the provided options helpful to varying degrees. However, more than half of the students thought it would be very helpful to know how the prospective major aligns with the UAE vision and the demand for jobs relevant to the major. Skills, job responsibilities, and the flexibility of the prospective jobs were found to be very helpful by 48.5%, 47.3%, and 44.7% of the students, respectively. The remaining pieces of information such as income, job nature, alum interview, related businesses, and related research were perceived as very helpful by fewer students.

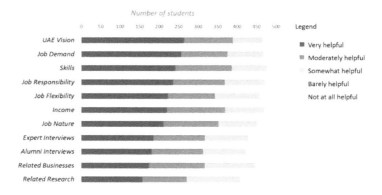

Figure 7. Information that could help future students decide on their major.

When asked if there was decision-support information other than what was suggested by the questionnaire, only a few students (N = 3) pointed out that internship information about the major would be helpful.

5.2. Correlative Analysis

To test the correlations amongst the influential factors, actions, and decision support factors, we used Pearson Correlation and ±0.5 as a cutoff indicating the minimum value to be considered as a significant correlation.

5.2.1. Influential Factors

Figure 8 shows the correlation heatmap amongst the 14 influential factors. Most correlations were generally weak (i.e., less than 0.5 and greater than −0.5). However, a few strong correlations emerged. The correlation between Initial Income and Future Income is 0.84, indicating that many students who choose a major because of its initial income also think the income will steadily grow. Further, the correlation between Passion and Suitable Skills is 0.65, suggesting that some students choose a major for which they have skills and passion. Finally, Business Opportunities and Future Income are highly correlated (0.61), showing that some students choose their majors because of the business opportunities and the growing income in the future.

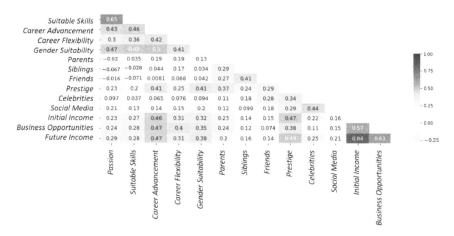

Figure 8. Influential Factors Correlation Heatmap.

5.2.2. Influential Actions

Concerning the influential actions students performed before deciding on their major (Figure 9), Internet Search and Brochures are strongly correlated (0.57), signaling that some students conducting an internet search to obtain information about college majors also read related brochures. Similarly, Internet Search is strongly correlated with Social Media (0.56), indicating that an internet search can be done in parallel with browsing social media content.

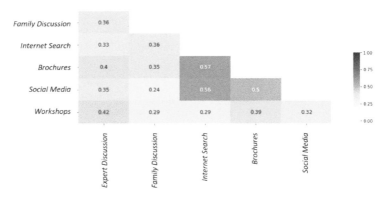

Figure 9. Influential Actions Correlation Heatmap.

5.2.3. Decision Support

At last, almost all the eleven-decision support information exhibited a moderate to a strong positive correlation, and some factors featured strong positive correlations of 0.7 and above (Figure 10). For instance, Job Demand strongly correlates with Job Responsibilities (0.74) and Income (0.7), indicating that many students desiring to know about job demand also want to know about job responsibilities and expected income. Further, Expert Interviews are highly correlated with Alumni Interviews, implying that many students who would like to view interviews with experts in the major domain also prefer to view interviews with alums of that major. It could be argued that some experts are also alums. However, in the survey, we defined alums as fresh graduates from the university.

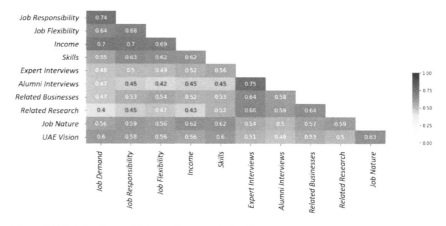

Figure 10. Decision Support Information Correlation Heatmap.

5.3. Confirmatory Factor Analysis (CFA)

We conducted a Confirmatory Factor Analysis (CFA) using SPSS AMOS to examine the relationship among three latent categories (influential factors, influential actions, and decision support) and their 31 initial, observable variables. As part of CFA, factor loadings (standardized regression weights) were assessed for each item with a 99% significance (p-value = 0.000). Numerous model revisions were performed from the original full model to fit the data. In the end, only 12 essential variables remained in the model, and 19 were removed (Figure 11) due to low factor loadings (<0.6). Further, Figure 11 demonstrates that three latent categories (influential actions, influential actions, and decision support) hold similar correlations, indicating no clear predominance of any category over the other two about college major decisions.

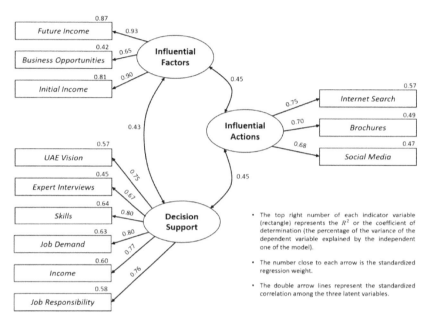

Figure 11. Confirmatory Factor Analysis Model.

Our analysis yielded a Chi-square value of 116.777 with 50 degrees of freedom and a *p*-value of 0.000. Since it does not exceed the alpha value of 0.05, the null hypothesis is rejected, indicating that the model does not fit the data adequately. It should be noted that problems with Chi-square, that is, it is sensitive to sample size, possibly leading to the null hypothesis rejection as the sample size increases. Therefore, additional testing was done before concluding the model fit. The result of our testing indicates that the Goodness of Fit (GFI = 0.963) and Tucker Lewis Index (TLI = 0.971) respect the 0.9 cutoff value revealing that the present data fits quite well with the proposed measurement model (Table 3). In conclusion, the three-factor model (Influential Factors, Influential Actions, and Decision Support) yielded a good fit for the data (Figure 11).

Table 3. Results of the Confirmatory Factor Analysis.

Measure	Estimate	Threshold	Interpretation	Cutoff Criteria			
CMIN	116.777	—	—				
DF	50	—	—	Measure	Terrible	Acceptable	Excellent
CMIN/DF	2.336	Between 1 and 3	Excellent	CMIN/DF	>5	>3	>1
CFI	0.978	>0.95	Excellent	CFI	<0.90	<0.95	>0.95
SRMR	0.041	<0.08	Excellent	SRMR	>0.10	>0.08	<0.08
RMSEA	0.052	<0.06	Excellent	RMSEA	>0.08	>0.06	<0.06
PClose	0.382	>0.05	Excellent	PClose	<0.01	<0.05	>0.05

CMIN: Chi-square value, DF: Degree of freedom, CFI: comparative fit index, SRMR: standardized root mean square, RMSEA: Square Error of. Approximation, PClose: a statistical significance test of the RMSEA.

We assessed the construct reliability using Composite Reliability (C.R.), a measure of internal consistency in scale items, similar to Cronbach's alpha. According to Table 4 their values range from 0.755 to 0.891, above the 0.70 benchmarks, indicating internal consistency. The convergent validity of scale items (the extent to which a measure relates to other measures of the same phenomenon) was estimated using Average Variance (AVE) whose threshold value is 0.50. Therefore, the scales used for the present study hold the required convergent validity.

Table 4. Discriminant Validity of the Latent Variables.

	CR	AVE	Decision Support	Influential Actions	Influential Factors
Decision Support	0.891	0.578	0.761		
Influential Actions	0.755	0.508	0.447 ***	0.712	0.454 ***
Influential Factors	0.873	0.702	0.434 ***		0.838

CR: Composite Reliability, AVE: Average Variance. *** Level of confidence of 99%.

5.4. Principal Component Analysis (PCA)

We conducted Principal Component Analysis (PCA) to arrive at a concise summary of the findings in this study. Table 5 shows the result of our analysis. Concerning the influential factors (personal, social, and financial factors) latent category, only the second component of PCA is key where all standardized regression weights are greater than 0.6 As such, Business Opportunities, Initial and Future income are the most critical reasons for students' major decisions. The remaining four PCA components (third, fourth, fifth and sixth) associated with these unobservable variables of our measurement model are irrelevant. Concerning the influential factors, we considered the fourth PCA component which indicated that Internet Search, Brochures, and Workshops are critical variables. At last, we considered component one of PCA to assess decision support variables. However further analysis with SPSS AMOS reduced the variable from 11 to 6, where Skills and Job Demand hold the highest loading factors (0.8). Further, how the major aligns with the UAE vision is critical for the students to decide on their major.

Table 5. Principal Component Analysis (PCA) of the study variables.

	Component					
	1	2	3	4	5	6
Personal Factors						
Passion	0.185	0.040	0.750	0.196	−0.148	0.122
Suitable Skills	0.232	0.046	0.778	0.158	−0.083	−0.037
Career Advancement	0.208	0.473	0.581	0.063	0.056	−0.079
Career Flexibility	0.101	0.203	0.601	0.049	0.208	0.038
Gender Suitability	0.157	0.273	0.708	−0.019	0.083	0.104
Social Factors						
Parents	0.074	0.205	0.047	0.238	0.636	−0.205
Siblings	0.008	0.033	0.027	0.021	0.749	0.118
Friends	0.017	0.036	−0.049	0.048	0.686	0.320
Prestige	0.142	0.352	0.218	0.170	0.507	0.247
Celebrities	0.071	0.155	−0.053	0.193	0.217	0.716
Social Media	0.072	0.095	0.162	0.232	0.064	0.694

Table 5. *Cont.*

	Component					
	1	2	3	4	5	6
Financial Factors						
Initial Income	0.182	0.801	0.140	0.211	0.068	0.120
Future Income	0.194	0.806	0.177	0.166	0.068	0.185
Business Opportunities	0.152	0.662	0.266	0.180	0.102	−0.033
Influential Actions						
Expert Discussions	0.067	0.145	0.048	0.583	0.253	0.081
Family Discussions	0.152	0.297	0.138	0.493	0.386	−0.275
Internet Search	0.237	0.175	0.220	0.631	−0.148	0.127
Brochures	0.144	0.196	0.096	0.727	−0.015	0.159
Social Media	0.163	0.046	0.226	0.587	−0.109	0.427
Workshops	0.035	0.019	−0.036	0.638	0.267	0.105
Decision Support						
Job Demand	0.751	0.337	0.055	−0.079	0.030	−0.086
Job Responsibilities	0.765	0.298	0.114	0.025	0.036	−0.122
Job Flexibility	0.743	0.259	0.130	0.027	−0.005	−0.036
Income	0.754	0.375	0.072	−0.007	−0.005	−0.062
Skills	0.728	0.135	0.268	0.136	−0.016	−0.088
Expert Interviews	0.785	−0.120	0.101	0.210	0.034	0.081
Alumni Interviews	0.738	−0.127	0.065	0.147	0.043	0.135
Related Businesses	0.757	0.020	0.074	0.132	0.086	0.146
Related Research	0.708	−0.080	0.138	0.254	0.032	0.184
Job Nature	0.764	0.132	0.121	0.116	−0.016	0.086
UAE Vision	0.738	0.154	0.158	0.011	0.064	0.077

5.5. Hypothesis Testing

Independent Samples *t*-tests were conducted to test the first five hypotheses. While for the last two hypotheses, the bivariate Pearson Correlation was used to measure the relationship strength and direction between the two variables. Moreover, we used an alpha level of 0.05 for all statistical tests.

5.5.1. Testing H1 (12-Year GPA Affects Students' Decision to Choose STEM Majors)

To examine the first hypothesis, we classified the college majors as either STEM (N = 188 respondents) or non-STEM (N = 303). STEM majors were defined as those belonging to: Engineering, Information Technology, Natural Science, Life Science, and Medicine. The major variable was then assigned a value of 1 if the student selected a STEM major and a value of 0 if they chose otherwise. After that, we calculated the average GPA score for each group. The H1 hypothesis's test results showed no statistically significant difference ($t492 = 1.623$, $p = 0.105$) between the average score (GPA) of students who selected STEM majors (M = 87.52, SD = ±8.80) and students who selected non-STEM majors (M = 86.14, SD = ±9.47).

5.5.2. Testing H2 (Expected Earning Affects Students' Decision to Choose STEM Majors)

The result of the test does not support the hypothesis ($t495 = 1.214$, $p = 0.225$) since there is no significant difference between the means of Future Income (one of the influential factors) of STEM students (M = 2.65, S.D. = ±1.13 Avg. score) and students of other majors (M = 2.52, S.D. = ±1.18 Avg. score).

5.5.3. Testing H3 (Business Opportunities Affect Students' Decision to Choose STEM Majors)

The result of testing the hypothesis shows that the availability of business opportunities is essential for students choosing STEM majors (M = 2.87, S.D. = ±1.19 Avg. score) compared to students of other majors (M = 2.55, S.D. = ±1.24 Avg. score), t495= 2.825 $p = 0.005$). Since the p-values for the hypothesis are smaller than the significance level, the H3 result has strengthened our hypotheses.

5.5.4. Testing H4 (Prestige Affects Students' Decision to Choose STEM Majors)

The result of the test strongly supports (t376.014 = 2.237, $p = 0.026$) the hypothesis that there is a statistically significant difference between STEM students' answers about prestige importance (M = 2.45, S.D. = ±1.36 Avg. score) compared to students of other majors (M = 2.17, S.D. = ±1.28 Avg. score).

5.5.5. Testing H5 (Career Advancement Affects Students' Decision to Choose STEM Majors)

The result of testing H5 supports the impact of career advancement on STEM students. There is a statistical difference (t495 = 3.823, $p = 0.001$) in students choosing STEM majors expecting career advancement (M = 3.28, SD = ±1.03 Avg. score) than other students of different majors (M = 2.92, SD = ±1.02 Avg. score).

5.5.6. Testing H6 (Career Flexibility Affects Female Students' Major Decisions)

The T-test results of the H6 show no difference (t495 = 0.167, $p = 0.867$) in the Career Flexibility factor between female students (M = 2.45, SD = ±1.24 Avg. score) and male students (M =2.50, SD = ±1.34 Avg. score).

5.5.7. Testing H7 (Students Who Are Passionate about a Certain Major Also Tend to Have the Right Skills for It)

In testing the hypothesis, we found a correlation between students' passion for the college major (M = 2.93, S.D. = ±1.06 Avg. score) and the skills needed for that major (M = 2.85, S.D. = ±1.04 Avg. score). The correlation is moderately positive and statically significant (r = 0.654, $p < 0.001$).

6. Discussion

6.1. What Factors Influence Students' Major Decisions?

This study aimed to investigate the factors influencing female students to choose their majors. The results show that most students (>70%) cited choosing a major suited for their gender and one where they expect career advancement. Concerning gender, our results are consistent with various studies showing that male and female students prefer different majors [30,31,33]. Indeed, some majors, such as nursing, are female-dominated [64], while STEM majors tend to be favored more by male students [32]. However, contrary to the extant literature on women desiring a flexible career, we did not find a significant indication for female students to choose their major based on career flexibility. This finding is a novel insight that must be investigated in future research.

Concerning career advancement, most studies shied away from addressing students' career aspirations when selecting their majors. A recent study showed that students understand the connection between majors and careers. However, less than half of them have a career plan when they select their major [65]. However, our results provide fresh insight into the relationship between projected career growth and major selection.

The results also show that students' passion and belief in their skills somewhat influence college major decisions. Intriguingly, our correlative analysis shows most students who choose their major based on passion also do so because they believe they have the right skills for the major. This finding is consistent with previous studies showing that students' interest in the major is a major driver for choosing that major [22,25,37,38]. Similarly, students' perception of their abilities has been cited as a crucial factor in college major decisions [28,39]. However, it is crucial to help students align their self-perceived skills with their goals when selecting their majors [8,21,23,37].

This research shows that financial factors are highly influential in students' college majors. Indeed, more than half of the students thought that initial income, growth of income, and availability of business opportunities were highly to moderately influential in their major decision. Unsurprisingly, the three factors (initial income, growth of income, and business opportunities) were highly correlated. Further, our Confirmatory Factor Analysis and Principal Component Analysis have shown that financial factors significantly influence students' major decisions. Our results are consistent with the literature, where students contemplate income [14,21], although they may not have realistic expectations about it [27]. However, according to our analysis, some personal factors (e.g., gender, career advancement, passion) were not significant

This research shows that social factors such as friends are not highly influential for most students. However, some moderate influence was found for the influence of prestige and social media. Concerning friends' influence, our results are in line with a study conducted in Saudi Arabia, a neighboring country [21], and other relevant studies conducted in the U.S. [22] and Sri Lanka [23]. However, our results differ from the findings reported in a study conducted in Poland [13], highlighting the influence of family members' opinions. Concerning prestige, our results agree with findings in other studies indicating that social status has a high impact on students joining a medical school in China [66] as well as undergraduate students in Saudi Arabia [21].

6.2. How Do the Students Choose Their Majors?

The study shows that by far, most students conduct an internet search and use social media to help them decide on their major and that it highly or moderately influences more than half of the students. Existing research on this topic is scarce. However, a recent study cites that students likely use social media and search for college major information on the internet [67]. Interestingly, our correlative analysis also indicates a high correlation between internet searches, social media, and brochures. The correlative analysis is supported by the Confirmatory Factor Analysis and Principal Component Analysis, which identified brochure reading, social media, and internet search as influential activities that students engage in before major-selection decisions. We found it surprising that brochures, a relatively old marketing method, are still impactful amongst Z-generation students.

In comparison, other activities, such as expert discussions and workshops, are less influential for most students. This insight could be helpful to decision-makers to invest in activities deemed significant for z-generation students. Consequently, the availability of college major information online is crucial for students. Future researchers are invited to investigate how students engage in major-selection decisions as some of our results are unique and could be challenged.

6.3. How Can We Support Future Students in Choosing Their Major?

This study shows that students value the availability of information to help them decide on their major. Most students rated most decision support options highly or moderately influential (Figure 7). However, our Confirmatory Factor Analysis and Principal Component Analysis show that students particularly appreciate information about major-related jobs in terms of demand, skills, income, and responsibilities. The correlative analysis reinforces the results as job demand and responsibilities are highly correlated with income. Further, students would also benefit from knowing how their jobs align with the UAE vision, and finally, interviews with experts in the domain are also considered helpful by many students. A study attempted to design a tool showing such information to the students [68], although the tool focused on IT students. Nevertheless, most students found the tool helpful. As such, future researchers are encouraged to study more closely what information is reliable and helpful for future students to decide on their major.

6.4. Influencers of STEM Students' Major Decisions

This research has focused on the factors influencing STEM students' major decisions and uncovered five findings. First, we did not find concrete evidence for the 12-year GPA affecting students' decision to choose STEM majors. This finding contradicts various studies highlighting that high GPAs are associated with STEM majors, such as [45,69]. Second, no statistical evidence was found for the effect of expected earnings on STEM majors. This finding is inconsistent with an existing study citing that an increase in expected wages for average graduates from STEM fields by ten percent raises the probability of choosing a STEM major by about four percent [70]. Third, we found significant statistical evidence showing that students choosing STEM majors rated business opportunities differently than others. We could not find a study that tested this hypothesis. Still, a related study has found that engineering (a branch of STEM) students exhibited more favorable attitudes toward entrepreneurship than other students [71]. Nevertheless, further investigation is needed to tackle this topic. Fourth, our results show that students choosing STEM degrees consider prestige more important. Existing studies such as [21] have cited prestige as a fact that students generally consider. However, this study contributes a unique insight into the relationship between social status and the desire to join STEM degrees. Fifth, our results point to significant evidence for the relationship between the expectation of career growth and the STEM degree choice. We find it unsurprising that students associated STEM majors with career advancement, considering the market demand for such majors and their possibilities for career growth.

7. Study Limitations

Several limitations may have affected the results of our study. First, the study was conducted at one university in the UAE at two campuses (Abu Dhabi and Dubai). As such, the surveyed students may not represent all the students at the same level in the UAE. Second, the study sample is dominated by female students. Despite the presence of a minority of male students in the survey, this study mostly represents female students. As such, future researchers may replicate the study with a more balanced number of female and male participants. Third, most of the participants are Emirati nationals, and only a few are international UAE-based students. Consequently, this study is not representative of all UAE-based students. Despite the limitations, the findings of the study should still be considered a valuable case study because of the interesting findings for decision-makers.

8. Conclusions

This research investigated the factors influencing mostly female UAE students at Zayed University to select their majors. Further, the study explored students' actions to help them form a major decision. Last, the study evaluated what information could be helpful to support future students with college major decisions. Our findings are as follows. Students are mainly influenced by financial factors such as initial and future income and business opportunities that their future major could unfold. Further, there is some influence of personal factors such as gender suitability and passion for the career. On the other hand, social factors such as parents, siblings, or friends are less influential for most students.

This research also identified that most students conduct internet searches, use social media, and read brochures, and such actions greatly influence most students. On the other hand, workshops and discussions with experts are mostly uninfluential or not done at all. In terms of information that could be helpful for college major decisions, students cited major alignment with the UAE vision and job-related information such as income, skills, and responsibilities.

This research uncovered interesting findings about students who chose STEM majors. Those students seem to be more influenced by the availability of business opportunities than others. Further, they cited prestige as a more important influencer on their decision than others. Finally, they are more influenced by the potential for career growth than others.

Author Contributions: Conceptualization, M.A.K., J.N. and H.A.K.; Methodology, M.A.K. and J.N.; Software, M.A.K. and J.N.; Formal analysis, M.A.K. and J.N.; Investigation, M.A.K., J.N., H.A.K., S.K. and S.A.; Data curation, M.A.K., H.A.K., S.K. and S.A.; Writing—original draft, M.A.K., J.N., H.A.K. and S.K.; Writing—review & editing, M.A.K., J.N., H.A.K., S.K. and S.A.; Visualization, M.A.K., J.N., S.K. and S.A.; Supervision, M.A.K., J.N. and H.A.K.; Project administration, M.A.K.; Funding acquisition, M.A.K. All authors have read and agreed to the published version of the manuscript.

Funding: This work was supported by Zayed University, UAE, under grant number R20131.

Institutional Review Board Statement: The study was approved by the Research Ethics Committee of Zayed University (Application No. ZU21_004_F).

Informed Consent Statement: Informed consent was obtained from the participants of this study.

Data Availability Statement: The datasets generated during and/or analyzed during the current study are available from the corresponding author on reasonable request.

Conflicts of Interest: The authors declare no conflict of interest.

References

1. Calderon, A. *Massfication of Higher Education Revisited*; RMIT University: Melbourne, Australia, 2018.
2. Hanushek, E.; Woessmann, L. Education and economic growth. *Econ. Educ.* **2010**, *60*, 67.
3. Peterson, P.L.; Baker, E.; McGaw, B. *International Encyclopedia of Education*; Elsevier: Amsterdam, The Netherlands, 2010; pp. 245–252.
4. Regulatory Authorities of Higher Education. The Official Portal of the UAE Government, 14 June 2022. Available online: https://u.ae/en/information-and-services/education/higher-education/regulatory-authorities-of-higher-education (accessed on 17 June 2022).
5. McMinn, M.; Dickson, M.; Areepattamannil, S. Reported pedagogical practices of faculty in higher education in the UAE. *High. Educ.* **2020**, *83*, 395–410. [CrossRef]
6. Ashour, S. Quality higher education is the foundation of a knowledge society: Where does the UAE stand? *Qual. High. Educ.* **2020**, *26*, 209–223. [CrossRef]
7. Emirates Competitiveness Council. *The Heart of Competiveness: Higher Education Creating the UAE's Future*; Policy in Action; Emirates Competitiveness Council: Dubai, United Arab Emirates, 2014.
8. Galotti, K.M. Making a "major" real-life decision: College students choosing an academic major. *J. Educ. Psychol.* **1999**, *91*, 379. [CrossRef]
9. Freedman, L. The developmental disconnect in choosing a major: Why institutions should prohibit choice until second year. *Mentor Acad. Advis. J.* **2013**, *2*. Available online: https://journals.psu.edu/mentor/article/view/61278/60911 (accessed on 25 December 2022).
10. Hastings, J.S.; Neilson, C.A.; Ramirez, A.; Zimmerman, S.D. (Un) informed college and major choice: Evidence from linked survey and administrative data. *Econ. Educ.* **2016**, *51*, 136–151. [CrossRef]
11. Altonji, J.G.; Blom, E.; Meghir, C. Heterogeneity in human capital investments: High school curriculum, college major, and careers. *Annu. Rev. Econ.* **2012**, *4*, 185–223. [CrossRef]
12. Bartolj, T.; Polanec, S. College major choice and ability: Why is general ability not enough? *Econ. Educ. Rev.* **2012**, *31*, 996–1016. [CrossRef]
13. Sojkin, B.; Bartkowiak, P.; Skuza, A. Determinants of higher education choices and student satisfaction: The case of Poland. *High. Educ.* **2012**, *63*, 565–581. [CrossRef]
14. Boudarbat, B.; Montmarquette, C. Choice of fields of study of university Canadian graduates: The role of gender and their parents' education. *Educ. Econ.* **2009**, *17*, 185–213. [CrossRef]
15. Mahani, S.; Molki, A. Factors influencing female Emirati students' decision to study engineering. *Glob. J. Eng. Educ.* **2011**, *13*, 26–31.
16. Šorgo, A.; Virtič, M.P. Engineers do not grow on trees. *Glob. J. Eng. Educ.* **2020**, *22*, 168–173.
17. Fernandes, C.; Ross, K.; Meraj, M. Understanding student satisfaction and loyalty in the UAE HE sector. *Int. J. Educ. Manag.* **2013**, *27*, 613–630. [CrossRef]
18. Davies, M.A.; Tikoo, S.; Ding, J.L.; Salama, M. Motives underlying the choice of business majors: A multi-country comparison. *Int. J. Manag. Educ.* **2016**, *14*, 50–61. [CrossRef]
19. Makhmasi, S.; Zaki, R.; Barada, H.; Al-Hammadi, Y. Students' interest in STEM education: A survey from the UAE. In Proceedings of the 2012 IEEE Global Engineering Education Conference (EDUCON), Marrakesh, Morocco, 17–20 April 2012.

20. Hammour, H. Influence of the attitudes of Emirati students on their choice of accounting as a profession. *Account. Educ.* **2018**, 27, 433–451. [CrossRef]
21. Aldosary, A.S.; Assaf, S.A. Analysis of factors influencing the selection of college majors by newly admitted students. *High. Educ. Policy* **1996**, *9*, 215–220. [CrossRef]
22. Charles, A.M.; Martha, A.H.; Priscilla, A.B. Influences on students' choice of college major. *J. Educ. Bus.* **2005**, *80*, 275–282.
23. Saranapala, I.S.; Devadas, U.M. Factors Influencing on Career Choice of Management and Commerce Undergraduates in National Universities in Sri Lanka. *Kelaniya J. Hum. Resour. Manag.* **2020**, *15*, 108. [CrossRef]
24. Yu, S.; Zhang, F.; Nunes, L.D.; Levesque-Bristol, C. Self-determined motivation to choose college majors, its antecedents, and outcomes: A cross-cultural investigation. *J. Vocat. Behav.* **2018**, *108*, 132–150. [CrossRef]
25. Sahin, A.; Waxman, H.C.; Demirci, E.; Rangel, V.S. An investigation of harmony public school students' college enrollment and STEM major selection rates and perceptions of factors in STEM major selection. *Int. J. Sci. Math. Educ.* **2020**, *18*, 1249–1269. [CrossRef]
26. Tan, L.M.; Laswad, F. Understanding students' choice of academic majors: A longitudinal analysis. *Account. Educ. Int. J.* **2009**, *18*, 233–253. [CrossRef]
27. Baker, R.; Bettinger, E.; Jacob, B.; Marinescu, I. The effect of labor market information on community college students' major choice. *Econ. Educ. Rev.* **2018**, *65*, 18–30. [CrossRef]
28. Bordón, P.; Canals, C.; Mizala, A. The gender gap in college major choice in Chile. *Econ. Educ. Rev.* **2020**, *77*, 102011. [CrossRef]
29. Montmarquette, C.; Cannings, K.; Mahseredjian, S. How do young people choose college majors? *Econ. Educ. Rev.* **2002**, *21*, 543–556. [CrossRef]
30. Verdín, D.; Godwin, A. Confidence in Pursuing Engineering: How First-Generation College Students' Subject-Related Role Identities Supports their Major Choice. In Proceedings of the 2021 IEEE Frontiers in Education Conference (FIE), Lincoln, NE, USA, 13–16 October 2021.
31. Wiswall, M.; Zafar, B. Determinants of college major choice: Identification using an information experiment. *Rev. Econ. Stud.* **2015**, *82*, 791–824. [CrossRef]
32. Lowinger, R.; Song, H.A. Factors associated with Asian American students' choice of STEM major. *J. Stud. Aff. Res. Pract.* **2017**, *54*, 415–428. [CrossRef]
33. Speer, J.D. The gender gap in college major: Revisiting the role of pre-college factors. *Labour Econ.* **2017**, *44*, 69–88. [CrossRef]
34. Cech, E.A.; Blair-Loy, M. The changing career trajectories of new parents in STEM. *Proc. Natl. Acad. Sci. USA* **2019**, *116*, 4182–4187. [CrossRef]
35. Peters, D. The Engineering Gender Gap: It's More than a Numbers Game. Available online: https://www.universityaffairs.ca features/feature-article/the-engineering-gender-gap-its-more-than-a-numbers-game/ (accessed on 17 December 2022).
36. Sterling, A.D.; Thompson, M.E.; Wang, S.; Kusimo, A.; Gilmartin, S.; Sheppard, S. The confidence gap predicts the gender pay gap among STEM graduates. *Soc. Sci.* **2020**, *117*, 30303–30308. [CrossRef]
37. Shaaban, K. Investigating the reasons for choosing a major among the engineering students in Qatar. In Proceedings of the IEEE Global Engineering Education Conference (EDUCON), Abu Dhabi, United Arab Emirates, 10–13 April 2016.
38. Ogowewo, B.O. Factors Influencing Career Choice Among Secondary School Students: Implications for Career Guidance. *Int. Interdiscip. Soc. Sci.* **2010**, *5*, 451–460. [CrossRef]
39. Betz, N.E.; Hackett, G. The relationship of mathematics self-efficacy expectations to the selection of science-based college majors. *J. Vocat. Behav.* **1983**, *23*, 329–345. [CrossRef]
40. Cho, J.; Jones, S.; Olsen, D. An exploratory study on factors influencing major selection. *Issues Inf. Syst.* **2008**, *9*, 168–175.
41. Gómez, J.; Tayebi, A.; Delgado, C. Factors That Influence Career Choice in Engineering Students in Spain: A Gender Perspective. *IEEE Trans. Educ.* **2021**, *65*, 81–92. [CrossRef]
42. Abbasi, M.N.; Sarwat, N. Factors inducing career choice: Comparative study of five leading professions in Pakistan. *Pak. J. Commer. Soc. Sci.* **2014**, *8*, 830–845.
43. Sharif, N.; Ahmad, N.; Sarwar, S. Factors influencing career choices. *IBT J. Bus. Stud.* **2019**, *15*, 33–46. [CrossRef]
44. Kori, K.; Altin, H.; Pedaste, M.; Palts, T.; Tõnisson, E. What influences students to study information and communication technology. In Proceedings of the 8th International Technology, Education and Development Conference, Valencia, Spain, 10–12 March 2014; pp. 1477–1486.
45. Moakler, M.W., Jr.; Kim, M.M. College major choice in STEM: Revisiting confidence and demographic factors. *Career Dev. Q.* **2014**, *62*, 128–142. [CrossRef]
46. Gonzalez, H.B.; Kuenzi, J.J. *Science, Technology, Engineering, and Mathematics (STEM) Education: A Primer*; Congressional Research Service, Library of Congress: Washington, DC, USA, 2012.
47. Mau, W.C.J. Characteristics of US Students That Pursued a STEM Major and Factors That Predicted Their Persistence in Degree Completion. *Univers. J. Educ. Res.* **2016**, *4*, 1495–1500. [CrossRef]
48. Wang, X. Why students choose STEM majors: Motivation, high school learning, and postsecondary context of support. *Am. Educ. Res. J.* **2013**, *50*, 1081–1121. [CrossRef]
49. Lee, A. Students with Disabilities Choosing Science Technology Engineering and Math (STEM) Majors in Postsecondary Institutions. *J. Postsecond. Educ. Disabil.* **2014**, *27*, 261–272.
50. Berger, M.C. Predicted future earnings and choice of college major. *ILR Rev.* **1988**, *41*, 418–429. [CrossRef]

61. Blom, E.; Cadena, B.C.; Keys, B.J. Investment over the business cycle: Insights from college major choice. *J. Labor Econ.* **2021**, *39*, 1043–1082. [CrossRef]

62. Åstebro, T.; Bazzazian, N.; Braguinsky, S. Startups by recent university graduates and their faculty: Implications for university entrepreneurship policy. *Res. Policy* **2012**, *41*, 663–677. [CrossRef]

63. Ucbasaran, D.; Lockett, A.; Wright, M.; Westhead, P. Entrepreneurial founder teams: Factors associated with member entry and exit. *Entrep. Theory Pract.* **2003**, *28*, 107–128. [CrossRef]

64. Colombo, M.G.; Piva, E. Start-ups launched by recent STEM university graduates: The impact of university education on entrepreneurial entry. *Res. Policy* **2020**, *49*, 103993. [CrossRef]

65. Breznitz, S.M.; Zhang, Q. Determinants of graduates' entrepreneurial activity. *Small Bus. Econ.* **2020**, *55*, 1039–1056. [CrossRef]

66. Pitt, R.N.; Zhu, L. The Relationship between College Major Prestige/Status and Post-baccalaureate Outcomes. *Sociol. Perspect.* **2018**, *62*, 325–345. [CrossRef]

67. Bray, S.; Palmer, S. Reasons stated by commencing students for studying engineering and technology. *Australas. J. Eng. Educ.* **2006**, 1–18. Available online: https://typeset.io/papers/reasons-stated-by-commencing-students-for-studying-2bdsd4vllt (accessed on 25 December 2022).

68. Kahn, S.; Ginther, D. *Women and Science, Technology, Engineering, and Mathematics (STEM): Are Differences in Education and Careers Due to Stereotypes, Interests, or Family?* Averett, S.L., Ed.; Oxford Handbooks Online: Oxford, UK, 2017.

69. Frome, P.M.; Alfeld, C.J.; Eccles, J.S.; Barber, B.L. Why don't they want a male-dominated job? An investigation of young women who changed their occupational aspirations. *Educ. Res. Eval.* **2006**, *12*, 359–372. [CrossRef]

70. Flabbi, L.; Moro, A. The effect of job flexibility on female labor market outcomes: Estimates from a search and bargaining model. *J. Econom.* **2012**, *168*, 81–95. [CrossRef]

71. Jiang, S.; Simpkins, S.D.; Eccles, J.S. Individuals' math and science motivation and their subsequent STEM choices and achievement in high school and college: A longitudinal study of gender and college generation status differences. *Dev. Psychol.* **2020**, *56*, 2137. [CrossRef]

72. Heilbronner, N.N. Stepping onto the STEM pathway: Factors affecting talented students' declaration of STEM majors in college. *J. Educ. Gift.* **2011**, *34*, 876–899. [CrossRef]

73. Forms, G. Understanding How UAE Students Select Their Majors. Available online: https://docs.google.com/forms/d/e/1FAIpQLSfhgKA3QZRyznVN5ZwZx2XBaYNJ4542jiPL7doT9s7Gp9S1iw/viewform (accessed on 2 September 2022).

74. McDowell, J.; Schaffner, S. Football, it's a man's game: Insult and gendered discourse in The Gender Bowl. *Discourse Soc.* **2011**, *22*, 547–564. [CrossRef]

75. Lehmann, C.R. *The Influence of Career Motivation on College Major Choice*; Rowan University: Glassboro, NJ, USA, 2019.

76. Yang, C.; Jin, X.; Yan, J.; Zhang, J.; Chen, C.; Cheng, Y.; Deng, G. An investigation of the intention and reasons of senior high school students in China to choose medical school. *BMC Med. Educ.* **2021**, *21*, 1–10. [CrossRef]

77. Pharr, J.M. *Facilitating the Choice of College Major Using the Consumer Decision Process, Content Marketing, and Social Media*; Georgia Southern University: Statesboro, GA, USA, 2022.

78. Kuhail, M.A.; Al Katheeri, H.; Negreiros, J. MyMajor: Assisting IT students with major selection. *Glob. J. Eng. Educ.* **2021**, *23*, 197.

79. Vaarmets, T. Gender, academic abilities and postsecondary educational choices. *J. Appl. Res. High. Educ.* **2018**, *10*, 380–398. [CrossRef]

80. Osikominu, A.; Feifer, G. Perceived Wages and the Gender Gap in Stem Fields. 2018, p. 11321. Available online: https://www.iza.org/publications/dp/11321/perceived-wages-and-the-gender-gap-in-stem-fields (accessed on 25 March 2022).

81. Dao, T.K.; Bui, A.T.; Doan, T.T.T.; Dao, N.T.; Le, H.H.; Le, T.T.H. Impact of academic majors on entrepreneurial intentions of Vietnamese students: An extension of the theory of planned behavior. *Heliyon* **2021**, *7*, e06381. [CrossRef] [PubMed]

Article

No Budge for any Nudge: Information Provision and Higher Education Application Outcomes

Sonia Ilie [1,*], Konstantina Maragkou [1], Ashton Brown [1] and Eliza Kozman [2]

[1] The Faculty of Education, University of Cambridge, Cambridge CB2 1TN, UK
[2] Behavioural Insights Team, Centre for Transforming Access and Student Outcomes (TASO), London SW1H 9EA, UK
* Correspondence: isi22@cam.ac.uk

Abstract: Despite increasing efforts to improve their access, students facing socio-economic disadvantages are still underrepresented in UK higher education. In this paper, we study whether behavioural nudging with information provision through text messages, embedded within a larger programme of widening participation activities, can be effective at increasing higher education application rates. We conducted two randomised control trials in which final year students in schools and further education colleges in areas with low higher education participation rates in the East of England region received a series of text messages that prompted thinking and/or action regarding the process of applying to higher education. We find null and statistically insignificant effects on application outcomes, suggesting that behavioural nudging in a setting where it is implemented as part of a more intensive widening participation programme is not effective at increasing higher education application rates. These results add to recent evidence regarding the potential impact of nudging in education by studying such interventions within a busy intervention space.

Keywords: randomised control trial; higher education outreach; higher education applications; widening participation; information provision

Citation: Ilie, S.; Maragkou, K.; Brown, A.; Kozman, E. No Budge for any Nudge: Information Provision and Higher Education Application Outcomes. *Educ. Sci.* **2022**, *12*, 701. https://doi.org/10.3390/educsci12100701

Academic Editor: Diana Dias

Received: 16 August 2022
Accepted: 6 October 2022
Published: 13 October 2022

1. Introduction

The need for policy interventions to raise higher education access and participation rates among people who face socio-economic disadvantages is widely acknowledged in the academic literature. Existing evidence from England, the context of our study, suggests that the socio-economic gap in higher education participation can be explained to a great extent by differences in prior attainment during secondary school, rather than by barriers arising at the point of entry to higher education [1]. At the same time, when people from less advantaged socio-economic backgrounds do participate in higher education, they are less likely to make optimal decisions in terms of choice of institution or course in comparison to their similarly achieving but more advantaged peers [2]. Both the higher education application processes and the decision-making around that are recognised as complex [3,4]. Such evidence highlights the need for policy interventions that can effectively support the attainment raising efforts of schools and colleges, potentially simplify processes and the information space around them, and provide gentle nudges to individuals to use such information as best as possible, about whichever post-compulsory education pathway they choose [5,6].

In England, the recent period has seen the implementation of a variety of outreach widening participation in higher education programmes and interventions. These interventions have attracted substantial governmental, institutional, and third-sector funding. With outreach and widening participation programming growing and diversifying, causal evidence of impact is increasingly important for improving funders' decisions regarding which programmes to prioritise, providers' decisions about the format and content of such programmes, and young people's decisions about which programmes to attend. This evidence, however, is often lacking [7] or faces the challenge of so-called 'black box' programmes. There is some evidence [7] that these 'black box' programmes, often encompassing a variety of interventions, are effective, especially when combining, for instance, the simplification of the application processes with individual support [8] but disentangling between their constituent parts is often difficult. Further evidence [5,9,10] suggests that particular types of interventions, specifically nudging programmes which provide participants with relevant information and seek to spark certain behaviours, are effective at improving both application rates and take-up of places in higher education. Even as very recent evidence finds small and inconsistent effects from nudge interventions [11], the provision of information is an established form of higher education outreach in the English context and there is some causal evidence [12] that, alongside further support, the provision of accurate information increases application rates, particularly to selective universities.

It is therefore essential to understand the impact of discrete and stand-alone interventions on higher education applications and access, especially if they are delivered in an otherwise busy intervention space. In this paper, we therefore present results from an experimental study evaluating the ways in which a behavioural nudging information-provision intervention has affected higher education application rates when deployed within a larger programme of higher education outreach in the East of England region.

1.1. Aims of the Paper

We report results from two randomised control trials (RCTs) designed to evaluate the effect of a light-touch information-providing (via text message) nudge intervention embedded within a larger programme of widening participation activities. The aim of the specific nudge intervention was to increase the probability of students applying to higher education. The trials, using the same experimental design in each of the two iterations of trialling, involved a total of 935 students in the final year of compulsory-age education, enrolled in 58 schools and colleges in the East of England region during the academic years 2017–2018 and 2018–2019.

The programme within which this intervention was embedded is the ongoing Take Your Place programme (hereafter, the programme) undertaken since 2017 by the Network for East Anglian Collaborative Outreach (neaco). The programme targets students living in socio-economically deprived geographic areas and delivers outreach activities in schools and further education colleges with high proportions of such students. The aim of the programme is to improve access to broadly defined higher education, by helping students explore their options and academic potentials. We return to a fuller description of the programme after discussing the relevant evidence background.

1.2. Evidence Background

The paper makes several contributions to the emerging literature that employs field experiments to examine nudging as a potential high-benefit and low-cost approach to improve educational outcomes. Although they have become increasingly popular in the field of behavioural economics, there is mixed evidence on the overall effectiveness of such nudging interventions [11]. Field experiments that provide information or reminders to students about the college application process and financial aid availability and eligibility, without the accompanying offer of professional assistance, typically have not led to higher rates of college access or success [13–15]. Using US data, Phillips and Reber [16] found no improvement in low-income students' higher education enrolment rates when they were provided with the information and support that higher-income students typically have. Similarly, Carrell and Sacerdote [17] found that providing students with information on the benefits of attending college had no impact on their attendance and persistence. More recently, Avery et al. [18] found null and negative effects of text message-based outreach on improving US students' college choices and outcomes at a national level, in contrast to positive and significant effects identified from the same intervention when distributed in specific school districts in Texas. In the German context, a separate study [19] found that information nudges increased higher education enrolment for students from a non-academic family background while decreasing (at least in the short-term) the enrolment intentions of students from academic backgrounds.

Overall, studies on nudging interventions in education appear to provide mixed evidence of the effectiveness of such approaches for higher education access and participation outcomes. A recent and comprehensive review of the nudging literature in education [6] suggests that nudging interventions *can* have broad and long-term effects on overall student outcomes but are not effective in all contexts or for all students. A key conclusion of that review highlights the importance of understanding the underlying behavioural mechanisms potentially resulting in application and access, and how closely interventions designed to impact these behavioural mechanisms match them. Furthermore, the broader evidence also suggests the importance of clarifying the conditions under which such intervention can facilitate behaviour change [20], including in terms of the wider context in which they are delivered.

Our focus on the effectiveness of a nudging intervention (delivered through text messages) on increasing university application rates, when the intervention is embedded within a wider range of widening participation activities, is a non-trivial contribution that we provide to this literature. Producing such evidence is important for informing education policy design and for understanding individual decision making. We suggest that by varying one aspect of a programme's provision, it is possible to capture the effectiveness and efficacy of specific programme components. This may contribute to the development of evidenced-based practices for widening participation and outreach practitioners. In addition, we verify the robustness of our empirical findings by repeatedly implementing the trial in two consecutive academic years and finding identical results.

We further contribute to the above debates by providing evidence within a context in which a lack of information, advice, and guidance may be a major driver of socio-economic inequalities in higher education applications. This is relevant both in terms of participation and access to selective institutions [2,21]. This is also relevant since credit constraints [22] and geographic isolation [23] continue to be factors that have been previously identified as equally important drivers of inequalities in higher education access among students from low socio-economic backgrounds in England. Such factors may be mitigated against by an income-contingent loan system that covers the entirety of students' tuition fees, and separately by increasing patterns of localisation, whereby students travel relatively short distances to reach a higher education institution [2]. Against this backdrop, generating evidence around the effectiveness of an outreach intervention, with a clear mechanism that may be delivered straightforwardly and at relatively low cost, is important.

Finally, we show evidence on the differential impact of the intervention by pre-determined student observable characteristics to facilitate previous findings that suggested that the impact of such interventions can be mostly effective on sub-groups of students.

2. The Intervention

The nudging intervention we explore in this paper has been delivered as part of one of the several regional partnerships under Uni Connect, a large-scale government supported initiative. We provide context to Uni Connect and the relevant evidence about its effectiveness below, before describing the specific regional Uni Connect partnership and its outreach programme. We then provide comprehensive information about the nudging intervention.

2.1. The National Context in England

Despite the increasing number of young people accessing higher education, young people facing socio-economic deprivation are still less likely to progress to higher education in England [24]. Factors which are associated with lower progression primarily focus on attainment at school [1], but also include being the first in the family to potentially attend higher education (an aspect associated with relatively less available knowledge of the higher education system) [25], and the economic circumstances of the household [26]. In addition to this, changing labour market conditions [27] and perceptions of their individual potential experiences in higher education [28] also contribute to changing intentions in relation to higher education applications [29].

To tackle these enduring inequalities, a large range of widening participation, fair access, and outreach programmes have been implemented in England. A relatively recent national programme is the government-funded Uni Connect initiative, looking to increase higher education participation across all types of higher education provision (from university to vocational routes) by taking a place-based approach and working regionally with universities, further education colleges, and schools, by delivering tailored programmes of outreach activity. Recent evidence [30,31] suggests that the impact of Uni Connect mirrors its complex nature. This large-scale evaluation work [30,31] takes in the full national programme and finds that both the range of interventions delivered and their relative impact vary by geography. It also finds that the overall impact of the programme is either negligible or has not been possible to causally attribute to the existence of the initiative. This is taken into consideration against a backdrop of recent disruptions and negative impacts from the pandemic and the associated public health crisis. While a further national-level evaluation is still underway, existing findings already suggest a need to disaggregate the constituent parts of Uni Connect activity, much like our present study does. Similarly, the current shift in direction for the next several years of Uni Connect towards attainment-raising interventions means that the earlier stages of the programme offered a unique opportunity to explore an intervention aimed at increasing application rates, rather than any other aspect of the higher education access process. Our study capitalises on this opportunity.

2.2. The Network for East Anglian Collaborative Outreach

The Network for East Anglian Collaborative Outreach (neaco) is one of the 29 regional partnerships under Uni Connect. The partnership has operated since 2017 in the East of England region with support from all universities and further education colleges in the region and delivers Take Your Place, its flagship outreach programme, in areas wherein the higher education participation of young people is low—and much lower than expected, given average attainment at age 16, and socio-economic composition. Students from these areas are classified as "target students" and represent the specific group whose progression to higher education is the key focus of this programme. A total of 106 schools and eight further education colleges were involved in the programme for the period under investigation in this paper.

The programme is special in that the overall approach adopted in the delivery of activities is based on a progressive framework that seeks repeated interactions with students. This is a key feature of the wider, national, and government-supported Uni Connect programme that for the past five years has dominated the higher education outreach landscape in England, alongside higher education provider- and third sector-driven activity. In participating schools and colleges, this translates into Take Your Place being delivered in a way that varies in each school or college, adapting to the needs of each educational setting, their environment, and the available resources.

There are two central foci for the outreach activity delivered by Take Your Place. The first prioritises the development of students' understanding and preparedness by focusing on the specific requirements, means, and option choices through which students can realise their aspirations for transitions between the key stages of the English educational system and into higher education. The second strand of activities is focused on passion and ambition, focusing on enabling students to explore, identify, and articulate their passions and aspirations, giving positive incentives for choosing post-16 and post-18 pathways. The activities delivered by the so-called Higher Education Champions (HECs), an outreach specialist usually embedded in schools and their college-based counterparts, range from information sessions and university campus visits to summer schools and community engagement opportunities.

At the time of the delivery of the first iteration of a behavioural nudging intervention explored in this paper (2017–2018) and the first trial, the delivery of Take Your Place was in its relatively early stages. By 2018–2019, the time of the second iteration of the intervention and the second associated trial, Take Your Place was far more established, both in terms of the scope and the range of activities being delivered. As a recent report for the programme illustrates [32], there continues to be substantial variation in the range of activities that the different schools and colleges engage in as part of Take Your Place, with levels of individual engagement with the programme monitored by the programme team and the target of separate analysis elsewhere. This is an important point as it relates to the potential of the nudging intervention to affect change in an increasingly busy intervention space, an issue we return to in discussing our design of the trial and the implications of our findings.

In addition to the in-school and in-college outreach activities provided by Take Your Place, in its first two years the programme also included a light-touch information-provision element.

This light-touch behavioural nudging intervention is the focus of the randomised control trials reported in this paper and is described below.

2.3. The Behavioural Nudging Intervention

In addition to progressive and sustained provision detailed above, the Take Your Place programme included a light-touch information-provision component. The objective of this behavioural nudging intervention was aligned with the programme's overarching aim, which is to improve the higher education application rates of participating students. The intervention aimed to do this through the provision of easily understandable information that students could act upon. A secondary aim of delivering this intervention was to enable the exploration of this type of information-provision nudging intervention in terms of its effectiveness.

The intervention was delivered in two consecutive school years (2017–2018 and 201–2019), with only minor differences between the two years, all relating to the accuracy of the information provided via text messages to individual participants: the specific dates and deadlines were updated, and the links to any online material shared to students were updated. Otherwise, the intervention was materially the same.

The content of the information related principally to the process of applying to higher education through the Universities and Colleges Admissions Service (UCAS). UCAS is the centralised national admissions system, where all universities and a number of other higher education providers are included. Individuals wanting to apply to university (or the other available types of higher education providers) make one single application through UCAS, to a total of up to five separate degree courses in each year. The intervention studied here provided participants with information about preparatory steps (e.g., drafting a personal statement, identifying appropriate degree courses), as well as practical issues (e.g., navigating the UCAS website and application portal, finding the required information and deadlines) and places where the students could go to find more information about any of the above aspects (such as signposting to teachers and staff of Take Your Place, providing links to relevant information web pages or videos hosted online).

A total of up to 14 text messages were administered to participants in the intervention. However, to recognise that participants may have applied to higher education prior to the deadline, and to avoid irrelevant information being sent to them, two text messages inviting a response were also sent, containing a simple yes/no question regarding whether the individual student had already applied to higher education. For all those responding positively, the text messages stopped, and the individual participants' outcome was recorded as having applied to higher education. Appendix A contains all the text messages that were sent to participants, excluding any links which are no longer available.

The timing of the delivery of the intervention was important, as it needed to align with the application window and relevant deadlines. It was administered starting the last week of October of each respective school year (2017–2018 for the first trial; 2018–2019 for the second trial) and ended in mid-January of the same school year (in the next calendar year), immediately after the application deadline, which regularly falls in the middle of January each year. As Appendix A indicates, the last text message was sent *after* the passing of the application deadline, signposting students to relevant information in terms of options available to them if they still wanted to apply to higher education for the relevant year.

Importantly, the text messages were personalised with the names of the individual participants, using a direct address ("Hi, [student name]!"). This followed evidence according to which personalisation was important in the provision of information in higher education outreach [12], and sought to create rapport with participants, which was hypothesised to increase the likelihood of action following the reception of the text messages.

A large team contributed to the development of the intervention, including staff on the neaco partnership and their institutional partners. The lead researcher was also involved in the set-up of the intervention through the provision of evidence in relation to various decisions (e.g., around personalisation).

3. Trial Design

To estimate the causal impact of the above nudging intervention on higher education application outcomes, two randomised control trials were implemented in each school year when the intervention was delivered (2017–2018 and 2018–2019). Each trial underwent the ethical approval process at the Faculty of Education University of Cambridge. The first of the two trials was jointly undertaken with researchers from the Behavioural Insights Team (BIT) and was registered by them (trial number 2017136). The latter team undertook a separate analysis of data pertaining to the first trial, were only briefly involved in the second trial, and did not undertake the full analysis of data as reported in this paper. We acknowledge their contributions to the first trial and thank them for their insights.

While the two trials were undertaken independently of each other, the testing of the intervention (materially the same across the two implementation years) allows us to pool the data across the two trials. This has implications for the power calculations (reported below), but we also explore the potentially different impacts of the intervention in each respective trial cohort in our later analysis. This is particularly relevant given the embedding of this intervention in the wider Take Your Place programme, which was at different stages of development in the two intervention years.

3.1. Outcome Measure

The outcome measure of interest is whether students applied to higher education via UCAS. This outcome measure was coded as binary, taking the value 1 if students had applied, and the value 0 if they had not applied. The outcome measure was collected with two procedures: first, from self-reported responses on whether they completed their application before the relevant deadline of the respective academic year; and second, with the help of on-the-ground staff, who obtained this information directly from the participants' schools and further education colleges. While there is evidence to support that student responses to this type of question are highly predictive of actual student application [29], the addition of the staff-provided data meant that the outcome measure could be collected from a high proportion of initial trial participants, contributing to very low attrition, as outlined later in this paper.

3.2. Trial Hypotheses

Each of the two trials operated under the same overall research hypothesis, according to which the text-based information-provision nudging intervention may encourage students in their final year of secondary education to apply to higher education via the standard UCAS route. We used a two-tailed test to test the non-directional hypothesis that the rate of application to higher education for students randomly allocated to receive the intervention was no different to that for students randomly allocated to the control condition.

3.3. Trial Characteristics

Both trials were based on individual-randomisation, balanced, two-arm (intervention and control) trials, run under an intention-to-treat approach. The intention-to-treat approach means that all participants randomly allocated to each of the trial conditions remained in that respective condition for the purpose of analysis (barring any missing data) regardless of the (unknowable) level of engagement with the intervention: that is students randomly assigned to the intervention condition were considered as part of this intervention condition even if they did not engage with any of the text messages. It was impossible to monitor engagement with, and immediate actions as a result of, the text messages because the participants' school and home lives were not monitored as part of these trials. They may have engaged in the behaviours suggested by the text messages immediately after receiving them, at a later point, or not at all; or they may have sought information or advice from their school or college. While clearly a limitation, this aligns with the commonly used intention-to-treat approach (analysing data according to the initial allocation result) we have also taken in this trial and means we are minimising the risk of over-stating our results.

We now outline the full experimental set-up and procedure. This applies to both trials.

3.3.1. Participant Recruitment

In the period under consideration for this study, the Take Your Place programme administered two large-scale surveys to students in schools and colleges participating in the wider programme. A separate section in each of these surveys invited final year students (those eligible to apply to higher education) to take part in the randomised control trial.

Detailed but simple information was provided to students as part of this recruitment process. Students were asked for fully informed consent to participate in a trial, with different students reached in the two consecutive years of the trials' implementation.

The information provided to students during this recruitment process included the trial aims, the randomisation procedure (explained as a 50–50 chance of receiving the text messages if taking part in the trial), and information about what the intervention would entail. The participants who consented to taking part were then invited to provide their phone numbers for the purposes of the text messages delivery.

The inclusion/exclusion criterion for the presentation of the recruitment information related to the participants' self-reported likelihood of applying to higher education. As part of the development of the text messages, it was decided that students expressing a very low likelihood of applying to higher education would not benefit from the text messages.

The students' likelihood to apply to higher education was gauged during the survey with a stand-alone 6-point Likert response scale question asking them to rate the likelihood of application at age 18/19 (the relevant age for a vast majority of students in the participating schools and further education colleges).The students were also asked if they had already applied to higher education. Based on the above questions, two formal exclusion criteria were used: first, the students who expressed that they had no intentions to apply to higher education were excluded from the sample eligible to take part in the trial. Second, all students who indicated that they had already applied to higher education were also excluded.

For the first trial, the survey was undertaken between September and early November 2017. A total of just over 21,300 students responded, with just over 4000 final year students invited to take part in the trial. A total of 531 students signed up.

For the second trial, the survey was undertaken between September and late October 2018. A similar number of total respondents was reached, and a total of 439 students signed up to the second trial.

There are two potential implications of this recruitment process. First, the external validity of the trials may be relatively low as participating schools (in the overall Take Your Place programme, and therefore also in the trials) were selected based on specific characteristics of the areas wherein the students lived. The second implication is that we are only able to estimate the impact of digital nudging among students who were willing to receive text messages, with findings not necessarily generalisable to the wider population of Take Your Place students. While this latter issue is important, it is also unavoidable from the perspective of ethical conduct of research and of trials, with prospective participants only recruited into the trial on the basis of full informed consent. To address this concern, we explored responses to a series of relevant learner survey questions (the same survey used for recruitment purposes) including self-reported knowledge of (higher) education options, knowledge of specific education or employment options, and knowledge of where to seek information about such topics, comparing responses between trial participants and trial non-participants in the relevant year group. While this full analysis is beyond the scope of this paper and will be reported elsewhere, we found no statistically significant differences between these two groups on the above variables. This suggests that the self-selected trial participants were not, at least for these observed variables, meaningfully different to the non-participants. We return to issues of external validity when we discuss the results of the trials in relation to the intervention set-up as part of the wider outreach programme.

3.3.2. Randomisation Procedure

Randomisation occurred after the participants had signed up to each respective trial as per the procedure above and it was carried out at the individual level. Randomisation was stratified by target student status (students living in areas where the rate of higher education progression was lower than expected given the average age (16) of attainment) and by student self-reported gender. This was conducted to ensure that any differences in higher education application likelihood by these two characteristics would not represent a bias in the trial.

Randomisation was carried out in statistical software (Stata) using a random number generator with a randomly chosen seed number, and it saw 50% of participants allocated to the intervention condition and 50% of participants allocated to the control condition, separately for each respective trial.

This randomisation approach generated an intervention and a control condition in each trial. While we were not able to monitor participant compliance with allocation, the distribution of text messages was carefully monitored, and no contamination errors at the distribution point were noted. It remains possible, though not highly probable, that the individuals in the intervention condition may have shared text messages, or information therein, with control group counterparts. However, as outlined above, the intervention was designed so that the text messages would build upon each other and follow a progressive and time-specific pattern. Therefore, unless participants in the intervention condition had 'leaked' all the messages and information to participants in the control condition, the intervention would not have been able to be engaged with as designed.

3.3.3. Attrition after Randomisation

A total of 970 eligible participants were recruited into the two trials. Data on the outcome measure (outlined below) were not available for a small number of these participants (3%), with 940 of the 970 (97%) participants across both trials presenting full data for analysis.

For the first trial, 515 participants of the 531 initially recruited were retained in the analysis. Attrition was similar for the control and intervention arms of this trial, at 3% each. For the second trial, 425 participants were retained in the analysis from the recruited total of 439, again with a balanced attrition per arm, at 3% each.

While attrition is always a concern in trials, due to the implications of the internal validity of the analysis, at 3%, the attrition rate for this trial is very low [33]. As such, we did not carry out any imputation checks; however, we did carry out a robustness test, as we detail in the Results section later in this paper.

3.3.4. Balance at Baseline

We examine whether our randomisation created balanced groups at baseline according to the observable characteristics of students. Table 1 below presents the descriptive statistics of the originally randomised sample and the magnitude of the differences between the intervention and control groups (column 3 in Table 1) for the pooled data and across both trials. The observed differences between the two groups are nearly equal to 0. We do not provide tests of statistical significance related to these mean comparisons because to do so would violate the logic of randomisation.

Table 1. Descriptive statistics and mean differences across intervention and control groups, stratification variables at baseline, and pooled data.

	Intervention		Control		Difference
	(1)		(2)		(1)–(2)
	Mean/(sd)	N	Mean/(sd)	N	Mean/(se)
Girl	0.58 (0.49)	484	0.58 (0.49)	486	0.00 (0.03)
Target student	0.33 (0.47)	484	0.33 (0.47)	486	0.00 (0.03)
Total N	970				

Note: The numbers presented in columns (1) and (2) are the mean values for the intervention and control groups. The numbers in parentheses are the standard deviations. The last column presents the mean differences (and the standard errors in parentheses) between the intervention and control groups for each variable.

We then move on to empirically examine the balance across the intervention and control groups for the analytical sample (after attrition, as outlined above). In Table 2, we show balance across the intervention and control groups for the sample with non-missing outcome data.

Table 2. Descriptive statistics and mean differences across intervention and control groups, stratification variables at analysis stage, and pooled data.

	Intervention		Control		Difference
	(1)		(2)		(1)–(2)
	Mean (sd)	N	Mean (sd)	N	Mean (se)
Girl	0.59 (0.49)	468	0.58 (0.49)	472	0.01 (0.04)
Target student	0.32 (0.47)	468	0.33 (0.47)	472	0.01 (0.04)
Total N	940				

Note: The numbers presented in columns (1) and (2) are the mean values for the intervention and control groups. The numbers in parentheses are the standard deviations. The last column presents the mean differences (and the standard errors in parentheses) between the intervention and control groups for each variable.

For the sample of students for whom we have outcome data and non-missing information on all other covariates, we observe no imbalance between trial arms across gender and target status, suggesting that the randomisation was balanced on these observable characteristics. This applies both to the initial baseline and to the post-attrition analytical sample.

3.3.5. Power Calculations

As part of the set-up of the trials, power analyses were conducted to judge the feasibility of detecting an effect of the intervention considering the likely response rate from the students. Given the lack of directly relevant evidence regarding the effect of such an intervention on university application rates at the time of the development of the trials, we calculated the sample sizes using a theorised minimum detectable effect size of 0.2. We assumed a conventional 80% statistical power (i.e., at least an 80% chance of detecting the main effect), and we also assumed that we could explain approximately 50% of the variance in the main outcome with the baseline variables we included, namely demographic characteristics (including 'target' student status and gender). The power calculation test to be run is two-tailed, as although the hypotheses are directional, it is important to statistically test for the eventuality of a negative effect. There parameters resulted in a required sample of 395 participants, half in the control group, and half in the intervention group. Were we to not meet the sample size requirements, a sample of 300 would yield a minimum detectable effect size of 0.229, and a sample of 200 one of 0.282, holding all other assumptions constant. All power calculations were performed in PowerUp! [34].

At the recruitment stage, keeping all other parameters the same as above, the achieved sample yielded a minimum detectable effect size of 0.172 for the first trial and a minimum detectable effect size of 0.190 for the second trial. When pooled, the minimum detectable effect size was 0.127, which is very good for education trials in England, many of which are (under-) powered for a 0.2 effect size [33].

At the analysis stage, we re-calculated the minimum detectable effect sizes. We used the same parameters as above, but instead of estimating the proportion explained variance from the covariates, we obtained this from a simple analysis, which put it at 13%. Together with the slight reduction in sample size, the at-analysis minimum detectable effect size was 0.231 for the first trial, 0.254 for the second trial, and 0.171 for the pooled sample.

3.4. Analytical Strategy

To obtain a causal effect of the information-provision nudging intervention on student outcomes, we compared post-intervention higher education applications by trial condition (intervention status) using the following OLS regression model for student i, in institution s, at year t:

$$Y_{i,s,t}^{Post} = \alpha + \beta_0 Y_{i,s,t}^{Pre} + \beta\, Treat_{i,s,t} + \delta' X_i' + \eta_s + \tau_t + \epsilon_{i,s,t},\ Y_{i,s,t}^{Pre} \neq 0$$

where:

- $Y_{i,s,t}^{Post}$ is a post-intervention binary measure of higher education application;
- $Y_{i,s,t}^{Pre}$ is a pre-intervention self-reported measure of intentions to apply to higher education;
- $Treat_{i,s}$ is a binary variable indicating whether the student was in the intervention or control group (0 = control; 1 = intervention);
- $'X_i'$ is a vector of individual characteristics (the stratification factors) at baseline;
- η_s are the institution fixed effects;
- τ_t is a dummy indicator of academic year (2017–2018 or 2018–2019);
- $\epsilon_{i,s,t}$ is a robust standard error clustered at the institution level.

It is important to note that participation to the trials was limited to students who expressed at least a mild intention to apply to higher education, that is, when $Y_{i,s,t}^{Pre} \neq 0$. To account for the fact that the wider outreach programme is an institution-level intervention and there is a clustering of students within institutions, we include institution-fixed effects and cluster all reported standard errors at the institution level. The coefficient of interest is β, which shows the impact of the individual-level random assignment to the nudging intervention on the probability of having applied to higher education before the deadline.

4. Results

First, we present the descriptive results for the outcome measure and the baseline measure of interest. Table 3 shows the rate of higher education applications for the intervention and control conditions for both trials, separately and pooled. In terms of the outcome measure of applications to higher education, and pooled across the two trials, 60% of the participants in the intervention group applied, compared to 59% of the control group. Additionally, for the pooled sample, the baseline intentions to apply (captured on a 6-point scale and used to recruit participants in the trials, with only those with at least a slight intention to apply to higher education being eligible) were also very similar across the two arms.

Table 3. Descriptive statistics for the higher education application outcome and baseline intentions to apply to higher education; pooled sample.

	Intervention		Control	
	Mean (sd)	N	Mean (sd)	N
Pooled data				
Applied to HE	0.60 (0.49)	468	0.59 (0.49)	472
Baseline intentions to apply	5.84 (1.77)	468	5.91 (1.81)	472
Trial 1				
Applied to HE	0.61 (0.49)	258	0.59 (0.49)	257
Baseline intentions to apply	5.34 (1.53)	258	5.24 (1.66)	257
Trial 2				
Applied to HE	0.59 (0.49)	210	0.58 (0.49)	215
Baseline intentions to apply	6.47 (1.84)	210	6.70 (1.69)	215

Note: The numbers presented in columns (1) and (2) are the mean values for the intervention and control group. The numbers in parentheses are the standard deviations.

We observed a very similar pattern when looking at the disaggregated data for the two trials, with the proportions of students applying to higher education in each of the respective intervention and control conditions across the two trials being very similar to each other.

In relation to the baseline intentions to apply (also in Table 3), these were fairly high across the board, and balanced by the intervention and control conditions. This mirrors evidence about the national sample of students engaged in Uni Connect, with only 11% of the learners in the analysis by the national evaluator relating to the relevant stage of the programme (by 2019) reporting that they were unlikely to apply to higher education [35]

We then applied the analytical strategy as outlined above. The results of the application of this strategy to the pooled trial data indicate that there is a very small but not statistically significant effect of the nudging intervention on higher education applications of students within schools and colleges participating in the wider outreach programme under consideration here.

Table 4 presents the estimates on the impact of the intervention on the higher education applications. These results refer to the pooled sample of students participating in the two trials presented in a sequential manner. In the first column (1), we show the row effect of the nudging intervention. In column two (2), we then add controls for individual-level characteristics. Finally, we add school-fixed effects for the results presented in column three (3).

Table 4. The impact of the text message nudging intervention on higher education application outcomes

HE Application	(1)	(2)	(3)
	Coefficient (se)	Coefficient (se)	Coefficient (se)
Intervention	0.01 (0.04)	0.01 (0.03)	0.01 (0.03)
Girl		0.11 ** (0.04)	0.08 (0.05)
Target student		0.02 (0.03)	−0.02 (0.03)
Constant	0.62 *** (0.04)	0.55 *** (0.09)	0.27 (0.23)
N	940	940	940
Number of clusters (schools)	57	57	57
Academic year	√	√	√
Institution-fixed effects			√

Notes: Pooled sample from trials 1 and 2. Standard errors clustered at institution level and reported in parentheses. Significance levels: * $p < 0.10$, ** $p < 0.05$, *** $p < 0.01$.

This third column represents the analysis as specified above and offers the main trial results. Tables 5 and 6 illustrate the results of the same analysis separately for the two trials. The estimated intervention effect is positive, yet very small and statistically insignificant, with an almost identical figure across all specifications (pooled, and separately for both trials, as seen in Tables 4–6). While target student status remains a statistically non-significant explanatory variable for higher education applications across all specifications of both the separate and the pooled analysis, for the first trial and for the pooled model, gender is statistically significantly (and positively) associated with higher education applications (intervention and target student status held constant), but only in the analytical specification without institution-fixed effects (column (2) in Tables 4 and 5 below). This is likely a result of a school/college-based variation in the overall rate of higher education application by gender, something that the institution-fixed effects capture (column (3)).

Table 5. The impact of the text message nudging intervention on higher education application outcomes, first trial (2017–2018).

HE Application	(1)	(2)	(3)
	Coefficient (se)	Coefficient (se)	Coefficient (se)
Intervention	0.02 (0.05)	0.02 (0.04)	0.02 (0.05)
Girl		0.16 ** (0.06)	0.08 (0.07)
Target student		0.02 (0.05)	−0.00 (0.05)
Constant	0.59 *** (0.05)	0.50 *** (0.06)	0.40 *** (0.04)
N	515	515	515
Number of clusters (schools)	57	57	57
Institution-fixed effects			√

Notes: Sample from trial 1 only. Standard errors clustered at institution level and reported in parentheses. Significance levels: * $p < 0.10$, ** $p < 0.05$, *** $p < 0.01$.

Table 6. The impact of the text message nudging intervention on higher education application outcomes, second trial (2018–2019).

HE Application	(1)	(2)	(3)
	Coefficient (se)	Coefficient (se)	Coefficient (se)
Intervention	0.01 (0.05)	0.01 (0.05)	0.02 (0.06)
Girl		0.06 (0.07)	0.04 (0.07)
Target student		0.01 (0.05)	−0.04 (0.05)
Constant	0.58 *** (0.07)	0.54 *** (0.08)	0.47 *** (0.06)
N	425	425	425
Number of clusters (schools)	29	29	29
Institution-fixed effects			√

Notes: Sample from trial 2 only. Standard errors clustered at institution level and reported in parentheses. Significance levels: * $p < 0.10$, ** $p < 0.05$, *** $p < 0.01$.

The outcome of the trial is therefore clear and consistent, showing no effect of the text messaging intervention on higher education applications.

4.1. Robustness Checks

We undertake two robustness checks to investigate how sensitive our estimates are to different specifications. First, we consider whether selective attrition between the treated and the control group students may bias our results. This is despite the fact that we observe very little variation in the overall rate of attrition by trial arm across the two trials. Therefore, in the first robustness check, we tested whether our results were similar when we replaced missing observations by assuming that all students for whom we had missing data in the intervention group applied to higher education, and that all the students for whom we had missing data in the control group did not apply to higher education. By running this analysis, we were able to examine whether, if we had managed to collect data for all the randomised sample and under the most optimistic assumptions about these missing data, we might have observed a significant effect of the intervention. The results are reported in Table 7 below, indicating that even under our most optimistic assumptions about missing data, we do not see an effect of the intervention on higher education applications.

Table 7. Robustness check for main trial result: 'most optimistic scenario' of all missing observations in intervention group applying to HE and all missing observations in the control group not applying to HE; pooled sample.

HE Application	(1)	(2)	(3)
	Coefficient (se)	Coefficient (se)	Coefficient (se)
Intervention	0.04 (0.03)	0.04 (0.03)	0.04 (0.03)
Girl		0.11 ** (0.04)	0.07 (0.05)
Target student		0.02 (0.03)	−0.01 (0.03)
Constant	0.59 *** (0.09)	0.53 *** (0.09)	0.43 *** (0.13)
N	970	970	970
Number of clusters (schools)	58	58	58
Institution-fixed effects			√

Notes: Pooled sample from trials 1 and 2. Standard errors clustered at institution level and reported in parentheses Significance levels: * $p < 0.10$, ** $p < 0.05$, *** $p < 0.01$. Missing dummy included for students with no data on attended institution.

For the second robustness check, we repeated our main estimations using conditional logistic regression to account for the dichotomous nature of our dependent variable (instead of the linear probability model used in the main analytical specification above). Table 8 presents the marginal effects from this analysis. Inevitably, the conditional logistic regression in column three (3), that is, when school-fixed effects are included in the estimation, results in a reduction in the sample size due to dropped observations when no variation in higher education applications was observed within schools. Even with that caveat, which further supports our choice of the OLS specification, we find no difference to the main results generated from our main analysis above when using this specification.

Table 8. Robustness check for main trial result: marginal effects (conditional) from logistic regression, pooled sample.

HE Application	(1)	(2)	(3)
	Marg. Eff. (se)	Marg. Eff. (se)	Marg. Eff. (se)
Intervention	0.06 (0.15)	0.06 (0.14)	0.05 (0.16)
Girl		0.46 ** (0.18)	0.36 (0.23)
Target student		0.06 (0.15)	−0.09 (0.17)
Constant	0.48 (0.40)	0.21 (0.38)	−1.13 (1.14)
N	940	940	890
Number of clusters (schools)	57	57	44
Institution-fixed effects			√

Notes: Pooled sample from trials 1 and 2. Standard errors clustered at institution level and reported in parentheses Significance levels: * $p < 0.10$, ** $p < 0.05$, *** $p < 0.01$. Missing dummy included for students with no data on attended institution.

As a result, the main findings of the trial remain unchanged, either under the alternative analytical specification, or when testing a best-case scenario attrition situation as in the first robustness check. This increases the confidence in our results.

4.2. Effect Heterogeneity

Finally, we explore whether the effect of the intervention may have been different for any of the two stratification factors, gender, and target student status. In Table 9, we show the results from the application of the main analytical strategy, but for disaggregated samples: target and non-target students, and, respectively, girls and boys, both across the pooled data.

Table 9. Robustness check for main trial result: marginal effects (conditional) from logistic regression; pooled sample.

HE Application	Target Student	Non-Target Student	Girls	Boys
	(1)	(2)	(3)	(4)
	Coefficient (se)	Coefficient (se)	Coefficient (se)	Coefficient (se)
Intervention	−0.07 (0.06)	0.06 (0.05)	0.03 (0.04)	−0.01 (0.05)
Constant	0.11 (0.35)	0.46 * (0.25)	0.51 * (0.29)	−0.37 (0.30)
N	307	633	549	391
Number of clusters (schools)	50	49	54	50
Covariates	√	√	√	√
Trial dummy	√	√	√	√
Institution-fixed effects	√	√	√	√

Notes: Pooled sample from trials 1 and 2. Sample disaggregated by Target/Non-Target Students; Girls/Boys. Standard errors clustered at institution level and reported in parentheses. Significance levels: * $p < 0.10$, ** $p < 0.05$, *** $p < 0.01$. Missing dummy included for students with no data on attended institution.

The results above suggest no evidence of a heterogeneous effects of the intervention on higher education application rates by the two groups (target/non-target student status, gender) under consideration in our experimental study. Taken together, these results therefore suggest the robustness of our analysis and its precise null results.

5. Discussion and Conclusions

In this paper, we have reported the results from two randomised control trials testing the effects of a light-touch behavioural nudging information-provision intervention on higher education applications in the English context. Given the existing evidence [13] on the use of behavioural nudging in the context of providing relevant educational information to (prospective) students, we hypothesised that the intervention, designed to work alongside the Universities and Colleges Admissions Service (UCAS) higher education application process in England, may encourage students who had at baseline expressed at least a mild intention to apply to higher education to realise this intention and apply to higher education.

We implemented two randomised control trials of the same intervention in consecutive school years, using individual-level random allocation to one of two experimental conditions in each trial: an intervention condition, receiving the intervention, and a control condition, not receiving the intervention.

The intervention was delivered as part of a wider programme of outreach and widening participation in the East of England region, which saw schools and further education colleges deliver, via staff employed by the programme, a wide-ranging set of outreach activities. From an ethical perspective, this means that students in the control group were not unfairly treated in relation to their opportunities to participate in potentially impactful outreach activities. However, from the perspective of the trials we have implemented, this means that we were in fact able to estimate what would amount to an *additional* effect of the nudging intervention. In that sense, the randomisation procedure, resulting as outlined above in balanced samples, may have also, in principle, ensured a balanced distribution of potential participation in these in-school activities; however, the business-as-usual approach of both experimental conditions may include a substantial amount of outreach intervention. While this represents a clear limitation of the trial, it also reflects the only possible real-world scenario for the delivery and testing of an outreach intervention: the

English policy and activity landscape around outreach that we have outlined above means many schools and colleges routinely are the place of many and diverse outreach and widening participation activities. Testing the nudging intervention in this context is a way to increase translational validity, even if it may work to potentially minimise the effect size of the intervention. Further research and evaluation around the Take Your Place programme will explore how variation by school/college, as well as by individual student, shapes later higher education outcomes for programme participants, and will look to understand the changes to self-reported knowledge, expectations, and intentions around higher education that may have occurred due to a participation (in various amounts) in Take Your Place.

As such, our main trial result of finding positive, very small, but statistically non significant results—essentially null results—is not necessarily surprising. This finding was robust both for statistical specification and for testing for the impact of (the very small) trial attrition, and it was consistent across each of the two trials separately as well as for the pooled data. Since the trial protocol was robustly implemented, attrition was low and the statistical power of the trial was good compared to other educational trials, which offers confidence that the null result is indeed a valid picture of the impact of this intervention, as delivered in the context of the wider outreach programme.

Although this embedding of a nudging intervention with an existing widening participation programme allowed for robust data collection, a high response rate, and a low attrition rate, nesting the intervention within the larger programme may therefore explain the lack of significant results.

This finding is particularly relevant given prior evidence [7] around so-called 'black box' interventions, where a variety of potential mechanisms for change may be at play at any one time, making it difficult to disentangle them. In that sense, our experimental study provides specific robust evidence regarding the impact (or rather, lack thereof) of a particular aspect of the wider outreach programme being delivered in the East of England region.

Moreover, our findings align with recent evidence that challenge the hypothesis that nudging may result in large effects [11] and offer further support to suggestions [36] that intensive guidance might be needed to change higher education application and enrolment behaviours. This is precisely what the wider programme, the focus of a larger-scale quasi-experimental evaluation currently underway, may have provided to some of the students participating in these two trials, potentially minimising the likely effect of the nudging intervention.

We are unable to provide definitive evidence regarding the interplay between this intervention and the wider programme in terms of their potential impact on higher education applications. However, the fact that each trial concludes with the same result, while being run when at different stages of the wider programme (in 2017–2018 in its first full year of implementation and therefore at an incipient stage; in 2018–2019 already embedded) may suggest that the level of other activity happening in the participating schools and colleges was not, overall, a factor affecting the potential effectiveness of the intervention. Our future research relating to Take Your Place will be able to explore this variation by school and college in greater depth.

We acknowledge two further limitations of our study, particularly in relation to issues of internal and external validity. First, the intention-to-treat approach to both trials means that we did not consider whether students had actually read, engaged, and acted upon the information provided to them via the text messages they had received. We were also not able to measure any 'leakage' or contamination from the intervention to the control group. While it is possible that students in the intervention group may have communicated with those in the control group (therefore minimising any intervention effect we may have been able to detect), this would have also meant that the recipients of the intervention had given the information at least some minimal thought and that the information would have prompted action, potentially cancelling out these two aspects. Future trials could make use of existing technology to measure actual levels of engagement (e.g., link clicks) with the information provided by the intervention. Future trials could also explore using alternative forms of communication of this intervention, with social media currently being a powerful vehicle for the communication of relevant information amongst young people.

From an external validity perspective, the recruitment into the trial of students who had expressed a non-negative (at least 'slightly likely') intention to apply to higher education means that the results are not immediately generalisable to the wider population of higher education-ready students in England. This is a common challenge of trials in education [33], but one that future trials may address by using rich administrative data present in England alongside national outreach and widening participation programmes which may offer the opportunity to generate representative samples and therefore more readily generalisable evidence.

The above limitations notwithstanding, the evidence we have generated with our experimental study is relevant for local policy-making purposes, including within the wider outreach programme within which the intervention was initially embedded. The null results are attributed to the implementation team leading the outreach programme, who decided not to continue its deployment and instead focus on intensive in-school outreach activity.

We also contend that the understanding of the intervention is useful for wider policy-making purposes, especially in a context of limited resources but continuing efforts to improve equity and fairness in higher education applications, access, and participation.

Author Contributions: Conceptualization (trial design): S.I. and E.K.; Formal analysis: All authors. Writing—original: S.I., K.M. and A.B.; Writing-revision: S.I. and K.M. All authors have read and agreed to the published version of the manuscript.

Funding: This research was funded by the Network for East Anglian Collaborative Outreach (neaco), which is funded by the Office for Students in England.

Institutional Review Board Statement: The studies received ethical approval from the Faculty of Education University of Cambridge.

Informed Consent Statement: Informed consent was obtained from all participants involved in the study.

Data Availability Statement: The data presented in this study cannot be shared and are not publicly available due to ethical considerations and the privacy and data protection restrictions governing their use.

Acknowledgments: This paper includes analysis from two randomised control trials conducted as part of a wider evaluation of the higher education outreach programme run by the Network for East Anglian Collaborative Outreach (neaco) in the East of England region. We also thank members of the neaco team. We also thank members of the Behavioural Insights Team who supported the initial development of the first trial and provided separate analysis for that trial.

Conflicts of Interest: The authors declare no conflict of interest.

Appendix A

Content of the information provided via text messages to participants randomly allocated to the intervention condition of each respective trial. Dates are indicative of when the text messages were sent and were consistent across the two trials.

Table A1. Text messages sent to intervention group participants (links removed from the below, as they differed slightly between the 2017–2018 and 2018–2019 iterations of the trial, as a result of websites to which participants were directed updating).

Date	Text in the Text Message
(0) Introduction, 31 October–2 November	Hi [student name], you signed up for the 'Take your place' project at [school/college name] and you have been selected! We will send you around 1 text each week with tips about what you can do next year. Reply STOP if you don't want to receive this extra support. Thanks!
(1) 31 October–2 November	Hi [student name], have you thought about applying to university? Now is a good time to research your options; speak to your teacher about how to apply! University can boost your career and you'll meet loads of new people—find out more here: [link]
(2) 7 November	Hi [student name], do you know what courses you can study at uni? There are so many options—make a plan to research 3 possible courses this week. Here is a useful link to get you started: [link]
(3) 14 November	Hi [student name], are you worried about the cost of going to uni? Help is at hand! Check out this video for info on the support available: [link]
(4) 21 November	Hi [student name], it's great that you're thinking more about your future! If you haven't already, set aside some time this week to register online to apply via UCAS: [link]
(5) 21 November (week of)	Hi [student name], we hope these messages are helpful. If you've already applied to higher education, reply YES.
(6) 28 November	Hi [student], have you found a course you want to apply for, and 5 different universities/colleges where it's offered? Why not make a list of what you need to do next—stick it on your fridge so you don't forget! If you are still choosing your courses there is more advice here: [link]
(7) 5 December	Hi [student name], now is a good time to write your personal statement. Remember to get straight into why you're interested in the subject, and really focused on the course—you can find top tips for different subjects at [link].
(8) 12 December	Hi [student name], just 4 weeks until applications close. Re-read your personal statement and ask yourself: did you begin with your strongest reason for wanting to study your subject of choice? Check these 14 common mistakes to avoid: [link]
(9) 19 December	Hello [student name] it's nearly time for Christmas! You've done some great work on your personal statement so far, well done. Remember to keep any description of extra-curricular activities short and explain what skill you gained from each. You should limit this part of your personal statement to one paragraph at the end.

Table A1. *Cont.*

Date	Text in the Text Message
(10) 2 January (after)	Happy New Year [student name]! Not long before applications close. If you've already applied to higher education, reply YES.
(11) 2 January	Hi [student name], if you're in the middle of filling out your UCAS application, check out their handy step-by-step guide [link] This week, make a plan to sit down and check you have ticked all the boxes!
(12) 9 January	Next week is the final deadline for your UCAS application. Make sure you have 5 choices in total and that you submit your application before 6 pm on the 15 of January. You can find useful guidance on filling out your application here: [link]
(13) 14 January—go out in the morning	Hello [student name], tomorrow at 6 pm is the UCAS 2018 deadline to apply to higher education. If you have any questions about your application, ask your teachers tomorrow!
(14) 16 January	Did you miss the application deadline? If you're not yet sure that higher education is the route for you, don't worry, you can still apply through Clearing later in the year. Contact the university or college directly and ask for advice.

References

Chowdry, H.; Crawford, C.; Dearden, L.; Goodman, A.; Vignoles, A. Widening participation in higher education: Analysis using linked administrative data. *J. R. Stat. Soc. Ser. A (Stat. Soc.)* **2013**, *176*, 431–457. [CrossRef]

Campbell, S.; Macmillan, L.; Murphy, R.; Wyness, G. Matching in the dark? Inequalities in student to degree match. *J. Labor Econ.* **2022**, *40*, 807–850. [CrossRef]

Dynarski, S.; Wiederspan, M. Student aid simplification: Looking back and looking ahead. *Natl. Tax J.* **2012**, *65*, 211–234. [CrossRef]

Budd, R. Undergraduate orientations towards higher education in Germany and England: Problematizing the notion of 'student as customer'. *High. Educ.* **2017**, *73*, 23–37. [CrossRef]

Sanders, M.; Chande, R.; Selley, E.; Team, B.I. *Encouraging People into University*; Department for Education: London, UK, 2017. Available online: https://www.bl.uk/britishlibrary/~||/media/bl/global/social-welfare/pdfs/non-secure/d/f/e/dfesc-encouraging-people-into-university-2017.pdf (accessed on 11 July 2022).

Damgaard, M.T.; Nielsen, H.S. Nudging in education. *Econ. Educ. Rev.* **2018**, *64*, 313–342. [CrossRef]

Younger, K.; Gascoine, L.; Menzies, V.; Torgerson, C. A systematic review of evidence on the effectiveness of interventions and strategies for widening participation in higher education. *J. Furth. High. Educ.* **2019**, *43*, 742–773. [CrossRef]

Herbaut, E.; Geven, K. What works to reduce inequalities in higher education? A systematic review of the (quasi-) experimental literature on outreach and financial aid. *Res. Soc. Stratif. Mobil.* **2020**, *65*, 100442. [CrossRef]

Castleman, B.L.; Page, L.C. Summer nudging: Can personalized text messages and peer mentor outreach increase college going among low-income high school graduates? *J. Econ. Behav. Organ.* **2015**, *115*, 144–160. [CrossRef]

9. Castleman, B.L.; Page, L.C. Parental influences on postsecondary decision making: Evidence from a text messaging experiment. *Educ. Eval. Policy Anal.* **2017**, *39*, 361–377. [CrossRef]

11. Szaszi, B.; Higney, A.; Charlton, A.; Gelman, A.; Ziano, I.; Aczel, B.; Goldstein, D.G.; Yeager, D.S.; Tipton, E. No reason to expect large and consistent effects of nudge interventions. *Proc. Natl. Acad. Sci. USA* **2022**, *119*, e2200732119. [CrossRef]

12. Sanders, M.; Burgess, S.; Chande, R.; Dilnot, C.; Kozman, E.; Macmillan, L. Role models, mentoring and university applications-evidence from a crossover randomised controlled trial in the United Kingdom. *Widening Particip. Lifelong Learn.* **2018**, *20*, 57–80. [CrossRef]

13. Bergman, P. Nudging technology use: Descriptive and experimental evidence from school information systems. *Educ. Financ. Policy* **2020**, *15*, 623–647. [CrossRef]

14. Bettinger, E.P.; Long, B.T.; Oreopoulos, P.; Sanbonmatsu, L. The role of application assistance and information in college decisions: Results from the H&R Block FAFSA experiment. *Q. J. Econ.* **2020**, *127*, 1205–1242.

15. Gurantz, O.; Pender, M.; Mabel, Z.; Larson, C.; Bettinger, E. Virtual advising for high-achieving high school students. *Econ. Educ. Rev.* **2020**, *75*, 101974. [CrossRef]

16. Phillips, M.; Reber, S. When "Low Touch" is Not Enough: Evidence from a Random Assignment College Access Field Experiment. UCLA CCPR Population Working Papers. 2018. Available online: http://papers.ccpr.ucla.edu/index.php/pwp/article/view/13/596 (accessed on 6 September 2022).
17. Carrell, S.; Sacerdote, B. Why do college-going interventions work? *Am. Econ. J. Appl. Econ.* **2017**, *9*, 124–151. [CrossRef]
18. Avery, C.; Castleman, B.L.; Hurwitz, M.; Long, B.T.; Page, L.C. Digital messaging to improve college enrolment and success. *Econ. Educ. Rev.* **2021**, *84*, 102170. [CrossRef]
19. Peter, F.H.; Zambre, V. Intended college enrolment and educational inequality: Do students lack information? *Econ. Educ. Rev.* **2017**, *60*, 125–141. [CrossRef]
20. Mertens, S.; Herberz, M.; Hahnel, U.J.; Brosch, T. The effectiveness of nudging: A meta-analysis of choice architecture interventions across behavioral domains. *Proc. Natl. Acad. Sci. USA* **2022**, *119*, e2107346118. [CrossRef]
21. Hoxby, C.M.; Avery, C. *The Missing "One-Offs": The Hidden Supply of High-Achieving, Low Income Students (No. w18586)*; National Bureau of Economic Research: Cambridge, MA, USA, 2012; Available online: https://www.nber.org/system/files/working_papers/w18586/w18586.pdf (accessed on 6 September 2022).
22. Callender, C.; Jackson, J. Does the fear of debt constrain choice of university and subject of study? *Stud. High. Educ.* **2008**, *33*, 405–429. [CrossRef]
23. Gibbons, S.; Vignoles, A. Geography, choice and participation in higher education in England. *Reg. Sci. Urban Econ.* **2012**, *42*, 98–113. [CrossRef]
24. Boliver, V.; Gorard, S.; Siddiqui, N. Using contextual data to widen access to higher education. *Perspect. Policy Pract. High. Educ.* **2021**, *25*, 7–13. [CrossRef]
25. Adamecz-Völgyi, A.; Henderson, M.; Shure, N. Is 'first in family' a good indicator for widening university participation? *Econ. Educ. Rev.* **2020**, *78*, 102038. [CrossRef]
26. Anders, J. The influence of socioeconomic status on changes in young people's expectations of applying to university. *Oxf. Rev. Educ.* **2017**, *43*, 381–401. [CrossRef]
27. Donald, W.E.; Ashleigh, M.J.; Baruch, Y. Students' perceptions of education and employability: Facilitating career transition from higher education into the labor market. *Career Dev. Int.* **2018**, *23*, 513–540. [CrossRef]
28. Harrison, N.; Waller, R. Challenging discourses of aspiration: The role of expectations and attainment in access to higher education. *Br. Educ. Res. J.* **2018**, *44*, 914–938. [CrossRef]
29. Anders, J.; Micklewright, J. Teenagers' expectations of applying to university: How do they change? *Educ. Sci.* **2015**, *5*, 281–305. [CrossRef]
30. Harding, S.; Bowes, L. Fourth Independent Review of Impact Evaluation Evidence Submitted by Uni Connect Partnerships. 2022. Available online: https://www.officeforstudents.org.uk/media/c304f005-89a1-4a5b-9468-b98eb7475ad4/cfe-review-of-impact-evidence-from-uni-connect-partnerships.pdf (accessed on 13 June 2022).
31. Office for Students. Uni Connect National Evaluation. Research Report OfS 2022.26. 2022. Available online: https://www.officeforstudents.org.uk/media/ebdc4bcd-148d-4d96-be5d-22a7d8660c51/uni-connect-evaluation-report-finalforweb.pdf (accessed on 13 June 2022).
32. Take Your Place Annual Report. 2021. Network for East Anglian Collaborative Outreach. Available online: https://www.takeyourplace.ac.uk/media/1369/neaco-annual-report-2021.pdf (accessed on 8 September 2022).
33. Connolly, P.; Keenan, C.; Urbanska, K. The trials of evidence-based practice in education: A systematic review of randomised controlled trials in education research 1980–2016. *Educ. Res.* **2018**, *60*, 276–291. [CrossRef]
34. Dong, N.; Maynard, R. PowerUp!: A tool for calculating minimum detectable effect sizes and minimum required sample sizes for experimental and quasi-experimental design studies. *J. Res. Educ. Eff.* **2013**, *6*, 24–67. [CrossRef]
35. Bowes, L.; Tazzyman, S.; Steer, R.; Birkin, G.; Telhaj, S. An Independent Evaluation of Uni Connect's Impact on Intermediate Outcomes for Learners. 2021 Office for Students Report. Available online: https://www.officeforstudents.org.uk/media/93132-a7-ef78-442d-bfc5-9d3c6bb42062/uc_wave_2-survey-findings_final_for_web.pdf (accessed on 9 September 2022).
36. Oreopoulos, P.; Petronijevic, U. *The Remarkable Unresponsiveness of College Students to Nudging and What We Can Learn from It (No. w26059)*; National Bureau of Economic Research: Cambridge, MA, USA, 2012 2019; Available online: https://www.nber.org/system/files/working_papers/w26059/w26059.pdf (accessed on 9 September 2022).

Article

The Higher Education Commitment Challenge: Impacts of Physical and Cultural Dimensions in the First-Year Students' Sense of Belonging

Diana Dias

School of Economic and Organizational Sciences, Lusofona University, 1749-024 Lisboa, Portugal; diana.dias@ulusofona.pt

Abstract: The students' perceptions and experiences about the organizational attributes of the higher education institution in which they are enrolled seem to have a strong influence on their integration, sense of belonging, and commitment to their new academic reality. The present paper focuses on the analysis of how first-year students build a sense of belonging and commitment to the higher education institution that welcomes them, focusing on institutional attributes that can act as (positive or negative) catalysts, such as physical and cultural dimensions. However, besides physical and cultural dimensions, it is crucial to consider its synergies with psychological, social, organisational, political, and axiological dimensions that have emerged as critical variables for contextualizing the analysis. The results suggest that the physical dimension nourishes the students' feelings of belonging, namely through the felt need to develop skills to manage their interaction with the spatial dimension of the institution that welcomes them. Moreover, newcomers' self-concept seems to be significantly increased by the feeling that they are now part of a cultural but also social elite. On the other hand, the feeling of integration seems to be supported basically on successful peer relationships. This perceived prestige of the higher education institution where they now belong represents, *a anteriori*, a crucial demand for the career management of the Bourdieu' "heirs," and, *a posteriori*, a real (and sometimes surprising) achievement for first-generation students.

Keywords: student experience; student engagement; organisational development; first-year experience; academic development

Citation: Dias, D. The Higher Education Commitment Challenge: Impacts of Physical and Cultural Dimensions in the First-Year Students' Sense of Belonging. *Educ. Sci.* **2022**, *12*, 231. https://doi.org/10.3390/educsci12040231

Academic Editor: James Albright

Received: 27 December 2021
Accepted: 13 March 2022
Published: 23 March 2022

Publisher's Note: MDPI stays neutral with regard to jurisdictional claims in published maps and institutional affiliations.

1. Introduction

Tavares [1] characterises Higher Education Institutions (HEIs) as "reflective, dynamic, flexible, resilient, learning realities". Based on their complex nature, the author advises a multifaceted and comprehensive analysis, considering different dimension, such as physical, psychological, social, organisational, political and cultural, and axiological dimensions.

The physical dimension refers to the infrastructures that encompass the buildings, their external and internal configuration, their design and architectural goal, and their layout and material resources. In fact, the design, disposition, and use of school buildings transmit educational and social values; thus, many of the psychological and social problems emerging in the educational community may be prevented, remedied, or even fixed through specific interventions in the physical surroundings [2–5].

The psychological and sociological dimension are also critical perspectives, as schools are only possible and justified by the people as members of the educational community. Thus, the psychological well-being depends on the capacity (and even need) of each student to connect with others. The relational issue is a core variable to any organisational analysis because the relationship conditions, for not only the processes but also of the results from the individual and the collective action.

Concerning the organisational dimension, the governance of HEIs, management strategies, and funding sources are the focus. On the other hand, the political and the cultural dimensions must also be considered. Ideologies remain the benchmark for the development of policies, shaping the institutional culture, grasped as a set of rules underlying an open system of human resources, where beliefs, expectations, concepts, and resources are compromised.

However, since the complementary nature of the institutional dimensions has already been highlighted, it is now important to highlight the transversal perspective: the axiological dimension. According to Tavares [1], the meaning of the changes carried out in the institutions must be reflected not only in the physical spaces, in their actors, in the curricula, and in all the organization and management systems (scientific, educational, research, or extension), but also in the surrounding community, considered at its different levels: micro, meso, exo, and macro.

Students' perceptions and experiences of the organisational attributes of the higher education institution they are enrolled in exert a strong influence in their integration into the academic universe. The present paper focuses on the analysis of the higher education institutional reality, emphasising the importance of the physical and cultural features of each institution that may act as catalysts of new students' integration. Thus, the physical, psychological and social, organisational, cultural and political, and axiological dimensions emerge as a relevant framework for analysis.

2. Literature Review

Student sense of belonging is critical to success in the first year of university, yet evidence about how and why various institutional factors influence engagement remains relatively rare. For many students, the transition from high school to HE is a hard hurdle [6,7]. They must learn how to deal with the new learning environment, build new relationships with peers and faculty, and grow into their new role as HE students [8,9].

Four phases are identified in the transition into the HE process [10]: preparation, encounter, adjustment, and stabilisation. In the preparation phase, students ponder about their course programme choice and choose where to enrol. Upon acceptance, students are confronted with a new learning environment and an academic culture. Through this encounter phase, they may experience some tension between their personal learning beliefs and behaviour and the new learning environment, with its own specific academic culture This tension impacts the development of their role as an HE student. Students develop their identity as HE students, adopt their perceptions and behaviour regarding the new learning environment, and ideally create a supportive network to feel at home and successfully cope with the demands and opportunities in HE [6,10]. This encounter phase usually takes place during the first weeks at HE. In the adjustment phase, the third phase of the transition process, amendments in attitude and behaviour take place gradually during the first year. Lastly, in the fourth and final phase in the transition process, students experience broadly what kind of behaviour leads to satisfying social and academic outcomes, and their attitudes and behaviour tend to stabilise [10,11].

First year students seem to be mostly concerned about two different but complementary issues: developing a sense of belonging in HE and building relationships with peers and faculty within it [12–15]. A sense of belonging refers to feeling at home at an HEI and that he/she fits in, that he/she is a member of one or more communities there, and that he/she is supported at the HE [16,17]. Developing a positive sense of belonging in HE seems crucial for the decision not to leave when one experiences difficulties in adapting to the new environment [18,19]. Previous studies have shown that students' interactions with peers and faculty are important for their experiences in HE. Such interactions can take place formally or informally, either inside or outside of a classroom setting [7,20].

Berger and Braxton [21] developed a model that focuses on organisational features as variables that influence student integration. According to this model, how students perceive and experience the organisational attributes of the higher education institution (HEI) they are enrolled in is a potential source of influence on their integration into the academic universe. The authors add that, more than and beyond the organisational features related to the structure of an HEI (such as size, selectivity, and ways of control), measures of organisational behaviour on campus influence how students make their academic integration. In this study, the authors argue that the traits students bring along when they join the institution affect the level of initial and subsequent commitment to it; this commitment, in turn, is positively affected by the level of integration into existing social communities in the HEI. Thus, the higher the level of subsequent commitment to the institution, the more likely the student is to remain in it [21]. Therefore, students' integration in HEIs is potentially influenced by how students experience their organisational attributes. According to the authors, organisational attributes, such as participation in organisational decision making, justice administration of policies, and communication, affect students' decision to stay or leave the institution. In this study, Berger and Braxton [21] include, in the model proposed by Tinto [19,22,23], variables that measure students' perceptions about the organisational attributes and seek to analyse the effects of these variables in students' integration.

3. Materials and Methods

The present paper reports a case study focus on first-year students enrolled in a programme of electrical engineering, who had been attending HE for six months, in a prestigious Portuguese university. In Portugal, Engineering studies are a very prestigious scientific field for HE candidates [24] and the access to them is highly competitive.

3.1. Participants

The sample was composed of 30 students, corresponding to 17.5% of the population. In terms of sampling procedures, the study sought to access a list of the total number of students enrolled in Electrical Engineering, rated according to their Grade Point Average. Despite the clear option for a qualitative approach, in the first moment, a probabilistic sampling method was elected, using a stratified random sample, to ensure the homogeneity of the sample distribution in terms of access grades, gender, age, and socio-cultural background.

The final sample of analysable data encompassed, therefore, 30 first year student interviews. Interviewees were 25 male students and 5 female students, which is similar to the gender distribution of the wider group. The students had a median age of 19 years, with a range of 18 to 20 years. The ethnic composition of the sample was 100% Caucasian. The analysis of social-educational indicators indicated the prevalence of students coming from families with a high educational level. All ethics issues were cautioned and all students signed informed consent statements.

3.2. Measurement

The chosen methods for data collection were two-fold: (i) semi-structured interview, and (ii) document analysis. Regarding the semi-structured interview, the literature advocates that this is a privileged way to capture and understand the richness, complexity, and meanings of students' choice process [25–28]. This kind of interview offered topics and questions to the interviewee, but they were carefully designed to elicit the interviewee's ideas and opinions on the topic of interest, as opposed to leading the interviewee towards preconceived choices. All the interviews were conducted, transcribed, and analysed in Portuguese.

The other method used was documental analysis, namely focusing on the institutional Guide to Strategic Development and the institutional strategic plan.

3.3. Data Analysis

Data analysis was performed through content analysis, using the Nvivo software. The choice of this tool was based on its versatility and flexibility to encompass the methodological orientation adopted for this research. Moreover, this software, while not being a statistical tool, took on a critical role in the efficiency of the data treatment, favouring the management and comparison of a considerable amount of non-structured data.

Transcripts were coded according to themes and analysed using a constant comparison approach [29]. The data were coded by paragraph and sentence, as proposed by Strauss and Corbin [30]. Data reduction in qualitative research is a necessary task and portions of transcripts have been selected to illustrate the respondents' views. Participants' own categories were tabulated, as suggested by Silverman [31].

4. Results

4.1. Physical Dimension

As previously stated, the physical dimension concerns the set of infrastructures composed of buildings, as well as their external and internal features. The analysis of the results from this study reveals that the main concern pointed out by the first-year students surveyed regarding this dimension regards classrooms conditions. In the newcomers words, the comfort and effectiveness of work devices in classrooms are particularly criticised. Daniel (The names used throughout this paper are fictitious) complains that "some classrooms do not have good conditions: the chairs and tables are damaged and too small for the number of students," while Sophie goes even further in her negative assessment "the classrooms are horrible. They are small and ugly. Only with a lot of goodwill can we have the minimum conditions." Moreover, while some students only criticise, others offer some proposals for change. Simon suggests that "classrooms, which are rather stuffy should be ventilated. And the air conditioning, which is always broken, should be fixed. In turn, Michael presents broader suggestions, such as "heating, improved and functional structures and good lighting."

However, the criticisms and suggestions regarding the physical space are not restricted to classrooms. As mentioned above, when students start this new stage of their academic life, one of the biggest impacts felt seems to have been a confrontation with a strange physical environment. Lloyd states: "I was a bit disappointed with the picture of it." Fabien also reflects on the impact of the external look on the institutional image: "I did not know that this was so old, almost falling apart ... It looks inconsistent since this is a Faculty of Engineering." In this discourse, the idea that the physical image of the institution should be related to its real purpose and social repercussion is evident.

When asked about the architectural changes they would propose for their new School all first-year students interviewed suggested some kind of intervention in the physical space, to promote not only the learning, but also the well-being of the entire academic community. Thus, students interviewed suggest significant infrastructural changes. Daniel is a refurbishing supporter: "I would make an overall renovation; for example, I would improve rooms, chairs, tables. I would have the facade of the main building painted." Diana agrees: "I think the main building is very beautiful. But it would need some good works."

The importance of the physical dimension to the students' well-being is so striking that some mention it spontaneously, as a way to measure their integration. Daniel and Bruce (respectively) justify their feeling of belonging through the skills attained in terms of controlling the spatial dimension: "I don't get lost any more. I know where things are" and "I now know the school well, the places." Displaced students further extend the physical influence to their feeling of integration, alluding to the city as a catalyst macro-structure for their well-being. The words of Mark about the city hosting his School are not nice: "The city is dark and very big. It's ugly; I wouldn't like to live here forever." The comparison proposed by Nelson is not the most flattering, either: "This food is like the city, tasteless and monotonous."

The lack of green areas and recreation spaces are also criticised by the interviewees ("having more green spaces, getting spaces where students can have fun, because there are people who do not like noise or do not like smoking ... ," Andrew). John calls for a new conception of space: "This is nice, but I would create larger and airy spaces," while Mitch and Alexis suggest the construction of a gymnasium, where they could develop sports activities ("I would build a gym. I was disappointed when I knew I could not play sports here," Mitch). Thus, the words of the interviewees are clear about the relationship between the institutional physical dimension and the subjective dimension of well-being. Others, however, are more pessimistic about the feasibility of improving the working conditions: "I would pull it down and build it again" (James) and "It's all very old. I would build it from scratch" (Edward).

The constraints inherent in the freshmen's socio-cultural and socio-economic background are not unrelated to the conceptualisation of these approaches. Furthermore, there is a much more critical stance on the part of children of middle-class families, compared with students from other social classes. David hopes that this soon will change for the better: "I think that something could be done, but it seems that we will move soon. I hope for the better. This place is hopeless." Charles agrees: "The School is very small and is outdated in architectural terms. I hope the situation will improve with the new School … " Fabien reflects on the urgent need to move to new facilities: "We needed to move to a more decent place." The transition to new premises will actually occur, but it does not provide, per se, guarantees of significant improvements in academic well-being. As Tavares (2003) advocates, the changes will have to ensure better basic and specific learning experiences, to encourage the acquisition of advanced communication tools that enable students to achieve as successfully as possible the different courses, the development of a feeling of autonomy, and the development of personal and interpersonal skills to ease their social and work integration.

In fact, many studies have revealed a significant relationship between quality of physical infrastructure and student achievement [32]. For students to learn to their full potential, scientific evidence suggests that the classroom environment must be of minimum structural quality and contain cues signaling that all students are valued learners. Indoor Environmental Quality is a popular theme in all sustainable development assessment tools aimed at increasing the comfort, health, and safety of a building's occupant and their most common indicators are: thermal, acoustic and noise comfort; ventilation and contamination level; and illumination and lighting [33]. According to Barrett et al. [34], thermal comfort is related to the learning progress, i.e., students usually perform better in the classroom where the temperature is easy to control. Ergonomic comfort is also an important factor and is concerned with the study of the adaptation of a man to the work, involving the physical environment and organizational aspects related to the activities performed on site. School furniture design demonstrates a close link between school desks, health problems, and discipline in class [34]. Nonetheless, a plethora of scientific evidence suggests that student learning and achievement is deeply affected by the environment in which this learning occurs. Improving student learning, achievement, and motivation requires attending to both the structural and symbolic features in the classroom.

4.2. Psychological and Sociological Dimensions

Considering that individuals and their relations are the key players of the school itself, the psychological and sociological dimensions are unavoidable in its analysis. The words of Mark reflect good prospects for the psychological dimension of the Faculty of Engineering: "It's good to be in the School of Engineering!" Students' narratives suggest that the self-concept of new students is significantly increased by the feeling that they are part of a reference group, which is the explicit goal of the institutional welcome events.

There is even the assumption that the interview itself might have worked as a mode of intervention to promote academic well-being. Adopting an eminently constructivist approach, it seems that pure and simple questioning of the students' feelings and thoughts about their way of life at the school may bring about benefits, not only from the fact that students feel heard, but also the opportunity for reflecting (and sometimes expressing) on some aspects of their daily lives. Mark asserts: "I've never bothered to think much about it, but I think the lessons are good, they train well." The perception of real utility was confirmed by some of the interviewees, who asked whether these interviews would continue the following years and whether it is a common process to ask students for suggestions.

The content analysis carried out on the narratives allows us to note the ubiquity of the interpersonal relationships and their crucial importance for the individual well-being Alexis states: "*Here the mood is great, people are fantastic.*" The feeling of integration seems to depend essentially on the relationships students establish with their peers. Andrew is explicit. "*I have colleagues whom I like, and this makes my integration.*" George also emphasises the importance of building relationships for his well-being: "*But when I have friends here, I think I'll feel better.*" This assertion is especially true when it comes to displaced students, to whom the establishment of new relationships emerges as a pressing need: "*My home community here is big. They give great help. They've been awesome, since the first day*" (Simon) Moreover, one of the big fears regarding the new university life is precisely building relationships. David, worried about facing the new relational configuration, is clear: "*What I feared most was the colleagues with whom I would share the house. Not here, we are all equal, it's different.*"

Social support is in fact important for students' first-year academic achievement Multiple studies found that students with better quality relationships with parents, faculty members, fellow students, and high school best friends had higher GPAs in the first year [35–37]. In addition, Goguen et al. [36] found that students who had conflicts with their best university friend achieved less in the first year, while conflicts with their best high school friend did not have a significant effect. After all, as Lloyd refers ("*I like being around here because I have my friends here*"), environmental comfort depends on the quality of the interactions developed.

4.3. Organisational Dimension

Although these are first-year students, they too recognise that the strategic objective of any HEI should be people-centred. Michael would like, precisely, for the Board of the Engineering School to know (and acknowledge) the point of view of its students "*Being closer to students and know their problems, their versions.*" This was one of the changes suggested by the interviewees in response to the request for proposals aimed at changing the school's community. However, if very few students interviewed stated that they would change nothing in the management of their School, the majority state their ignorance regarding the governing bodies: "*I don't know. I cannot comment on what I'm not familiar with*" (Michael). It is again Michael who reflects on the losses on this situation: "*I don't know the work of the Board. That's bad . . .*" Accordingly, Andrew even suggests: "*I don't know them. That is, I'd change that. They should make themselves known.*"

David, apparently, already knows the members of the Board and even advises them to "*be less 'full of themselves' because they feel the best.*" Michael's initial idea, which proposed a closer relationship between the governing bodies and the students, is often referred to by other colleagues. Seth thinks they should "*intervene more actively in issues of tuition, being on the students' side.*" Daniel takes the opportunity to criticise one of the measures of the Board he disagreed with: "*I think the Director was wrong by posting a notice showing up against the student demonstrations. All people have the right to express themselves.*" In this regard, students from the middle-class take on a much more critical stance, while students from the upper-class choose to express their ignorance regarding the Board and its activities. The students from the lower classes tend to be especially vocal, mainly about a closer relationship between governing bodies and students, in addition to greater availability of technical material in practical classes. The trend maintains: the importance of relationships to the lower classes, fierce criticism of the middle-classes, and a distant silence from the upper classes.

Despite these different standpoints, most proposals offered by students point towards two main mottos. On the one hand, they signal the need to increase the availability of technical and technological equipment in the classroom ("*In the electronics field there should be more material,*" Nick). On the other hand, there is the proposal for more direct intervention in the teaching strategy adopted ("*More attention to how classes are taught,*" Liam).

Taking up the respondents' words, the proposals in the pedagogical field put forth by them can be categorised into: (i) strategic pedagogical measures (*"I'd reformulate the evaluation period,"* Fabien; *"I'd increase practical classes,"* Alexis), and (ii) intervention with the faculty (*"I would make the salaries of teachers depending on student evaluations. I think it would be a good idea. Things would work differently,"* Sophie).

Regarding proposals within the scope of the more administrative functions, there are many different answers, which encompass most of the services and facilities of an essentially bureaucratic and logistical support nature provided by the school. The cafeteria seems to be the focus of major criticism, which extends not only to the diversity (*"Food should be more diversified,"* Andrew) but also the quality of food (*"Food. It's disgusting. It should be improved,"* Mark). The protagonists of these critiques are essentially displaced students and/or from lower classes, perhaps, therefore, more subject to the regular use of the canteen. The friendliness of the staff seems to be another target point of possible changes. While Anne points out that the difference in treatment that she feels concerning faculty and student populations (*"I'd make them nicer to the students . . . As for teachers, they are very pleasant"*), Sophie seems resigned to the situation: *"Sometimes, they could be nicer, but that's the way it is . . . "* Concerning the service itself, the slowness seems to be the most mentioned topic (*"fewer queues,"* James suggests), although Daniel also adds a positive critique: *"They are slow but efficient."* Another suggestion shared by several freshmen has to do with the strategy of disseminating information, which, in their words, seems not to be the most effective: *"More logic for the signs display"* (Joseph).

Finally, a highlight ought to be made to the criticism, yet often repeated, about the bureaucracy surplus they face in their first year as HE students: *"The paperwork: they are a nuisance"* (Peter) and *"It's all very bureaucratic. There are still many obstacles"* (Liam).

4.4. Cultural and Political Dimension

In the specific case of the institutional culture underlying the institution under analysis, attention should be placed on its plea for the quality and recognition that it holds, as a leading HEI in the area of Engineering. It is that institutional culture, which extends to all elements of the educational community, that seems to be indisputably acknowledged and accepted by the majority, made clear by the freshmen's words: *"It is being part of an elite of the best"* (Joshua); *"It's to be VIP"* (Guy). This idea of superiority that is recognised in comparison with the other HE students, and with society in general, seems to have been fairly well integrated by the new students, who, only a few months after having joined the Faculty of Engineering, state that they feel integrated into a group with which they not only identify but also to which they are proud to belong. Their words leave no room for doubt as to the position of superiority: *"Being a student at this school is to be a bit superior to others"* (Andrew), *"Being a student of this school is to be a student of an institution of prestige earned by its requirement. It's not for all"* (Anne). Similarly, their speeches confirm the pride of belonging to this institution: *"I am very proud because of the prestige of this university"* (Nick); *"It's to have the privilege of knowing the most renowned teachers in the country and even some from abroad, and of learning from them as much as possible"* (Fabien); *"Being a student here is a privilege, because it is one of the best Engineering Schools"* (Diana). Mark even acknowledges behavioural and attitudinal idiosyncrasies to those who attend or have attended this specific school: *"There is a way of doing things peculiar of his school—a more relaxed one because we are the best."*

It is interesting to note that it was specifically the prestige of this higher school that seems to have been an essential factor to the vocational (and strategic) option of the Bourdieu' "heirs." However, six months after their enrolment, it is mainly the first-generation students that appeal to the prestige of this Faculty, predicting a spread of that prestige for themselves as members of that institution. The identity as a HE student seems to become diluted in the face of the more specific status of an Engineering student, and the future professional status significantly influences their attitudes to the reference group: *"Being an engineer is a sign of pride, is a sign that you understand what you do"* (Mitch); *"Being an engineer is something spectacular. Not having to explain: is a kind of pride"* (Alexis). Andrew's words are also significant: *"The place also forces us to stand for the Faculty of Engineering, we mus be united."*

However, the whole widespread wave of pride for the prestige of the School they belong to did not convince all respondents and not even all first-generation students. Nick while acknowledging the prestige of the Faculty of Engineering, has with it a relationship based on a pragmatic and utilitarian principle: *"For me, this Faculty is a means and not an objective. I take from it what interests me: the knowledge and the degree. The rest is scenery."* In turn, David, making use of irony that characterises much of his speech, reflected as follows *"Now it would be nice to say that it is quite proud and stuff, right? I don't go around jumping nor am I here forced. It's like going to the restaurant, looking at the menu and choosing the mos expensive dish, as people say it is very good. Only when it comes to the table you know what it is And only after you eat it you know it was really good. This school was the dish I chose, now we wil see . . . "*

4.5. Axiological Dimension

To explore the axiological dimension, the Strategic Plan issued by the University which this Faculty is part of, was analyzed. This document shows visible concerns with holistic and axiological education, inasmuch as that it defines its mission as follows: "to create scientific, cultural and artistic knowledge, high quality education strongly anchored in research, social and economic value of knowledge and the active participation in the advancement of the communities around it. The University [. . .] is an education, research and development institution committed to the full training of citizens, respecting thei rights and actively involved in the progress of their communities" (University Strategic Plan, 2011, p. 4). In this same document, the aim of educating for the values is furthe strengthened by considering the main components of its mission: "The University [. . .] is today a national cultural, artistic, technological and scientific reference, and known also for the production and dissemination of knowledge. The University [. . .] is, therefore, a mobiliser and a driver of the socioeconomic and cultural development of the country" [38

With regard specifically to the School of Engineering, it may be observed that, in its strategic plan, the institutional mission is embodied in the training of world-class engineering professionals, supported by excellent research and development, addressing the scientific, technical, ethical, and cultural aspects. It continues, stressing that, "in addition to a solid technical and scientific training, the School of Engineering will seek to give them a set of competencies and values, especially the capacity for initiative, learning and problem solving, as well as intellectual integrity and sense of responsibility and solidarity, preparing them for professional success" [39].

If the discursive intentions, whether institutional or political, seem united in the defence of the axiological component as the foundation for HE, students themselves—and particularly the freshman respondents—also seem aware of their fundamental importance Considering the words of George on the hopes that his father lays on him, and which clearly take on the defence of values such as respect and responsibility: *"He always says: 'you'll be one of those engineers that know what they do, not like some I know, that have a lot of theory in thei minds, but do not lay their hands to anything.' He also says that I have to respect people who are long in the profession, even if they do not hold a degree, because they have the degree of life."* It is the same value of respect, along with honesty, that is mentioned by George to describe the main features of a successful engineer: *"It's about understanding what you do, being supportive of people with whom you work and not being the kind 'hand over the money.'"* Among the students who appeal to moral and ethical values as key factors to professional competence, it is worth noting that the vast majority come from the middle, lower-middle, and low classes It could be hypothesised that these social backgrounds are those which would be more aware of these values and, therefore, would instil them on their children, insofar that they possibly would have felt disadvantaged by their absence, in their own work.

On the other hand, indifference or even opposition to values taken as universally accepted, such as justice or respect for others, are pointed out as negative symptoms o the systemic organisation in which they operate. Anne points to the peer competition as a situation to be avoided: *"In other* [Schools], *such as Medicine, it is a competition that kills them."* Hazing is, for some, also a paradigmatic example of indifference to the basic values of interpersonal relationships. Sean states: *"I felt humiliated, mistreated . . . I was not used to being treated like that."* For him, the major objective of hazing complies with the incorrect values: *"I think they are avenging of what others did to them, but we aren't to be blamed. It is a kind of revenge."*

5. Discussion and Conclusions

The aim of the present paper was the analysis of the HE institutional reality with a focus on the impacts of physical and cultural dimensions in the first-year students' sense of belonging. There was an interest in focusing on the diverse institutional dimensions that may act as catalysts (positive, thus facilitating, or negative, thus hindering) of the integration of new students, namely in their institutional commitment construction process. Thus, the physical, psychological, social, organisational, political and cultural, and axiological dimensions emerged as a relevant framework for analysis. This paper explored each of these dimensions of institutional analysis, using them as reading grid of the reality perceived by freshmen. All these dimensions are unavoidable as real levers for the freshmen integration process, within the institutional academic and social environment.

The physical dimension takes on great importance, insofar that it functions as a way to measure students' integration, fostering their feeling of belonging through the skills attained in terms of controlling the spatial dimension. Moreover, specific groups of students seem to be more sensitive to the physical dimension than others. On the one hand, displaced students extend the physical influence on their feeling of integration, describing the city as a catalyst macro-structure for their well-being. On the other hand, children of middle-class families seem to be more critical to a material environment that they expect to work as a lever for upward social mobility. In fact, the physical dimension of the host institution seems to work as a real catalyst for the newly arrived students' sense of belonging. The magnificence of the buildings, the quality and quality of pedagogical resources, the well-being of the classrooms, and even their decoration seem to have, in the perception of the interviewed students, a significant impact on the way they are proud to belong there. The literature in the field of education is clear about the pedagogical advantages of schools that take care of the health, safety, and comfort of their students, considered basic principles for a quality education. The spatial configuration aggregates or separates, promotes concentration or conviviality. More than functional schools, the governance of educational institutions must be attentive and promote safe, comfortable spaces with the necessary conditions of luminosity, temperature, and cosiness so that the student feels comfortable and chooses to stay there longer. Furthermore, the external signs of greatness, grandeur, and even seniority contribute to the institutional reputation and, consequently, to the feeling of pride in belonging. In the specific case of higher education, this effect of the physical/spatial dimension can be intended precisely to act as a positive catalyst for students' sense of belonging, endorsing meaningly to their commitment to the institution.

Concerning the psychological dimension, new students' self-concept emerges significantly increased by the feeling that they are part of, more than a reference group, an elite. Furthermore, regarding the sociological dimension, interpersonal relationships are crucial for the students' well-being, given that the feeling of integration seems to rely basically on the relationships they establish with their peers.

From the organisational viewpoint, students recognise that the strategic objective of any HEI should be people centred. Students from the lower classes tend to be especially demanding, mainly about a closer relationship between the governing bodies and students, while the upper-class students choose to express their ignorance regarding the Board and its activities. It is possible to identify a trend: the importance of relationships to the lower-classes, fierce criticism of the middle-classes, and a distant silence from the upper-classes' students. Some of them do not question any factors that might in any way overshadow the prestige that was the basis of their vocational options. Others, apparently more demanding, strongly criticise an institution from which they expect the possibility of being the bridge to a higher lifestyle than their parents'. Others are concerned, above all, with the interpersonal integration as a catalyst for their institutional integration.

Moreover, in the organisational dimension, strategic pedagogical changes emerge with critical relevance, namely related to the need to envisage students as institutional protagonists. Regarding the more administrative functions, most of the services are a target of criticism, with special emphasis on the bureaucratic and logistical support.

In terms of the cultural and political dimension, the prestige that brands the HEI under analysis is recognised and accepted by all elements of the educational community. This idea of superiority seems to have been well incorporated by new students, who not only identify with the reference group, but also are proud to belong to it. This perceived prestige represented, *a anteriori*, a crucial vocational (and strategic) demand for the Bourdieu' "heirs," and, *a posteriori*, a conquest to the first-generation students, who foresee a spread of that prestige for themselves as members of that institution. In fact, the institutional culture, which in this case intentionally contributed to the creation of a feeling of upward social mobility, seems to have an effective effect on creating a sense of belonging and commitment to the institution. For students who come from families of high sociocultural status, entering this school is yet another evidence of their personal and social value, which confirms and reaffirms their social status. For first-generation students in higher education, entering this school represents the social climb not only of the student himself, but also of the family of origin, which, by cultural contagion, also ends up developing a feeling of upward social mobility.

To explore the axiological dimension, the HEI analysed shows visible concerns with the holistic and axiological education, with its aim to educate for the values in a framework of human, cultural, scientific, ethical, and technical training, in the context of diversified processes of teaching and learning and complementary activities aimed at the development of attitudes and skills, as well as the dissemination of knowledge. This axiological component is embodied and valued by students themselves, and particularly by freshmen from the middle, lower-middle, and low classes.

After analysing the students' narratives and institutional documents, a set of institutional initiatives aimed at the promotion of mechanisms to facilitate better integration of the new students emerge as significant. However, some issues that relate to the "unspoken," underlying the official nature of the purpose of the integration activities, ought to be addressed.

The massification of HE is real and tangible. One of the most obvious consequences is, undoubtedly, the emergence of new and diverse publics. The HEI analysed did, naturally, accept among its many years of history young people who, a decade or two ago, would have no viability to pursue a degree. The socio-economic and socio-cultural dispersion of the sample from this study proves that. New dimensions for the devices to manage the dichotomy between the real juvenile dispersion and the students' dispersion expected by this School are, therefore, necessary. The management of students' expectations in the face of students' realities emerges as a critical need.

If new students are not the expected ones, at least let us try to make them whom they are expected to be. This could be an underlying theme to moments such as the welcome ceremony for new students, which officially receives the newcomers and emphasises the institutional prestige over the centuries. It is explicitly conveyed to freshmen that their enrolment in this institution makes them part of an elite. If the heterogeneity characterises the population that enrols for the first time in the School of Engineering, relevant features of the attempts to homogenise those who attend it may be found, through a whole effort to build an identity framework that aims at creating feelings of belonging, pride, and group cohesion. All the ceremonies associated with the welcome of its new students, including a speech that appeals to the most distinguished alumni, seems an obvious attempt on the part of the School of Engineering to ensure an elitist position against other HEIs, weaving, from the outset, a web, with corporatism (both in its many positive and also negative aspects) certainly as one of the main features.

However, the welcome ceremony takes just one side of a multifaceted strategy of the School of Engineering towards maintaining a place overlooking the rest of the educational landscape. The expectations risen on new students, regarding the prestige and excellence of the Faculty of Engineering, are prior to their enrolment, which is just a confirmation that verges on the Pygmalion effect. The expectations instilled especially by parents and high school teachers (many of whom are alumni of the Faculty of Engineering) create, from the outset, a golden structure that will shape the way they view and analyse the HEI at the beginning of their university path. The "snowball effect" seems to play an important role here, to which the actual quality of education provided by the institution is certainly not unrelated to. Marketing may be significant, but the "product" itself also deserves a credit reference.

The results of these strategies seem obvious by their effectiveness, in the words of the respondents: "Being a student at the School of Engineering is being a student of an institution of prestige earned by its high level of demand" (Anne).

It does not fit the purposes of this article to provide a complete answer regarding the issue that attending a degree with the seal of the School of Engineering may turn its students into an elite. In fact, it is important to recognize the limitations of this study, since, as it is a case study, it focuses on a limited number of students, on a specific institution, and on a particular program. We assume that qualitative research is an exploratory methodology. Its focus is on the subjective character of the analysed object, trying to understand the student's behaviour and studying their particularities and individual experiences, among other aspects. In addition to understanding and interpreting behaviours and trends, this methodology sought to identify hypotheses for a problem and discover the perceptions and expectations of its actors. Thus, it would be important to extend this exploration to more students, namely from other schools with cultural and physical dimensions different from those studied, in order to assess the results found here. However, it seems indisputable that the self-concept of new students is significantly increased by the feeling that they are part of a reference group, and if the psychological, sociological, and even axiological dimension are important to construct a sense of belonging to the institution, the physical and cultural dimension play a critical role as positive catalyst for the commitment that the student establishes with the institution that welcomes him. The issue is whether this recently restructured self-concept is strong enough to manage possible academic or relational failures (*"This is not an ordinary school. I came here because I deserved. It is a responsibility,"* Fabien).

Thus, if the institution does not have full control over the mechanisms that shape the profile of their incoming student population, it must, then, look after their output profile.

Funding: This research received no external funding.

Institutional Review Board Statement: The study was conducted in accordance with the Declaration of Helsinki, and approved by the Ethics Committee of Universidade Europeia (date of approval: 31 July 2020).

Informed Consent Statement: Informed consent was obtained from all subjects involved in the study.

Conflicts of Interest: The authors declare no conflict of interest.

References

Tavares, J. *Formação e Inovação no Ensino Superior [Training and Innovation in Higher Education]*; Porto Editora: Porto, Portugal, 2003.

Alexander, S. E-learning developments and experiences. *Educ. Train.* **2001**, *43*, 240–248. [CrossRef]

Higgins, S.; Hall, E.; Wall, K.; Woolner, P.; McCaughey, C. *The Impact of School Environments: A Literature Review*; Design Council: London, UK, 2005.

Azemati, H.; Aminifar, Z.; Pourbagher, S. Effective Environmental Factors on Designing Productive Learning Environments. *Arman. Archit. Urban Dev.* **2018**, *11*, 1–8.

5.   Pourbagher, S.; Azemati, H.R.; Saleh Sedgh Pour, B. Acceptance and challenging analysis of Factors Affecting Users' Stress in UniversityLearning Environments. *J. Archit. Thought* **2021**, *5*, 201.
6.   Gale, T.; Parker, S. Navigating change: A typology of student transition in higher education. *Stud. High. Educ.* **2014**, *39*, 734–753. [CrossRef]
7.   Pascarella, E.T.; Terenzini, P.T. *How College Affects Students: A Third Decade of Research*; Jossey-Bass, An Imprint of Wiley: Indianapolis, IN, USA, 2005; Volume 2.
8.   Wilson, E.J.; Elliot, E.A. Brand meaning in higher education: Leaving the shallows via deep metaphors. *J. Bus. Res.* **2016**, *69*, 3058–3068. [CrossRef]
9.   Sanne, P.; Germie, V.D.B.; Chris, K.; Arne, P.; Geert, J.S.; Eva, M. Differences between adolescents in secure residential care and non-residential educational facilities. *J. Soc. Work* **2021**, 14680173211009712. [CrossRef]
10. Coertjens, L.; Brahm, T.; Trautwein, C.; Lindblom-Ylänne, S. Students' transition into higher education from an internationalperspective. *High. Educ.* **2017**, *73*, 357–369. [CrossRef]
11. Christie, F. Careers guidance and social mobility in UK higher education: Practitioner perspectives. *Br. J. Guid. Couns.* **2016**, *44*, 72–85. [CrossRef]
12. Zagenczyk, T.J.; Gibney, R.; Few, W.T.; Scott, K.L. Psychological contracts and organizational identification: The mediating effect ofperceived organizational support. *J. Labor Res.* **2011**, *32*, 254–281. [CrossRef]
13. Palmer, M.; O'Kane, P.; Owens, M. Betwixt spaces: Student accounts of turning point experiences in the first-year transition. *Stud. High. Educ.* **2009**, *34*, 37–54. [CrossRef]
14. Tett, L.; Cree, V.E.; Christie, H. From further to higher education: Transition as an on-going process. *High. Educ.* **2017**, *73*, 389–406. [CrossRef]
15. Walton, G.M.; Cohen, G. A question of belonging: Race, social fit, and achievement. *J. Personal. Soc. Psychol.* **2007**, *92*, 82–96. [CrossRef] [PubMed]
16. Hausmann, L.R.; Schofield, J.W.; Woods, R.L. Sense of belonging as a predictor of intentions to persist among African American and White first-year college students. *Res. High. Educ.* **2007**, *48*, 803–839. [CrossRef]
17. Hurtado, S.; Carter, D.F. Effects of college transition and perceptions of the campus racial climate on Latino college students' sense of belonging. *Sociol. Educ.* **1997**, *70*, 324–345. [CrossRef]
18. Christie, H.; Munro, M.; Fisher, T. Leaving university early: Exploring the differences between continuing and non-continuing students. *Stud. High. Educ.* **2004**, *29*, 617–636. [CrossRef]
19. Tinto, V. *Completing College: Rethinking Institutional Action*; University of Chicago Press: Chicago, IL, USA, 2012.
20. Hagenauer, G.; Volet, S.E. Teacher–student relationship at university: An important yet under-researched field. *Oxf. Rev. Educ.* **2014**, *40*, 370–388. [CrossRef]
21. Berger, J.B.; Braxton, J.M. Revising Tinto's interaccionalist theory of student departure through theory elaboration: Examining the roleof organizational attributes in the persistence process. *Res. High. Educ.* **1998**, *39*, 103–119. [CrossRef]
22. Tinto, V. *Leaving College: Rethinking the Causes and Cures of Student Attrition*; The University of Chicago Press: Chicago, IL, USA, 1987.
23. Tinto, V. Dropout from higher education: A theoretical synthesis of recent research. *Rev. Educ. Res.* **1975**, *45*, 89–125. [CrossRef]
24. Amado-Tavares, D. *O Superior Ofício de Ser Aluno: Manual de Sobrevivência Do Caloiro*; Edições Sílabo: Lisbon, Portugal, 2008.
25. Denzin, N.K.; Lincoln, Y.S. (Eds.) *Handbook of Qualitative Research*; Sage: Thousand Oaks, CA, USA, 1994.
26. Merriam, S.B. *Qualitative Research. A Guide to Design and Implementation*; Jossey-Brass: San Francisco, CA, USA, 2009.
27. Savenye, W.C.; Robinson, R.S. Qualitative research issues and methods: An introduction for educational technologists. In *Handbook of Research for Educational Communications and Technology*; AECT: Bloomington, IN, USA, 1996; pp. 1171–1195.
28. Willig, C. Introducing qualitative research in psychology. In *Adventures in Theory and Method*; Open University Press: Philadelphia, PA, USA, 2001.
29. Glaser, B.G. *Basics of Grounded Theory Analysis: Emergence vs. Forcing*; Sociology Press: Mill Valley, CA, USA, 1992.
30. Strauss, A.; Corbin, J. *Basics of Qualitative Research: Grounded Theory Procedures and Techniques*; Sage: London, UK, 1990.
31. Silverman, D. *Doing Qualitative Research: A Practical Handbook*; Sage: Thousand Oaks, CA, USA, 2000.
32. Cheryan, S.; Ziegler, S.A.; Plaut, V.C.; Meltzoff, A.N. Designing Classrooms to Maximize Student Achievement. *Policy Insights Behav. Brain Sci.* **2014**, *1*, 4–12. [CrossRef]
33. Alyami, S.H.; Rezgui, Y. Sustainable Building Assessment Tool Development Approach. *Sustain. Cities Soc.* **2012**, *5*, 52–62. [CrossRef]
34. Barrett, P.; Davies, F.; Zhang, Y.; Barrett, L. The Impact of Classroom Design on Pupils' Learning: Final Results of a Holistic Multilevel Analysis. *Build. Environ.* **2015**, *89*, 118–133. [CrossRef]
35. Dika, S.L. Relations with faculty as social capital for college students: Evidence from Puerto Rico. *J. Coll. Stud. Dev.* **2012**, *53*, 596–610. [CrossRef]
36. Goguen, L.S.; Hiester, M.A.; Nordstrom, A.H. Associations among Peer Relationships, Academic Achievement, and Persistence in College. *J. Coll. Stud. Retent.* **2011**, *12*, 319–337. [CrossRef]

37. Yazedjian, A.; Toews, M.L.; Navarro, A. Exploring parental factors, adjustment, and academic achievement among White and Hispanic college students. *J. Coll. Stud. Dev.* **2009**, *50*, 458–467. [CrossRef]
38. University of Porto. Strategic Plan and Broad Lines of Action. University of Porto 2011–2015. 2011. Available online: https://sigarra.up.pt/up/pt/conteudos_service.conteudos_cont?pct_id=18777&pv_cod=56piP'HapWhQB (accessed on 19 November 2021).
39. Faculty of Engineering. Strategic Plan of the Faculty of Engineering 2005–2009. Available online: https://sigarra.up.pt/feup/pt/web_base.gera_pagina?p_pagina=p%c3%a1gina%20est%c3%a1tica%20gen%c3%a9rica%201001 (accessed on 19 November 2021).

Article

Student Academic and Social Engagement in the Life of the Academy—A Lever for Retention and Persistence in Higher Education

Maria José Sá

CIPES–Centre for Research in Higher Education Policies, 4450-137 Matosinhos, Portugal; mjsa@cipes.up.pt

Abstract: Research studies worldwide have focused on higher education dropout, persistence, and success. Given the profound changes in higher education that have taken place in recent decades, higher education institutions need to compete for students by attracting, retaining, and, ultimately, graduating them. Thus, higher education institutions increasingly offer actions that aim to foster student success. While a smooth and supported process of student transition from secondary to tertiary education is one of the key variables in higher education student retention and paramount for preventing student dropout, the student's overall experience in higher education plays a pivotal role in their performance and success. This paper focuses specifically on higher education students' academic and social involvement, notably through their engagement in extracurricular activities and decision-making processes, which are perceived as critical mechanisms in their persistence in higher education. The study used a qualitative approach with the analysis of four Portuguese higher education institutions. Data were collected through in-depth interviews with students and institutional leaders, complemented with document analysis, and explored through content analysis. The results reveal that, from the wide range of opportunities for involvement offered to students by the higher education institution, activities of an academic nature are the most sought after by students to complement their educational experience. However, students perceive involvement in extracurricular activities in general as critical, both to their overall education and preparation for the labor market and to an easier integration into the institutional environment. Hence, student involvement in cultural or recreational activities, alongside their involvement in institutional decision-making bodies and associative movements, is a privileged way of complementing students' academic training and is perceived by them as important in their overall education, both as professionals and as individuals.

Keywords: student experience; student engagement; higher education; extracurricular activities

Citation: Sá, M.J. Student Academic and Social Engagement in the Life of the Academy—A Lever for Retention and Persistence in Higher Education. *Educ. Sci.* **2023**, *13*, 269. https://doi.org/10.3390/educsci13030269

Academic Editor: Billy Wong

Received: 25 January 2023
Revised: 23 February 2023
Accepted: 1 March 2023
Published: 3 March 2023

1. Introduction

The major reconfigurations that the Higher Education (HE) arena worldwide has been subject to over the past decades (in particular with the massification of this educational level, the increasing scarcity of resources, especially in financial terms, and the institutional competition for students) have caused a shift in the way higher education institutions (HEIs) relate with their public [1,2]. Thus, the academic community, governmental structures, and HEIs have come to focus on the issues related to how students seek HE and, once in the system, how they integrate, perform, become academically involved, and attain success. In this context, one of the HEIs' major concerns is related to student retention and dropout rates.

The literature, both seminal and more recent, acknowledges the transition from high school to higher education as one of the most complex in students' educational paths [3–16]. This challenging transition may affect their performance and, ultimately, their success in HE [17]. Among HEIs' concerns is, therefore, that this process runs with minimum incidents and as smoothly as possible for first-year students, as this is the year with the highest dropout rate, in part due to students' difficulties in adapting to the higher education context [13,18].

After the process of transitioning from secondary to tertiary education is completed and students persist, they continue to face many complex challenges throughout their educational path in higher education. The purpose of this study is to get an insight into the factors that, from both the students' and institutional leaders' standpoints, influence their overall experience in HE and which reflect on their path, performance, and academic success. The literature identifies one of these factors as student involvement, also often described as academic and social integration. There is a well-documented direct and positive relationship between students' academic and social involvement as well as their persistence and graduation in the literature [19–22].

According to Astin [11,12,23–25], one of the first researchers to address this topic and the author of a seminal work, students' involvement in the life of the academy plays a paramount role in their retention. His Theory of Student Involvement seeks to explain the dynamics that underlie students' change and development [23]. Using the author's own terms, "students learn by becoming involved" [24] (p. 133).

This paper presents part of the results of a broader study that seeks to obtain a deeper understanding of students' perceptions about their success in HE as a result of their overall experience in the HEI and focuses specifically on students' involvement in extracurricular activities and institutional decision-making processes as a mechanism to enhance their overall experience in HE.

The concept of student involvement in the life of the academy is not a novelty, and the literature offers a wide array of studies addressing this topic [11,12,19–21,23,24,26–32]. According to Astin [12,25], students' involvement consists of the amount of physical and psychological energy they invest in their academic experience; highly involved students devote a considerable amount of their time and energy to their studies, spend a good part of their time on campus, participate in campus activities, and interact with their peers and faculty. Conversely, students with a low degree of involvement neglect their studies, spend very little time on campus, do not participate in extracurricular activities, and have very sporadic contact with peers and faculty. The concept of engagement used by the author involves a behavioral component, as "[...] It is not so much what the individual thinks or feels, but what the individual does, how they behave, that defines and identifies involvement" [12] (p. 519).

Although Astin [11,23,25] ascribes high relevance to the role of the institutional environment by providing students with opportunities and possibilities to engage socially and academically with ideas, people, or activities, the author places the student at the center of this process. The author [9,11,20,22,23] argues that the change will occur to the extent that students capitalize on the opportunities offered to them and take an active attitude of involvement. Thus, students' change and potential development are not only effects of the organizational environment but also mainly a result of the quality of their commitment and involvement in the opportunities offered by the HEI [6,19,26]. According to Astin's [12] Theory of Student Involvement, for a curriculum to reach the expected goals, it should enable students to apply effort and investment in terms of energy so that the desired learning and development can occur, emphasizing their active participation in the learning process. Students' time is envisaged in this theory as the most important institutional resource, as the attainment of developmental goals on the part of the students is a direct consequence of the time and effort they commit to academic activities.

Bergmark and Westman [33] sustain that this engagement may take the form of joint participation, notably with faculty and other stakeholders, in developing partnerships, co-creating curriculum, and acting as agents of educational change. Student engagement, both at the academic and social level, may thus foster their overall development and the feeling of belonging [33]. Moreover, this active institutional and social participation and engagement is also critical in the development of transversal competences by HE students (such as communication, teamwork, research, problem-solving, leadership, creativity, critical thinking, and time management), which are paramount in personal enhancement and professional preparedness [34,35]. In the same vein, Bergmark and Westman [33] maintain that student participation influences their engagement and motivation to attain the knowledge and competences that will be critical in their future profession.

Based on Astin's Theory of Student Involvement [12,24], Berger and Milem [36] argue that the more involved students are in the life of the HEI, the more likely they are to interact with and be affected by the environment of the campus. Moreover, the campus organizational environment and students' perceptions of that environment directly influence the extent and types of student involvement [36]. This involvement is not limited, naturally, to students' participation in academic activities but far exceeds these limits and is materialized, to a large extent, in their involvement in extracurricular activities of a more social or recreational nature [37].

The literature on this topic acknowledges and emphasizes the relevance of students' social experiences in their integration into the institution and their subsequent commitment to it, e.g., [6,9,19,21,30,36,38–40], among others. Spady [41], in his seminal work, posits that students' integration into the life of the institution depends on their ability to successfully respond to the demands of both the social and the academic systems in which they are placed. The efficacy of this process results, according to the author, in the students' higher satisfaction, which leads, in turn, to a higher level of institutional commitment and, thus, to an increased likelihood that they persist. This assumption is shared by Tinto [8–10], who advocates that the degree of students' interaction with the academic and social environment of the HEI determines their conduct in terms of persisting in or dropping out of the institution. In line with Tinto [8,9], Braxton et al. [42] argue that the higher the level of social integration, the higher the subsequent level of commitment to the institution.

Acknowledging the central importance of HE students' involvement in their academic experience, Kahu [29] offers a model that, like Astin's [12] Theory of Student Involvement, places the student in the center of the teaching and learning process, pointing out the complexity of factors influencing their involvement, and perceiving students' involvement as a psychosocial process, influenced by institutional and personal factors. Among them, the author highlights the students' relationships with peers, faculty, and non-teaching staff; motivation; and the students' personalities, among many other factors [29]. Building on this model, Kahu and Nelson [43] emphasize that an engaged student better attains not only scientific knowledge and competences but also academic success and personal development. Furthermore, the authors upgrade Kahu's [29] model by analyzing student transitions. They conclude that the interactions between the students' individual traits and the institutional factors are critical for student engagement, highlighting the importance of a close relationship between the HEI and its students. Furthermore, these personal and institutional factors do not function separately, and there is a need for interaction between them to enhance student engagement [43].

Also based on Astin's [24] Theory of Student Involvement and on its prerogative that students' academic and social involvement plays a central role in shaping their outcomes, Berger and Milem [36] argue that the more involved students are in the life of the academy, the more likely they are to interact with and be affected by the environment of the campus. Still, according to the authors, the organizational environment of the campus and students' perceptions of that environment have a direct influence on the extent and types of students' involvement in academic and social activities. The more positive the students' perception of the organizational environment, the greater their likelihood of participating in various academic and social activities promoted and made available by HEIs and, at the same time, persisting in the institution. Subsequent studies have achieved similar conclusions, thus showing the centrality of the relationship between the institutional environment and students' engagement in different kinds of activities, as well as the fact that the student experience is enhanced with their participation in academic and social activities inside and outside the classroom, e.g., [44–48].

Moreover, student participation and engagement in institutional decision-making bodies may also be a booster for a fulfilling overall experience of HE students. The activities that allow for this involvement encompass rather simple ones, such as informal strategies inside and outside the classroom, and more structured and broadened ones, such as the active participation of students in "institution-level systems for student representation" [49] (p. 688), where they may be heard at the formal institutional level and be effective actors in the institutional decision-making process. Pascarella and Terenzini [6] argue that if students' involvement and commitment are key pieces of this puzzle, then HEIs should focus on ways and mechanisms they can use to keep their students involved and committed. According to the authors, this is possible by promoting academic, social, and extracurricular dynamics and offers that might foster students' involvement and commitment to their individual goals and the HEI as a whole. On the other hand, students' involvement in the life of the academy is potentially influenced by the way they experience the HEI's organizational attributes. Organizational attributes such as participation in organizational decision-making, justice in policy administration, and communication may affect students' decisions to persist in or drop out of the institution [50].

Considering the above, it is safe to ascertain that student engagement is a variable with relevant weight in the definition of higher education student success [51,52]. Furthermore, student engagement and participation influence student retention [53]. The study aimed to assess the degree of importance of extracurricular activities in higher education students' integration and adaptation to the HEI as well as the role they ascribe to these activities in their overall development. Given the goal of the study, the following research questions guided the research:

1. How do students mobilize and get involved in extracurricular activities, and to what extent do these actors understand this involvement as relevant to their academic experience?
2. How do students and HEIs view their participation in institutional decision-making?

2. Materials and Methods

2.1. Research Design

To obtain the perceptions of the institutional actors involved and, therefore, meet the goal of the study mentioned above, the methodology chosen for this research study is qualitative, and the multiple case study methodology was used. As argued by Baxter and Jack [54], this methodological approach enables the exploration of a phenomenon in the context in which it occurs, using a wide range of data collection sources. Moreover, qualitative methods are better suited to grasping and interpreting the meanings [55–57], that is, specifically in this research study, how students perceive and represent their academic experience in terms of integration in the HEI. The qualitative approach allows for obtaining a thorough and detailed understanding of the phenomena studied in their own context and based on the perceptions of the actors involved in them [56].

2.2. Participants

The sample of this study is composed of 58 academic actors, including students and institutional leaders, from four Portuguese HEIs (two universities and two polytechnic institutes, all from the public subsystem). Concerning students, the study sample is composed of 40 HE students. For the selection of participants from the four HEIs, the following criteria were considered: the nature of the study program (1st and 2nd cycle, or degree and master's degree); the nature of knowledge (hard-pure, soft-pure, hard-applied e soft-applied [58]); and gender. Of the 40 participant students, 21 (52.5%) are undergraduate students, and 19 (47.5%) are graduate students. The participants are 19 male and 21 female students. The analysis of social-economic-educational indicators reveals the prevalence of students coming from middle-class families and whose parents have compulsory education qualifications (in Portugal, the 12th grade).

As for the institutional leaders, the sample is composed of 18 institutional actors that have some level of influence on the institutional decision-making process (e.g., Vice/Pro-Rectors and Vice-Presidents that deal with issues concerning quality, training, education, organization, and academic activities). Moreover, the Student Ombudsman, students representatives on the Pedagogical Council, and presidents of Student Unions are also part of the sample. The sample selection sought to reflect the heterogeneity of the wider group by following the sample section criteria mentioned above.

Contrary to the sample of institutional leaders, the sample of students was not defined a priori. According to the literature [59,60], it is common for the size of the sample to take shape as the study progresses until no new categories, themes, or explanations emerge from the data, at which point theoretical and empirical saturation is reached. In the study, data saturation was reached with the 40th interview. The strategy adopted in the design of the sample consisted of a sampling procedure according to which the researcher has access to informants through other informants, which gives rise to a "snowball" sample [61,62]. The selection of undergraduate and postgraduate students aimed to obtain the perceptions of both groups regarding the integration processes and the involvement in extracurricular activities, as students from each group have distinct features and hence may perceive these processes differently.

The mean age of the students is 23.28 (σ 2.82), with the maximum age being 35 and the minimum age being 19. Regarding the distribution of the sample by age range, more than half of the students in the sample (60%) are between 21 and 25 years old; 22% of the students are between 18 and 20 years old; 10% of students are between 31 and 35 years old, and 8% are between 26 and 30 years old.

2.3. Data Collection Tools

Data collection tools are threefold: (1) semi-structured interviews with students; (2) semi-structured interviews with institutional leaders; and (3) document analysis to allow for data triangulation. Tables 1 and 2 detail the questions of the semi-structured interview with students and institutional leaders that specifically concern student integration, adaptation, and engagement, which were generated based on the literature review.

Table 1. Questions from the semi-structured interview with students.

Dimensions	Questions	
	1st Cycle (Bachelor's)	2nd Cycle (Master's)
Integration/adaptation to the HEI	• Do you like the HEI you enrolled in? • How would you describe the environment surrounding the HEI? • How do you consider the opening hours and operation of the services? • How was your experience regarding hazing? Do you think that it helped you integrate into the HEI?	• Do you like the HEI you enrolled in? • How would you describe the environment surrounding the HEI? • How do you consider the opening hours and operation of the services?
Adaptation to the study program	• Do you like the program you are enrolled in? • Do you believe it is well structured/organized and its subjects have quality and relevance? • Do you believe there is a link between curriculum content and professional opportunities? • How much of your time and energy do you devote, on average, to your studies? • In terms of time management, do you believe that the workload allows you to prepare yourself in academic terms?	
Involvement in extracurricular activities	• Are you a part of any academic association? • Do you get involved in cultural, recreational and/or sporting activities at the HEI?	
Relationship with peers	• How would you describe your relationship with your peers in academic and social terms (i.e., inside and outside the classroom)?	
Relationship with teachers	• Do you think there is a good relationship between teachers and students? • Do you believe contact with teachers inside and outside the classroom is easy? • Do you believe teachers show the availability of time to support/interact with students?	
Attainment of educational goals	• Do you expect, with your overall experience in HE, to attain the goals you set when you came here?	• Do you expect, upon the conclusion of the master's, to attain the goals you set when you came here?

Table 2. Questions of the semi-structured interview with institutional leaders.

Interviewees	Dimensions	Questions
Heads of HEIs	Internal structures, policies and practices	• What is the HEI's vision of the student? • How is institutional communication carried out with students on subjects of interest to them (they knowledge they have about academic and social rules, etc.)? • What is the level of student participation in organizational decision-making on the development of social and academic rules? • What actions are taken to listen to students about their experience at the HEI? • In terms of the physical structure of the institution, how do you assess the quality of the facilities (in terms of curricular and extracurricular activities)? • What actions are carried out by the HEI to integrate new students?
	Curricular and co-curricular programs, policies and practices	• Regarding students' involvement in academic life, whether in academic or social terms, what are the opportunities, stimuli, and possibilities for this involvement to be effective?
Student Ombudsman	Student support	• What kind of problems do students bring with them when they come to you? • In what ways does this body address these requests? • What type of students seek the Ombudsman's help the most? • How often do students use this support?
	Integration of new students	• Are there any initiatives carried out by this body to welcome and integrate new students? • What is, specifically and in practice, the support provided by the Student Ombudsman to new students?
	Organizational structure	• How would you characterize the institution in terms of (a) study spaces/classes and (b) leisure spaces? • How do you characterize the environment on campus? • How do you envision student participation in institutional decision-making?
	Relationship with the HEI	• How do you characterize the relationships that students establish in this institution in terms of (a) the relationship between peers, whether in academic or social terms; (b) the relationship with teachers, inside and outside the classroom; and (c) the relationship with the various services and non-teaching staff?
President of the Student Union (SU)	Student support	• What are the motivations for students to join the SU? • What kind of problems do students bring when they seek the SU? • How does the SU address these requests? • What kind of students are most interested in the SU? • In what academic year are the students enrolled who most seek SU for support in solving problems?
	Integration of new students	• What initiatives does the SU carry out to welcome and integrate new students? • What is the support provided by the SU to new students?
	Curricular and extracurricular activities	• What activities does the SU promote to support students on their academic path? • What kind of extracurricular activities does the SU carry out? • What is the participation of students in these activities?
	Organizational structure	• How would you characterize the institution in terms of (a) study spaces/classes and (b) leisure spaces? • How do you characterize the environment on campus? • How do you envision student participation in institutional decision-making?
	Relationship with the HEI	• How do you characterize the relationships that students establish in this institution in terms of (a) the relationship between peers, whether in academic or social terms; (b) the relationship with teachers, inside and outside the classroom; and (c) the relationship with the various services and non-teaching staff?
Student Representative in the Pedagogical Board (PB)	Role and goals	• What is the role of the student representative with the PB? • In personal terms, how do you see your role in the PB?
	Representingstudents	• What motivated you to apply for this position? • What are your skills and powers as a student representative with the PB? • What are the advantages for students of having their representative at the PB? • What problems/issues do you, as a student representative, carry to PB meetings? • Is there feedback from you to the students you represent? If so, how is this feedback provided?
	Relationship with the HEI	• How do you characterize the relationships students establish in this institution in terms of their (a) relationship with the HEI in general, the various services, and non-teaching staff; and (b) academic or social relationships between peers?

2.4. Procedure

One of the data collection sources used was document analysis, which consists of "[…] a systematic procedure for reviewing or evaluating documents—both printed and electronic" [63] (p. 27). This tool allowed the gathering of information that enables data triangulation, thus increasing the trustworthiness of the study [64]. In this study, documents made available by the HEIs were analyzed, namely their strategic plan, activities report, and other documents, as well as the HEIs' website on the Internet. The second source consisted of in-depth interviews with students and institutional leaders, which took place on the premises of the HEIs analyzed. The interviews started by providing the participants with information on the goals of the study. Subsequently, respecting the ethical principles of the research, the interviewees were assured of the anonymity and confidentiality of the data they would convey [65]. The interviews were audio-recorded after authorization from the interviewees and transcribed in full for later analysis.

2.5. Data Analysis

The research technique used in the analysis of the collected data consists of content analysis, which enables the compression of a large amount of words and text into fewer content categories based on explicit coding rules [66]. In this study, according to the methodological approach used, a set of categories coded a priori have been built based on the critical review of literature carried out on the dimensions and factors affecting HE students' academic and social experiences. However, the categorization initially created was not intended to be closed; data analysis allowed the establishment of emerging categories, i.e., categories that, according to their relevance to the study, have been incorporated into the categorical system throughout the data analysis. The data were coded by paragraph and sentence, as proposed by Strauss and Corbin [67]. Table 3 depicts the themes, categories and sub-categories that form the categorical system that deals specifically with student integration into and engagement with the life of the academy.

Table 3. Themes, categories, and sub-categories of the study.

Dimension	Theme	Categories	Sub-Categories
Individual		Integration	• Integration/adaptation to the HEI • Integration/adaptation to HE
Organizational	Internal structures, policies and practices	Vision of the student	• Student follow-up practices • Participation of students in institutional decision-making • Student support mechanisms • Quality of the physical structure for (a) academic activities and (b) social/leisure activities
Academic Experience	Interpersonal	Curricular and co-curricular programs, policies and practices	• Opportunities, incentives and possibilities for academic and social involvement
		Relationship/interaction with teachers and peers in the classroom	
Social Experience	Interpersonal	Relationship/interaction with teachers and peers	• Affective dimension • Instrumental dimension • Limited to the classroom • Beyond the classroom • Depending on the teachers
		Involvement	• Academic activities • Cultural activities • Leisure/sports activities • Non-involvement
		Social integration/adaptation	• Integration by peers • Integration by the HEI
Functional Experience		Operational interaction	• Bureaucratic processes and procedures • Student suitability
		On-campus spatial orientation	• Spatial orientation within the campus
		Institutional Environment	• Human dimension • Physical dimension
		Relationship/interaction with non-teaching staff	• Affective level of interactions • Functional level of interactions

Following Saldaña [68], data coding began when the first interviews and institutional documents were analyzed in the pre-coding phase. In the second phase (or first coding cycle), the codes were refined and organized into categories and sub-categories through a deeper analysis of the data. Finally, in the third phase (or second coding cycle), the data were compared and consolidated.

3. Findings

Students' involvement and commitment are pivotal in their academic and social developmental processes [12,19,26,36,48], and HEIs have part of the responsibility for this process. This responsibility has to do with promoting dynamics and the production of offers at the academic, social, and extracurricular levels that can promote such involvement and commitment, both with students' personal goals and with the HEI [6,50]. Considering the learning process as global and comprehensive, HEIs should rethink the organizational structures so that it is possible to incorporate and capitalize on the students' experiences that occur outside the classroom, trying to connect the formal and informal learning contexts, and taking themselves as organizations focused on learning rather than on instruction [6].

The models that analyze HE students' experiences argue that their participation in extracurricular activities plays a relevant role, on the one hand, in their involvement with the institution and, on the other hand, in their willingness to seek the achievement of their personal goals and targets. This phenomenon has clear consequences in terms of the students' likelihood to persist in or drop out of their studies in a given institution or even in HE [6,12,19–21,26,27,31,36,69,70].

The analysis of the students' narratives regarding their involvement in extracurricular activities allowed the identification of four sub-categories: (1) involvement in academic activities; (2) involvement in cultural activities; (3) involvement in recreational/sports activities; and (4) involvement in associative activities. Moreover, the institutional perspective on this topic is also analyzed.

3.1. The Students' Perspective

3.1.1. Involvement in Academic Activities

Academic events are the most frequently mentioned ones by respondents and those that come first on the list of their preferences in terms of involvement in extracurricular activities. Students state that whenever they have the opportunity, they participate in lectures, workshops, conferences, and seminars, especially if they fall within the scope of their educational field, as they perceive these moments as relevant contributions to their academic preparation and overall education. These students perceive that these educational moments may be a lever for networking, for closer contact with their future professional area, and for a first approach to the labor market and the opportunities therein. One student states: "I regularly participate in events of an entrepreneurial nature because I know I'll have to work for a boss at first, but I do not see myself doing that for the rest of my life, and I know that I have to take the initiative and get the most enjoyment from it" (undergraduate student). This stance reflects a logic of preparation to attain personal and professional goals in the future. Students see these events as opportunities to grasp what is happening in the labor market insofar as "[. . .] people who come here to speak in these lectures are either starting a business or already run one and come here to share their experience with us, which is always an added-value" (undergraduate student).

3.1.2. Involvement in Cultural Activities

The second group of activities preferred by the students surveyed regards cultural events, such as plays, music concerts, and cinema. They perceive these activities as also educational opportunities, but mainly as moments where they can interact with others and strengthen their social relationships outside the classroom. As a graduate student states, "I participate in some cultural activities because I think it's good to foster team spirit [. . .] I think it brings people together". However, it is stressed rather frequently that, depending on time management and the availability of financial resources, these activities lose out to the more academic ones, such as lectures and workshops, for example.

The analysis of the perceptions of the institutional leaders surveyed regarding students' involvement in cultural activities reveals that they clearly acknowledge the educational value of these activities and, thus, they seek, through the promotion of diversified actions, to engage their students in activities that are "[. . .] structured and that develop in students a sense of responsibility and commitment" (Vice-Rector). The institutional acknowledgement of students' involvement in such initiatives is subsequently "[. . .] endorsed in the diploma supplement ("The Diploma Supplement is produced by higher education institutions according to standards agreed by the Commission, the Council of Europe and the United Nations Educational, Scientific and Cultural Organization (UNESCO). It is also part of the Europass framework transparency tools. The Diploma Supplement is designed as an aid to support the recognition of academic qualifications. The Diploma Supplement is an important tool of the European Higher Education Area for graduates to ensure that their degrees are recognized by higher education institutions, public authorities and employers in their home countries and abroad. It does, however, not represent a Curriculum Vitae or a substitute for the original qualification" [71]; it is an activity that the student carried out without receiving any money but that has contributed to his/her education" (Vice-Rector) According to this leader, the endorsement in the Diploma Supplement of activities in which students participated and had active involvement is an institutional validation of such participation as a complementary form of education. It is stated that this "[...] is a way of saying that we value their engagement in these activities, and also that we believe that this is also education, not in the strict academic sense, but educational activities during the academic period" (Vice-Rector).

3.1.3. Involvement in Recreational/Sports Activities

A third group of activities consists of recreational or sports events, which are attractive to some students and in which they participate whenever they have the opportunity to do so. Some of these activities include sports tournaments, football games, dinners, and parties with friends. Similarly to what happens with cultural activities, these social events are perceived as privileged moments to interact and strengthen ties with colleagues and friends. In short, social events of a more recreational nature are perceived by these students not only as moments of relaxation but also as opportunities to strengthen ties of friendship established with peers.

3.1.4. Involvement in Associative Activities

For some of the students interviewed, participation in associative activities—student unions, student study groups, and academic choirs, among others—is also perceived as a positive form of active involvement in the life of the academy. It also functions as a way to attain social and professional tools that will be useful for them in the future. On the other hand, the assumption of responsibilities as representatives of their peers in the institution's management bodies is also referred to as relevant to their experience in HE.

For these students, the extracurricular activities made available by the institution play a relevant role in their experience in HE because, as they state, "[...] there is much more to life than university" (graduate student). They perceive these activities as developmental moments because, according to a student, "[...] these events add to my education and help me feel integrated into the academic community" (graduate student). These students believe that these moments always provide some kind of learning, and they are also acknowledged as privileged ways of student integration into the academic community.

Although most students interviewed mention that they participate, to a greater or lesser extent, in extracurricular activities as part of their educational process, there is a small group of students who have the opposite behavior—very low adhesion or even non-adhesion. The most commonly cited reasons for this social behavior have to do mostly with financial constraints and time availability, but also because these students do not see their involvement in these activities as a priority, choosing to study instead. Another reason given was the obvious lack of interest in these activities.

From the set of extracurricular activities that the HE students affirm that they engage in, the analysis of the narratives allowed for the identification of the four sub-categories described above. Figure 1 provides an overall view of these four sets of extracurricular activities as well as their relative relevance, as depicted by the different sizes of the circles.

These results are in line with previous studies that reveal the participation of students in extracurricular activities has benefits for student learning and career development [37], as well as the attainment of both technical and transversal skills [33,72]. Furthermore, participation in extracurricular activities has a significant influence on the engagement levels of students when compared to those who do not get involved in these activities [73]

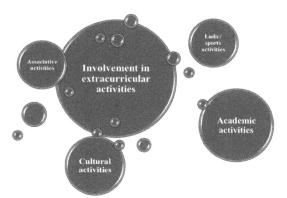

Figure 1. Students' involvement in extracurricular activities. Source: The author's production.

3.2. The Institutional View

In line with the students' perceptions, institutional leaders understand the student's path as multifaceted, extending beyond the academic or curricular component and viewing students' participation in extracurricular initiatives as relevant to their overall education. Therefore, HEIs encourage the participation of their students in voluntary, cultural, recreational, and sports activities, among others. However, the analysis of the institutional leaders' narratives points towards the perception of a low level of involvement and participation of students in the extracurricular activities offered by the institution and academic groups. The argument that students have a very heavy academic load, which does not allow them to set aside some of their time to participate in this type of activity, is used by some of these leaders, who recognize the need to "[. . .] have a more active raw material, but I also recognize that time is not enough for everything" (Vice-President). Furthermore, these leaders also refer to the Bologna Process as "[. . .] taking much more of students' time, often preventing them from taking a more active part in these activities" (Vice-President). However, this justification is not consensual, and it is even refuted by other leaders, who claim that students' academic loads are not, currently, "[. . .] different from it was 30 or 40 years ago" (Pro-Rector) and that "[. . .] the fact that students claim that they have a very intense academic load is no reason not to be present" (President of the Student Union). The institutional leaders' vision regarding the involvement of students in non-curricular activities is that sometimes it is difficult to attract them.

In addition to the possible time scarcity that leads students to not participate regularly in extracurricular activities, institutional leaders put forward other reasons for this behavior, specifically: (i) the personalities of those responsible for boosting such events; (ii) the current social trend for the reduced demand for cultural goods; (iii) certain scientific areas seen as more absorbing in terms of time devoted to study; (iv) the physical distance between the place where these activities take place and the residence of some of the students; (v) the reconfigurations in terms of HE students' profiles; and (vi) the new and different ways in which students relate to involvement in extracurricular activities, compared to students from previous generations. While acknowledging the existence of the insufficient adhesion of the students to these initiatives, some of the institutional leaders mention that, in certain kinds of actions, this insufficiency does not occur. Given that HEIs have a wide offer in terms of activities, the understanding is that there are possibilities for all students' needs, tastes, and availability.

In sum, according to institutional leaders' perceptions, students' participation in extracurricular activities is generally low, falling very often short of expectations. However, in some scientific areas that interest students, or given the possibility of personal and overall development, these actors end up engaging in actions that, while not being part of the courses' syllabus, are envisaged as educational opportunities offered by their institution.

4. Conclusions

The analysis of the interviewees' narratives allows for the conclusion that students' academic experience cannot be disconnected from their social and functional experience in the HEI. This stance confirms the importance, described in previous studies [22,24,26,30,33,37,50,74,75], of students' involvement in educational activities beyond the classroom boundaries. Corroborating literature, participants in this study posit that student life cannot be limited to class attendance and the preparation of papers and exams—this experience should be complemented with recreational or, at least, less formal activities. These can be materialized mainly in extracurricular activities, such as the participation in seminars, workshops, and conferences with perceived relevance to the enhancement of students' curriculum and as a complement to their education, but also in other activities, such as the participation in decision-making bodies and associative activity. Students perceive these activities as being a vehicle par excellence for the attainment and/or development of transversal competences, seen as an added value in their overall education, sometimes at the expense of one or two points in the final grade, which are seen as a small price to pay for the competences they have attained through their active participation in the life of the academy.

Most institutional actors who participated in this study believe, similarly to the students interviewed, that the students' involvement in extracurricular activities, i.e., more cultural or recreational activities, as well as their involvement in institutional decision-making bodies and associative movements, are privileged ways of complementing students' academic training and are perceived by them as pivotal in their overall education, both as professionals and as individuals. Furthermore, students' participation and involvement in decision-making bodies, such as the Pedagogic Councils or the General Councils, or in academic movements, such as student unions or student study groups, is understood as an excellent vehicle for students to attain competences that can be used later on, in the labor market. The issue of grades is even sidelined when compared to the attainment of transversal competences, especially by students involved in decision-making dynamics and bodies.

On the side of the HEIs, the involvement of students in institutional decision-making processes is also seen as central. Besides allowing students' involvement in making decisions that directly affect them, this is also a way to prepare them for their future professional lives through the attainment of participation and decision-making competences, among others. Students' engagement in extracurricular activities works, or should work, in conjunction and complementarity with the academic activities in the sense of students' overall education, while contributing to their degree of commitment to the HEI, their persistence in the institution and, ultimately, their graduation. Thus, the results from this study, while revealing the relevance students ascribe to their integration in the HEI, namely through their engagement in extracurricular activities of a diverse nature, may assist institutional policymakers in defining and improving strategies for their students' integration and development.

This study is not without limitations. The first is due to the methodological approach chosen. The choice of a qualitative methodology prevents generalizations, inasmuch as the purpose of qualitative research is not to generalize the results but rather to describe, interpret, and ascribe meaning to the subjects' positioning concerning a given situation [76]. This is the main disadvantage of using qualitative approaches, as they do not allow the generalization of the results of studies with the same degree of certainty that quantitative approaches do. Moreover, the results of these studies cannot be tested to verify whether they are statistically significant or due to chance [77]. Moreover, qualitative research can provide answers to specific research questions that quantitative research cannot [78]. The second limitation concerns the number of cases studied and their geographic location. This study was limited to four case studies in northern Portugal, albeit the choice of the HEIs to be studied tried to obey some criteria that could make these cases, in some way, "representatives" of the Portuguese reality—by selecting a classic university, a new university, a large polytechnic institute, and a small polytechnic institute. The third limitation is that this study encompassed only the public sub-sector of Portuguese HE, so it remains to analyze the reality of private HE. We believe that, while some of the dimensions of analysis used in this study would deliver similar results, others would possibly show relevant differences.

Funding: This research was funded by FCT—FOUNDATION FOR SCIENCE AND TECHNOLOGY, I.P., grant number UIDB/00757/2020 of CIPES—Centre for Research in Higher Education Policies, by national funds through FCT/MEC. The APC was funded by *Education Sciences*.

Institutional Review Board Statement: The study was conducted in accordance with the Declaration of Helsinki, and approved by the Review Board of CIPES–Centre for Research in Higher Education Policies (protocol code 05/2022 of 28 December 2022).

Informed Consent Statement: Informed consent was obtained from all subjects involved in the study.

Data Availability Statement: The data presented in this study are available on request from the corresponding author. The data are not publicly available due to privacy restrictions.

Conflicts of Interest: The author declares no conflict of interest.

References

1. Pucciarelli, F.; Kaplan, A. Competition and strategy in higher education: Managing complexity and uncertainty. *Bus. Horiz.* **2016**, *59*, 311–320. [CrossRef]
2. Siemens, G.; Matheos, K. Systemic Changes in Higher Education. In *Becoming an Open Scholar*; Kimmons, R., Ed.; EdTech Books, 2022. Available online: https://edtechbooks.org/open_scholar/systemic_changes (accessed on 13 February 2022).
3. Spady, W.G. Dropouts from higher education: An interdisciplinary review and synthesis. *Interchange* **1970**, *1*, 64–85. [CrossRef]
4. Ajjawi, R.; Dracup, M.; Zacharias, N.; Bennett, S.; Boud, D. Persisting students' explanations of and emotional responses to academic failure. *High. Educ. Res. Dev.* **2019**, *39*, 185–199. [CrossRef]
5. Aljohani, O. A comprehensive review of the major studies and theoretical models of student retention in higher education. *High. Educ. Stud.* **2016**, *6*, 1–18. [CrossRef]
6. Pascarella, E.T.; Terenzini, P.T. *How College Affects Students. Vol. 2. A Third Decade of Research*; Jossey-Bass: San Francisco, CA, USA, 2005.
7. Sosu, E.M.; Pheunpha, P. Trajectory of university dropout: Investigating the cumulative effect of academic vulnerability and proximity to family support. *Front. Educ.* **2019**, *4*, 1–10. [CrossRef]
8. Tinto, V. Dropout from higher education: A theoretical synthesis of recent research. *Rev. Educ. Res.* **1975**, *45*, 89–125. [CrossRef]
9. Tinto, V. *Leaving College: Rethinking The Causes and Cures of Student Attrition*, 2nd ed.; The University of Chicago Press: Chicago, IL, USA, 1993.
10. Tinto, V. Through the eyes of students. *J. Coll. Stud. Retent. Res. Theory Pract.* **2017**, *19*, 254–269. [CrossRef]
11. Astin, A. *Preventing Students from Dropping Out*; Jossey-Bass: San Francisco, CA, USA, 1975.
12. Astin, A. Student involvement: A developmental theory for higher education. *J. Coll. Stud. Dev.* **1999**, *40*, 518–529.
13. Sá, M.J. 'Welcome to Wonderland'. Integration rituals and ceremonies for higher education first-year students, and lessons for institutions. *Eur. J. High. Educ.* **2021**, 1–16. [CrossRef]
14. Dias, D.; Sá, M.J. The impact of the transition to HE: Emotions, feelings and sensations. *Eur. J. Educ.* **2014**, *49*, 291–303. [CrossRef]
15. Dias, D.; Sá, M.J. Initiation rituals in university as lever for group cohesion. *J. Furth. High. Educ.* **2014**, *38*, 447–464. [CrossRef]
16. Amado-Tavares, D. *O Superior Ofício de Ser Aluno: Manual de Sobrevivência do Caloiro [The Superior Craft of Being a Student: Freshman's Survival Manual]*; Edições Sílabo: Lisboa, Portugal, 2008.
17. Thompson, M.; Pawson, C.; Evans, B. Navigating entry into higher education: The transition to independent learning and living. *J. Furth. High. Educ.* **2021**, *45*, 1398–1410. [CrossRef]
18. Chrysikos, A.; Ahmed, E.; Ward, R. Analysis of Tinto's student integration theory in first-year undergraduate computing students of a UK higher education institution. *Int. J. Comp. Educ. Dev.* **2017**, *19*, 97–121. [CrossRef]
19. Anzivino, M.; Rostan, M. University student participation in out-of-class activities. In *The University as a Critical Institution?* Deem, R., Eggins, H., Eds.; Sense Publishers: Rotterdam, The Netherlands, 2017; pp. 185–216.
20. Browning, B.R.; McDermott, R.C.; Scaffa, M.E.; Booth, N.R.; Carr, N.T. Character strengths and first-year college students' academic persistence attitudes: An integrative model. *Couns. Psychol.* **2018**, *46*, 608–631. [CrossRef]
21. Tinto, V.; Pusser, B. *Moving from Theory to Action: Building a Model of Institutional Action for Student Success*; National Postsecondary Education Cooperative (NPEC): Washington, DC, USA, 2006.
22. Xerri, M.J.; Radford, K.; Shacklock, K. Student engagement in academic activities: A social support perspective. *High. Educ.* **2018**, *75*, 589–605. [CrossRef]
23. Astin, A. Student involvement: A developmental theory for higher education. *J. Coll. Stud. Pers.* **1984**, *25*, 297–308.
24. Astin, A. *Achieving Academic Excellence: A Critical Assessment of Priorities and Practices in Higher Education*; Jossey-Bass: San Francisco, CA, USA, 1985.
25. Astin, A. *What Matters in College? Four Critical Years Revised*; Jossey-Bass: San Francisco, CA, USA, 1993.

26. Bowden, J.-H.; Tickle, L.; Naumann, K. The four pillars of tertiary student engagement and success: A holistic measurement approach. *Stud. High. Educ.* **2019**, *46*, 1207–1224. [CrossRef]
27. Collaço, C.M. Increasing student engagement in higher education. *J. High. Educ. Theory Pract.* **2017**, *17*, 40–47.
28. Kahn, P.E. Theorising student engagement in higher education. *Br. Educ. Res. J.* **2014**, *40*, 1005–1018. [CrossRef]
29. Kahu, E.R. Framing student engagement in higher education. *Stud. High. Educ.* **2013**, *38*, 758–773. [CrossRef]
30. Kahu, E.R.; Picton, C.; Nelson, K. Pathways to engagement: A longitudinal study of the first-year student experience in the educational interface. *High. Educ.* **2020**, *79*, 657–673. [CrossRef]
31. Kuh, G.D.; Kinzie, J.; Buckley, J.A.; Bridges, B.K.; Hayek, J.C. *What Matters to Student Success: A Review of the Literature (Commissioned Report for the National Symposium on Postsecondary Student Success: Spearheading a Dialog on Student Success)*; National Postsecondary Education Cooperative (NPEC): Washington, DC, USA, 2006.
32. Tani, M.; Gheith, M.H.; Papaluca, O. Drivers of student engagement in higher education: A behavioral reasoning theory perspective. *High. Educ. Int. J. High. Educ. Res.* **2021**, *82*, 499–518. [CrossRef]
33. Bergmark, U.; Westman, S. Student participation within teacher education: Emphasising democratic values, engagement and learning for a future profession. *High. Educ. Res. Dev.* **2018**, *37*, 1352–1365. [CrossRef]
34. Brouwer, J.; Jansen, E. Beyond grades: Developing knowledge sharing in learning communities as a graduate attribute. *High. Educ. Res. Dev.* **2019**, *38*, 219–234. [CrossRef]
35. Sá, M.J.; Serpa, S. Transversal competences: Their importance and learning processes by higher education students. *Educ. Sci.* **2018**, *8*, 126. [CrossRef]
36. Berger, J.B.; Milem, J.F. Organizational behavior in higher education and student outcomes. In *Higher Education: Handbook of Theory and Research*; Smart, J.C., Ed.; Agathon Press: New York, NY, USA, 2000; pp. 268–338.
37. Han, A.; Kwon, K. Students' perception of extracurricular activities: A case study. *J. Adv. Educ. Res.* **2018**, *3*, 137–147. [CrossRef]
38. Bean, J.P.; Eaton, S.B. A psychological model of college student retention. In *Reworking the Student Departure Puzzle*; Braxton, J.M., Ed.; Vanderbilt University Press: Nashville, TN, USA, 2000; pp. 48–62.
39. Klemenčič, M.; Chirikov, I. How do we know how students experience higher education? On the use of student surveys. In *The European Higher Education Area*; Curaj, A., Matei, L., Pricopie, R., Salmi, J., Scott, P., Eds.; Springer: Dordrecht, The Netherlands, 2015; pp. 361–379.
40. Swail, W.S.; Redd, K.E.; Perna, L.W. *Retaining Minority Students in Higher Education. A Framework for Success*; ASHE-ERIC Higher Education Report; Association for the Study of Higher Education: Washington, DC, USA, 2003.
41. Spady, W. Dropouts from higher education: Toward an empirical model. *Interchange* **1971**, *2*, 38–62. [CrossRef]
42. Braxton, J.M.; Doyle, W.R.; Hartley, H.V.; Hirschy, A.S.; Jones, W.A.; McClendon, M.K. *Rethinking College Student Retention*; Jossey-Bass: San Francisco, CA, USA, 2013.
43. Kahu, E.R.; Nelson, K. Student engagement in the educational interface: Understanding the mechanisms of student success. *High. Educ. Res. Dev.* **2017**, *37*, 58–71. [CrossRef]
44. Day, I.N.Z.; van Blankenstein, F.M.; Westenberg, P.M.; Admiraal, W.F. Explaining individual student success using continuous assessment types and student characteristics. *High. Educ. Res. Dev.* **2018**, *37*, 937–951. [CrossRef]
45. Jones, W.A. The impact of social integration on subsequent institutional commitment conditional on gender. *Res. High. Educ.* **2010**, *51*, 687–700. [CrossRef]
46. Littlepage, B.; Hepworth, D. Influence of social integration on class success. *J. Contin. High. Educ.* **2016**, *64*, 162–171. [CrossRef]
47. Matthews, K.E.; Andrews, V.; Adams, P. Social learning spaces and student engagement. *High. Educ. Res. Dev.* **2011**, *30*, 105–120 [CrossRef]
48. Wilkins, S.; Butt, M.M.; Kratochvil, D.; Balakrishnan, M.S. The effects of social identification and organizational identification on student commitment, achievement and satisfaction in higher education. *Stud. High. Educ.* **2015**, *41*, 2232–2252. [CrossRef]
49. Young, H.; Jerome, L. Student voice in higher education: Opening the loop. *Br. Educ. Res. J.* **2020**, *46*, 688–705. [CrossRef]
50. Smith, L.J.; Chenoweth, J.D. The contributions of student organization involvement to students' self-assessments of their leadership traits and relational behaviors. *Am. J. Bus. Educ.* **2015**, *8*, 279–288. [CrossRef]
51. Sá, M.J. 'The secret to success'. Becoming a successful student in a fast-changing higher education environment. *Eur. J. High Educ.* **2020**, *10*, 420–435.
52. Coates, A.; Matthews, K.E. Frontier perspectives and insights into higher education student success. *High. Educ. Res. Dev.* **2018**, *37*, 903–907. [CrossRef]
53. Kirk, G. Retention in a Bachelor of Education (Early childhood studies) course: Students say why they stay and others leave. *High. Educ. Res. Dev.* **2018**, *37*, 773–787. [CrossRef]
54. Baxter, P.; Jack, S. Qualitative case study methodology: Study design and implementation for novice researchers. *Qual. Rep.* **2008**, *13*, 544–559. [CrossRef]
55. Denzin, N.K.; Lincoln, Y.S. *The Handbook of Qualitative Research*, 4th ed.; Sage Publications: Thousand Oaks, CA, USA, 2011.
56. Merriam, S.B. *Qualitative Research. A Guide to Design and Implementation*; Jossey-Brass: San Francisco, CA, USA, 2009.
57. Willig, C. Interpretation in qualitative research. In *The SAGE Handbook of Qualitative Research in Psychology*; Willig, C., Rogers, W.S., Eds.; Sage Publications: London, UK, 2017; pp. 276–290.
58. Becher, T.; Trowler, P.R. *Academic Tribes and Territories*, 2nd ed.; McGraw-Hill Education: Berkshire, UK, 2001.

9. Saunders, B.; Sim, J.; Kingstone, T.; Baker, S.; Waterfield, J.; Bartlam, B.; Burroughs, H.; Jinks, C. Saturation in qualitative research: Exploring its conceptualization and operationalization. *Qual. Quant.* **2018**, *52*, 1893–1907. [CrossRef]
10. Low, J. A pragmatic definition of the concept of theoretical saturation. *Sociol. Focus* **2019**, *52*, 131–139. [CrossRef]
11. Heckathorn, D.D. Snowball versus respondent-driven sampling. *Sociol. Methodol.* **2011**, *41*, 355–366. [CrossRef] [PubMed]
12. Kline, T.J.B. Sample issues, methodological implications, and best practices. *Can. J. Behav. Sci.* **2017**, *49*, 71–77. [CrossRef]
13. Bowen, G.A. Document analysis as a qualitative research method. *Qual. Res. J.* **2009**, *9*, 27–40. [CrossRef]
14. Morgan, H. Conducting a qualitative document analysis. *Qual. Rep.* **2021**, *27*, 64–77. [CrossRef]
15. Denzin, N.K.; Lincoln, Y.S. *The Sage Handbook of Qualitative Research*, 5th ed.; Sage Publications: Thousand Oaks, CA, USA, 2017.
16. Krippendorff, K. *Content Analysis: An Introduction to Its Methodology*, 4th ed.; Sage Publications: Thousand Oaks, CA, USA, 2018.
17. Strauss, A.L.; Corbin, J. *Basics of Qualitative Research: Grounded Theory Procedures and Techniques*, 2nd ed.; Sage Publications: Thousand Oaks, CA, USA, 1998.
18. Saldaña, J. *The Coding Manual for Qualitative Researchers*, 2nd ed.; Sage Publications: Thousand Oaks, CA, USA, 2013.
19. Bargmann, C.; Thiele, L.; Kauffeld, S. Motivation matters: Predicting students' career decidedness and intention to drop out after the first year in higher education. *High. Educ.* **2021**, *83*, 845–861. [CrossRef]
20. Almeida, L.; Soares, A.P.; Ferreira, J.A. Questionário de Vivências Académicas (QVA-r): Avaliação do ajustamento dos estudantes universitários [Questionnaire of Academic Experiences (QVA-r): Assessment of university students adjustment]. *Avaliação Psicológica* **2002**, *2*, 81–93.
21. Hassan, K. Investigating conditions for student success at an American university in the Middle East. *High. Educ. Stud.* **2014**, *4*, 62–74. [CrossRef]
22. Buckley, P.; Lee, P. The impact of extra-curricular activity on the student experience. *Act. Learn. High. Educ.* **2021**, *20*, 37–48. [CrossRef]
23. Munir, S.; Zaheer, M. The role of extra-curricular activities in increasing student engagement. *Asian Assoc. Open Univ. J.* **2021**, *16*, 241–254. [CrossRef]
24. European Commission. Diploma Supplement. Available online: https://ec.europa.eu/education/diploma-supplement_en (accessed on 12 May 2022).
25. Pike, G.R. The convergent and discriminant validity of NSSE scalelet scores. *J. Coll. Stud. Dev.* **2006**, *47*, 551–564. [CrossRef]
26. Crabtree, B.F.; Miller, W.L. (Eds.) *Doing Qualitative Research*, 2nd ed.; Sage Publications: Thousand Oaks, CA, USA, 1999.
27. Atieno, O.C. An analysis of the strengths and limitations of qualitative and quantitative research paradigms. *Probl. Educ. 21st Century* **2009**, *13*, 13–18.
28. Busetto, L.; Wick, W.; Gumbinger, C. How to use and assess qualitative research methods. *Neurol. Res. Pract.* **2020**, *2*, 2–10. [CrossRef] [PubMed]

Article

Educational Challenges of Higher Education: Validation of the Information Competence Scale for Future Teachers (ICS-FT)

Gerardo Gómez-García [1,*], Francisco-Javier Hinojo-Lucena [1], Francisco-Domingo Fernández-Martín [2] and José-María Romero-Rodríguez [1]

[1] Department of Didactics and Scholar Organization, University of Granada, 18071 Granada, Spain; fhinojo@ugr.es (F.-J.H.-L.); romejo@ugr.es (J.-M.R.-R.)
[2] Department of Evolutive Psychology, University of Granada, 18071 Granada, Spain; fdfernan@ugr.es
* Correspondence: gomezgarcia@ugr.es

Abstract: The irruption of information and communication technologies has brought about an abrupt change in the demands placed on future professionals. In this sense, in recent years, information competencies have gained importance in university education from a cross-cutting perspective which advocates as its main purpose the training of young people in information search, evaluation, processing and communication skills, especially through a digital network. Based on this idea, the present work aims to develop the Information Competence Scale for Future Teachers (ICS-FT), in order to measure the level of self-perceived skills in this area. For this purpose, a work design is presented below concerning an empirical validation, divided into different phases: the validation of content, construct and reliability, which has taken as a pilot sample a total of 259 university students studying the degree of Primary Education. The results of the validation determined the optimal conditions of content, construct and reliability that allowed the application of this scale as a generic approach to determine the level of competence in the information skills of future teachers.

Keywords: information competencies; digital literacy; information literacy; higher education; future teachers

Citation: Gómez-García, G.; Hinojo-Lucena, F.-J.; Fernández-Martín, F.-D.; Romero-Rodríguez, J.-M. Educational Challenges of Higher Education: Validation of the Information Competence Scale for Future Teachers (ICS-FT). *Educ. Sci.* **2022**, *12*, 14. https://doi.org/10.3390/educsci12010014

Academic Editor: Peter Williams

Received: 5 November 2021
Accepted: 21 December 2021
Published: 29 December 2021

1. Introduction

In recent years, the irruption of technology has monopolized a compendium of modifications that have produced an abrupt change in the way we understand daily processes. Specifically, since its emergence, the Internet has become one of the most major pastimes used by the population, and more specifically, when exercising both generic and advanced information queries and searches [1,2]. This is due, to a greater extent, to the number of possibilities offered by this resource and the multitude of variants it offers the user with just a "click" [3]. As a consequence, from the educational landscape, a substantial paradigm shift is taking place, reorienting teaching/learning processes and reconsidering the role of students, teachers, future demands and demands that revolve around these factors [4].

In this characteristic context of the information society in which we find ourselves, the need for future professionals to possess information competencies is a priority common to all disciplines, all learning environments and all levels of education [5]. Its acquisition is already justified in different educational plans, and its correct development encourages university students to have a greater understanding of knowledge, in order to possess a greater metacognitive capacity and, in short, to assume greater control over their own learning process [6].

The "Conferencia de Rectores Universitarios Españoles of ICT" (Crue-ICT) Joint Commission and Rebiun [7] define information competencies as "the set of knowledge, skills, attitudes and behaviors that enable individuals to recognize when they need information, where to locate it, how to evaluate its suitability, and how to use it appropriately according to the problem at hand" (p. 6). In view of the constant change that revolves around the current context, the relevance of training in information skills, as well as the general promotion of information literacy in the population, is presented as one of the challenges that contemporary society must face in educational terms [8]. Especially, this skill becomes more relevant in different education professionals, whose objectives include training their students to have a critical spirit and responsible attitude towards the functions of locating, evaluating, configuring and communicating information [9,10].

This term is closely related to that of digital competence in teaching. The development of digital competence has become one of the most demanding educational challenges faced by the educational community. In this sense, digital training constitutes one of the lines of action for the promotion and fulfilment of the objectives proposed by the Agenda 2030 for Sustainable Development [11]. This training takes as its main reference the following conceptual framework: The European Digital Competence Framework for Citizens [12] (DIGCOMP). The digital competence is distinguished by five dimensions that structure the concept: 1—Information and Information Literacy; 2—Communication and Collaboration; 3—Digital Content Creation; 4—Digital Security; and 5—Problem Solving. Specifically, when reference is made to information literacy, the specialized literature refers to the ability to "identify, locate, obtain, store, and organize digital information, data and digital content, assessing their purpose and relevance for teaching tasks". Likewise, there are complementary definitions that understand this concept as the ability to think critically and give reasoned opinions on any information we find and use [13]. As far as the training of future teachers is concerned, the latest research shows low levels of information literacy skills [14,15], content creation [16,17], or skills in informational and digital communication and collaboration [18,19].

Upon reaching university, students require basic training to interact with the informational process, since the development of their skills is not enough to be able to locate, access, retrieve, evaluate, and critically use information autonomously [20]. Throughout their university careers, there are many situations in which these competencies are required, and not having adequate training leads to unsatisfactory results, and thus to a deficit in this type of knowledge. Therefore, the justification of this concept in educational terms is agreed upon regarding the importance of achieving an integration in the university curricula of this discipline. This is considered common and transversal to all formative degrees in any type of subject [21] in order to promote a comprehensive learning that augurs a better and greater professional development [22]. In this sense, Cortés et al. (2004) cited by Gallardo and Lau [23], point out a series of priority informational skills to work on during the university stage:

(a) Understanding of the structure of knowledge and information: identifying the information cycle (generation, processing, organization and dissemination).
(b) Determine the nature of an information need: be able to identify and communicate your information needs.
(c) Develop effective strategies to search for and find information: carry out an orderly search process to ensure success in obtaining information.
(d) Information retrieval: develop strategies for effective information retrieval from different sources.
(e) Analyze and evaluate the information: determine the scope and depth of the information.
(f) Integrate, synthesize and use information: incorporate previous knowledge and make the corresponding transfers in different disciplinary fields.
(g) Presenting the results of the information obtained: understanding the information obtained and being able to express it adequately.
(h) Respect intellectual property and copyrights: behave ethically in the use and application of information.

Thus, there are several studies that analyzed the level of informational skills in different university students. From the implementation of intervention programs, substantial improvements were encouraged in aspects such as formal data searches in official [24,25] and informal repositories [26]; in the writing of academic papers [27], the citations and referencing of scientific sources [28,29]; critical thinking and autonomous learning [30–32]; quality assessment of electronic sources [33]; or in shaping new scholarly elaborations and their communication [34]. Accordingly, the benefits of working on these competencies within university education are noted [35].

With regard to instruments related to the evaluation of self-efficacy in these competencies, it is necessary to highlight those that were referents when configuring the competencies established in this work. (i) Firstly, there is the IL-HUMASS 21 scale [36], which was designed for a population of students, librarians and teachers based on four dimensions (information seeking, evaluation, processing and communication/dissemination) and three self-report dimensions (motivation, self-efficacy and favorite source of learning). (ii) Secondly, there is the information literacy self-efficacy scale (ILSE), developed by Kurbanoglu et al. [37], which measured these competencies in terms of seven basic skills: (a) Defining the need for information; (b) Initiating the search strategy; (c) Locating and accessing resources; (d) Evaluating and understanding information; (e) Interpreting, synthesizing and using information; (f) Communicating information; and (g) Evaluating the product and the process. Undoubtedly, these are two rigorously configured instruments that were used in multiple investigations and taken as references for the elaboration of the questionnaire used in the present work.

With regard to the justification of this instrument, its configuration is intended to be useful for students who are in the process of becoming future teachers in order to self-evaluate their level of information competencies. To this end, the wording of the items is simple, and the number of items configured is brief, following the recommendations of experts [38,39] regarding the development of questionnaires aimed at a young population in order to obtain more rigorous results.

Therefore, the main objective of this work is to construct and empirically validate a self-perception instrument for the development of the information competencies of university students.

2. Materials and Methods

The present study was developed following a cross-sectional, correlational, quantitative design [40], framed in the validation of an ad hoc scale through a content and internal consistency analysis [41]. To this end, the study was divided into different phases (Figure 1) from its initial configuration to the final drafting of the instrument and subsequent statistical validation [42]. Therefore, two large stages can be distinguished. The first is linked to the process of developing the instrument and the second to its validation.

2.1. Sample

A total of 259 university students studying for a degree in Primary Education at the University of Granada (Spain) participated in the pilot study. The age range was between 18 and 15 years, with a mean age of 23.29 years (SD = 3.49), of which 63.3% were female and 36.7% male. A greater number of women were included in the study due to the fact that, generally, for teacher training degrees, the female population is more prevalent [43]. The sample selection procedure was based on a non-probabilistic or convenience sample [44]. On the other hand, the sample size was greater than 200 cases, above the minimum threshold established in different simulation studies to set up structural equation models [45]. See the details at Appendices A and B.

2.2. Instrument Development and Content Validation

Firstly, an exhaustive review of the literature on the topic in question was carried out. From this point, in accordance with Wilson [46], the operational definition of information competencies was drafted. In this case, the definition expressed by the (CRUE-ICT) Joint Commission and Rebiun [7] was taken as the main definition. Next, the drafting of the scale items took place. Throughout, the main priority was that the items were simple, and specific references to their configuration were followed [42,47]. Likewise, the type of scale chosen in this case was Likert type 7 with a frequency response type (1 = never/7 = always)

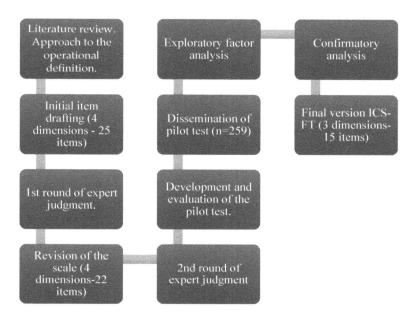

Figure 1. Phases carried out to validate the ICS-FT scale.

Consequently, content validation was carried out through expert judgments [38]. The expert judges were asked to evaluate, in a total of two rounds, different aspects of the measurement scale, the questionnaire items, and an overall assessment of the questionnaire [39], as well as the pilot scale presented in this work. Therefore, the overall assessment was made up of a qualitative analysis (analyzing the degree of comprehension, adequacy of the wording according to the target population, etc.) and a quantitative assessment (scale 1 to 10), in order to evaluate the degree of belonging to the object of study, i.e., to what extent each of the items should form part of the scale. As for the panel of the expert judges, it was composed of four university professors belonging to the branch of Didactics and School Organization. Specifically, they worked within the lines of research related to educational technology, digital competence, continuing teacher training and inclusion of information and communication technologies (ICT) in the classroom. They had an extensive curriculum in terms of research activity, as well as in the validation of multiple scales, several of which are similar in nature to those presented here (especially those associated with digital competence in teaching and development). On the other hand, the degree of understanding by the target population in the pilot study was also assessed by means of an open-ended item in which the participants of the study could show those strengths or weaknesses they considered important in order to improve the wording of the scale items.

2.3. Data Analysis

In the first instance, an exploratory factor analysis was performed using the principal components method. The factors obtained were orthogonally rotated using the Varimax method with Kaiser normalization. Then, following the recommendations of Muthén and Muthén [48], the characteristics of the data distribution were analyzed: descriptive statistics and linearity or normality of the extracted factors. Likewise, possible differences in the distribution of data according to gender were analyzed using the Mann–Whitney U test and the Kruskal–Wallis H test for independent samples. Spearman's bivariate correlation analysis technique was applied to analyze the links between the dimensions.

Once the number of factors was determined, finally, confirmatory analysis was carried out to check whether the theoretical measures of the model were consistent through the modeling of diagrams and the use of structural equations [49]. In summary, the aim was to check whether the data obtained fit the hypothetical model produced by the exploratory factor analysis. Finally, the reliability of the scale and of the different dimensions configured were analyzed using Cronbach's alpha coefficient. The different analyses were performed with the SPSS v.25 and AMOS v.24 statistical packages.

3. Results

In the first instance, with regard to content validity, Table 1 shows the qualitative assessment of the scale expressed by the expert judges. These contributions were useful for making significant modifications to the different items that made up the final version of the scale, and for clarifying some conceptual issues, as in the case of identifying the need for information (judge 1), clarifying items by including examples (judge 3), or using a simple vocabulary in order to adapt the instrument to the target population (judge 4).

Table 1. Qualitative assessment of expert judgment.

Experts	Report
Expert 1	It is necessary to specify whether students are aware of when they need information on a certain topic, in order to cover in greater depth all the aspects expressed in the operational definition of the construct.
Expert 2	Some items need to be reworded to make them easier for university students to understand.
Expert 3	I would specify the different formats through which information can be presented (audio, social network, video, textual, etc.). Similarly, when referring to social networks, I would allude to all of them.
Expert 4	I would replace the word sex with gender. I would also change the word "biases" to "errors" when referring to information that may not be correct, to improve understanding by undergraduates.

Secondly, the results of the quantitative assessment of the scale items (Table 2) showed that, in general, all the items were considered optimal by the committee of experts. Those items that received an average score equal to or lower than 7 were eliminated, as was the case with items 3 and 5 and 20.

Table 2. Qualitative assessment of expert judgment.

Item Reference	Expert 1	Expert 2	Expert 3	Expert 4	Mean
I.1	8	9	9	8	8.5
I.2.	7	8	8	8	7.75
I.3.	7	7	6	7	6.75 (Retired)
I.4.	9	9	10	10	9.5
I.5.	6	7	6	6	6.25 (Retired)
I.6.	8	7	8	7	7.5
I.7.	9	9	10	10	9.5
I.8.	9	9	9	9	9
I.9.	9	9	10	9	9.25
I.10	9	9	10	9	9.25
I.11	9	9	9	9	9
I.12	9	9	9	9	9
I.13	8	8	8	8	8
I.14	8	8	8	8	8
I.15	9	8	9	8	8.5
I.16	8	8	8	8	8
I.17	9	9	8	9	8.75
I.18	8	9	9	9	8.75
I.19	7	8	8	7	7.5
I.20	6	7	6	6	6.25 (Retired)

On the other hand, with respect to the evaluation of comprehension by the study sample based on the item open to suggestions, no suggestions for profound improvement were suggested, indicating only that the comprehension of the scale was optimal.

3.1. Factor Analysis

For the grouping of the questionnaire items into second-order dimensions, the principal component extraction method with Varimax rotation was applied. A three-dimensional solution was fixed. Table 3 shows the rotated component solution with the respective communalities. Factor 1 defines the information evaluation competencies. It is made up of six items that explain 19.87% of the total variance. Factor 2 refers to the information search and communication skills. It is made up of four items that explain 17.51% of the total variance. Factor 3 evaluates competency in information processing and elaboration, explaining 17.29% of the total variance with five items. The total variance explained by the three factors is 54.66%. In short, of the 17 total items resulting from the content analysis, after the application of the exploratory factor analysis, the scale obtained a total of 15 items distributed in three factors.

Table 3. Matrix of rotated components and factorial weight.

	Factor 1	Factor 2	Factor 3	Factorial Weight
I.1. I double check about the veracity of the information I check.	**0.799**	0.097	0.073	0.615
I.2. I compare a piece of information in several sources to verify its accuracy.	**0.791**	0.219	0.162	0.630
I.3. I am able to identify if a piece of information has mistakes.	**0.705**	0.085	0.321	0.548
I.4. I am able to identify if the resources of a piece of information are up to date.	**0.627**	0.472	0.104	0.456
I.5. I am able to identify if a piece of information is useful for my learning process.	**0.489**	0.333	0.448	0.537
I.6. I share the information after I have checked its reliability.	**0.436**	0.362	0.203	0.557
I.7. I use specialized resources (such as scientific databases) to look up for specialized information about a topic.	0.201	**0.718**	0.029	0.580
I.8. Before I present a piece of information, I share the sources I have used.	0.235	**0.715**	0.118	0.417
I.9. I index the pieces of information I use following a specific scientific citation, such as APA.	−0.048	**0.682**	0.384	0.362
I.10. I acknowledge what it implies to share fake information.	0.263	**0.491**	0.229	0.700
I.11. I am able to write a text with a clear structure (such as an instruction, its development, and a conclusion).	0.109	0.079	**0.782**	0.652
I.12. I am capable of acknowledging the main ideas of a text.	0.115	0.067	**0.721**	0.626
I.13. I am capable of selecting the right format to present a piece of information, (whether it is text, audio, image, or video).	0.229	0.269	**0.650**	0.607
I.14. I am capable of distinguishing the veracity of the pieces of information I receive from different sources (such as emails, news on social media, etc.).	0.242	0.385	**0.499**	0.551

Table 3. *Cont.*

	Factor 1	Factor 2	Factor 3	Factorial Weight
I.15. When facing a problem, I am capable of knowing where and how to look for information that I need.	0.307	0.366	**0.435**	0.362
Variance		2.980	2.626	2.593	8.199
% Variance		19.865	17.509	17.288	54.662

The Kaiser–Meyer–Olkin test (KMO = 0.89) indicates that there is a high correlation between the variables. Barlett's test of sphericity was significant ($\chi 2 = 1344.02$; gl = 105, $p < 0.001$) indicating that a factor analysis was appropriate.

Therefore, once the factors and variance percentages were extracted, we proceeded to analyze the characteristics of the data distribution. The results of the normality test indicated that the data did not follow a normal distribution. In this sense, the use of a U-Mann–Whitney test was advocated, which determined that men and women had a similar level of competence in the four second-order dimensions (Table 4).

Table 4. Descriptive analysis by gender.

	Male (n = 95)			Female (n = 164)			U Mann–Whitney		
	M	SD	Me	M	Dt	Me	Z	p	d
Factor 1	5.73	0.93	5.83	5.66	0.83	5.83	−0.849	0.396	0.05
Factor 2	6.02	0.98	6.25	6.03	0.86	6.25	−0.409	0.682	0.03
Factor 3	6.10	0.71	6.20	6.23	0.59	6.40	−1.388	0.165	0.09

Table 5 shows that the competency of evaluating information is directly and significantly associated with the competency of working with information sources and with the competency in comprehension and elaboration of texts. The latter two are significantly related. Age is not related to any of the second-order dimensions.

Table 5. Spearman's Rho correlations.

		Factor 1	Factor 2	Factor 3
Factor 2	Rho	0.545		
	p	<0.001		
Factor 3	Rho	0.600	0.537	
	p	<0.001	<0.001	
Age	Rho	−0.063	0.087	−0.099
	p	0.316	0.162	0.111

3.2. Reliability Analysis

The reliability analysis (Table 6) shows that the first factor has a high Cronbach's alpha coefficient compared to a moderate-high value for factor 3 and a moderate value for factor 2. The lowest level of competence is found in information evaluation skills.

Table 6. Descriptive statistics and reliability of factors.

	M	SD	α
Factor 1	5.69	0.87	0.83
Factor 2	6.02	0.91	0.70
Factor 3	6.18	0.64	0.75

3.3. Confirmatory Analysis

In order to validate the factor structure extracted after the exploratory factor analysis, a confirmatory factor analysis was carried out using the maximum likelihood assumption. The model consists of fifteen observed variables explained by three second-order dimensions that correspond to those specified after the exploratory factor analysis. The structure of the model and the standardized solution is presented in Figure 2.

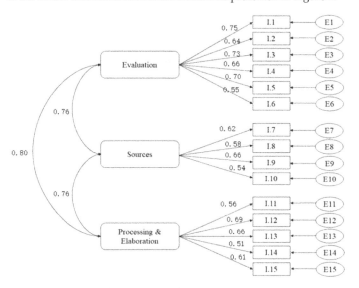

Figure 2. SEM model of the ICS-FT scale.

The chi-square index of absolute goodness-of-fit of the model to the data ($\chi287 = 224.336$; $p < 0.001$) shows that there is a significant discrepancy between the data and the model. The coefficient $\chi2/gl = 2.579$ is above 2, which is in line with what was reported for the chi-square value, which indicated that the model does not fit the data perfectly. However, the CFI = 0.89 and NFI = 0.84 have values close to 0.90, while the RMSEA = 0.078 is less than 0.08. These three indicators do show that the model is appropriate for explaining the data from the proposed structure.

Figure 2 shows that the second-order dimensions are highly correlated. In turn, each of these dimensions explains, according to the standardized regression coefficients, a significant proportion of the variance of the observed variables. In short, it can be affirmed that the model is adequate for explaining the factor structure of the observed variables; although, future research of this structure should be refined in order to achieve a better fit to the data.

4. Discussion

Information literacy has become one of the main challenges of the information society. With the arrival of the Internet in our lives, and the large amount of time we spend interacting with digital networks, this subject has become very important in the transversal training of young university students in order to promote sustainable processes of search, evaluation, processing and communication of information skills [5]. In this context, the information competence scale for future teachers was configured in order to measure the levels of information competence for those university students who are in their initial training period for their profession and are able to self-diagnose their level of information competence in this discipline. It is a discipline common to all areas of knowledge, but in the case of the future teacher, it is even more important, since he/she is in charge of transmitting knowledge to a new generation whose interaction with digital and informative media is daily and continuous [14].

For this purpose, this work was framed in an empirical validation design grouped around different phases [42]: initial design and content analysis through expert judgment [38], configuration of the pilot test and dissemination to the target population, and construct (exploratory and confirmatory factorial) and reliability analysis. Finally, and after all these procedures, a scale of 15 items grouped into three dimensions was obtained: (I)—Competences in information evaluation; (II)—Information search and communication skills; and (III)—Competencies in information processing and elaboration. There are three dimensions that comprise the basic processes understood at the time of information collection: Firstly, there is the evaluation of the information coming from the digital network, in order to know how to locate information correctly; secondly, there is a deepening work in specialized sources, in order to be able to classify the sources of information according to the quality of the information offered; and finally, from this information, it is necessary that future teachers are able to elaborate their own information from the specialized information so that emphasis is placed on the process of creation, elaboration and the processing of the information. Although it is true that the scale is brief, it is intended to establish a generic view of the students' self-perceived level of this set of skills and abilities. Therefore, from its application in populations, it can elucidate initial approaches to promoting educational interventions in this regard and promote an improvement in competency indexes. Likewise, it is a scale that, unlike several of its predecessors [36,37], is not contextualized in the library landscape, in favor of establishing the focus on transversal actions of an academic nature carried out by any university student, and in this case, more specifically, of future teachers.

The results obtained in the present study showed that the scale obtained favorable scores in terms of its internal structure, as well as in terms of reliability indices. Likewise, the analyses presented did not reflect significant differences in the self-perceptions of the pilot population studied in terms of the variables gender and age, which according to Haladyna and Rodriguez [41], is a positive index in favor of the scale. Likewise, the SEM model obtained from the data distribution indicated high levels of correlation and covariance between the constructs that make up the scale, which is another factor in favor of the scale [49].

5. Conclusions

In recent years, the exponential increase in information and communication technologies has become an empowering phenomenon that has made the Internet the main option for searching and interacting with information. As a result, today's society needs future professionals who are able to identify, evaluate and critically communicate the information they find on the digital network. In education, there is a demand for teachers and professors who are experienced in digital competence, and more specifically, in information literacy, in order to continue fostering future generations trained in critical thinking and with the skills to search, locate, evaluate, process and communicate information. Therefore, from this work, we tried make progress towards this goal; towards a prospective work, in which information literacy becomes important in the training of the future teachers, understood as one of the current and future challenges that the educational system must face during the digital boom and digital transformation that is happening in today's society. However, these types of competencies should be considered as transversal to all areas of knowledge.

Finally, with regard to future lines of research, it is necessary for the scientific community to continue investigating the level of informational competence presented by future professionals in different disciplines of knowledge, as well as to develop intervention programs in this area to promote an improvement in information searches, selection and evaluation, elaboration and communication skills. It is, therefore, one of the challenges that Higher Education must address, in order to ensure that future generations of young people present competencies in accordance with the needs demanded by today's 21st century Society.

Author Contributions: Conceptualization, G.G.-G. and F.-J.H.-L.; methodology, G.G.-G. and F.-D.F.-M.; validation, G.G.-G., F.-D.F.-M. and J.-M.R.-R.; formal analysis, G.G.-G.; investigation, G.G.-G., J.-M.R.-R.; data curation, F.-D.F.-M.; writing—original draft preparation, G.G.-G.; writing—review and editing, G.G.-G. and F.-D.F.-M.; visualization, G.G.-G.; supervision, F.-J.H.-L. All authors have read and agreed to the published version of the manuscript.

Funding: This work belongs to the doctoral thesis work funded through the Ministry of Education (Reference FPU2017-05952), as well as the project entitled: Development of informational competence of university students in a period of uncertainty promoted by the COVID-19 (ref: PPJIB2020.21) funded by the University of Granada.

Acknowledgments: To the AREA research group of the University of Granada. To Fátima León Medialdea as official translator of the manuscript.

Conflicts of Interest: The authors declare no conflict of interest.

Appendix A. Information Literacy Scale for University Students (ICS-US)

1. I double check about the veracity of the information I check.
2. I compare a piece of information in several sources to verify its accuracy.
3. I am able to identify if a piece of information has mistakes.
4. I am able to identify if the resources of a piece of information are up to date.
5. I am able to identify if a piece of information is useful for my learning process.
6. I share the information after I have checked its reliability.
7. I use specialized resources (such as scientific data bases) to look up for specialized information about a topic.
8. Before I present a piece of information, I share the sources I have used.
9. I index the pieces of information I use following a specific scientific citation, such as APA.
10. I acknowledge what it implies to share fake information.
11. I am able to write a text with a clear structure, (such as an instruction, its development, and a conclusion).
12. I am capable of acknowledging the main ideas of a text.
13. I am capable of selecting the right format to present a piece of information, (whether it is text, audio, image, or video).
14. I am capable of distinguishing the veracity of the pieces of information I receive from different sources (such as emails, news on social media, etc.).
15. When facing a problem, I am capable of knowing where and how to look for information that I need.

Appendix B. Information Literacy Scale for University Students (ICS-US) (Spanish Version)

1. Me cuestiono sobre la veracidad de una información cuando la consulto.
2. Comparo una misma información en diferentes fuentes para comprobar si es cierta.
3. Soy capaz de identificar si una información contiene errores.
4. Soy capaz de determinar si una información que contiene un recurso está actualizada.
5. Soy capaz de evaluar si una información es útil para mi proceso de aprendizaje.
6. Comparto una información una vez comprobada su veracidad.
7. Accedo a portales especializados (bases de datos científicas, repositorios oficiales, etc.) para consultar información específica sobre un contenido.
8. Comunico las fuentes consultadas utilizadas a la hora de presentar una información.
9. Referencio las fuentes de información siguiendo alguna tipología de citación científica (p.ej: APA).
10. Conozco los riesgos existentes en torno a compartir una información falsa.
11. Soy capaz de elaborar un texto propio con un estructura clara (p.ej: introducción; desarrollo, conclusión).
12. Reconozco en un texto las ideas principales que trata de transmitir.

13. Soy capaz de diferenciar el formato más adecuado para presentar una información (texto, audio, imagen, vídeo, etc.).
14. Soy capaz de diferenciar aquellas informaciones que recibo (emails; sms; noticias en redes sociales, etc.) en función de la veracidad que le otorgo.
15. Al tener que hacer frente a un problema, decido dónde y cómo encontrar la información que necesito.

References

1. Alonso, A.; Gewerc, A. Alfabetización mediática en la escuela primaria. Estudio de caso en Galicia. *Rev. Complut. Educ.* **2018**, *29*, 407–422. [CrossRef]
2. García-Valcárcel, A.; Salvador, L.; Casillas, S.; Basilotta, V. Evaluación de las competencias digitales sobre seguridad de los estudiantes de Educación Básica. *Rev. Educ. Distancia* **2019**, *19*, 1–34. [CrossRef]
3. Ricoy, M.C.; Sánchez-Martínez, C.; Feliz-Murias, T. Credibility versus fake news in digital newspapers on tablets in primary education. *Cultura y Educación* **2019**, *31*, 296–325. [CrossRef]
4. Martínez, L.D.; Hinojo, F.J.; Aznar, I. Aplicación de las Tecnologías de la Información y la Comunicación (TIC) en los Procesos de Enseñanza-Aprendizaje por parte de los Profesores de Química. *Inf. Tecnol.* **2018**, *29*, 41–52. [CrossRef]
5. Gómez-Pablos, V.B.; Muñoz-Repiso, A.G.V.; Martín, S.C.; González, M.C. Evaluación de competencias informacionales en escolares y estudio de algunas variables influyentes. *Rev. Complut. Educ.* **2020**, *31*, 517–528. [CrossRef]
6. Irving, C.; Crawford, J. From secondary school to the world of work: The experience of evaluating information literacy skills development at Glasgow Caledonian University (GCU). *J. eLit.* **2005**, *2*, 137–143.
7. Comisión Mixta CRUE-TIC & REBIUN. Competencias Informáticas e Informacionales (CI2) en los Estudios de Grado 2012. Available online: https://www.rebiun.org/sites/default/files/2017-11/CI2_estudios_grado_2012.pdf. (accessed on 5 September 2021).
8. Gómez-García, G.; Hinojo, F.J.; Aznar, I.; Romero, J.M. Análisis sobre la productividad en torno a la alfabetización informacional en la etapa de Educación Superior. *Texto Livre Ling. Tecnol.* **2021**, *14*, e33694. [CrossRef]
9. Oliveira, C.; Lopes, J.; Spear-Swerling, L. Teachers' academic training for literacy instruction. *Eur. J. Teach. Educ.* **2019**, *42*, 315–334. [CrossRef]
10. Wilson, C. Media and Information Literacy: Pedagogy and Possibilities. *Comunicar* **2012**, *39*, 15–22. [CrossRef]
11. Alonso-García, S.; Aznar-Díaz, I.; Cáceres-Reche, M.-P.; Trujillo-Torres, J.-M.; Romero-Rodríguez, J.-M. Systematic Review of Good Teaching Practices with ICT in Spanish Higher Education. Trends and Challenges for Sustainability. *Sustainability* **2019**, *11*, 7150. [CrossRef]
12. Ferrari, A. *DIGCOMP: A Framework for Developing and Understanding Digital Competence in Europe*; Publications Office of the European Union: Luxembourg, 2013.
13. Sales, D. Definición de alfabetización informacional de CILIP, 2018. *Ann. Doc.* **2020**, *23*. [CrossRef]
14. Trujillo Torres, J.M.; Gómez García, G.; Ramos Navas-Parejo, M.; Soler Costa, R. The development of information literacy in early childhood education teachers. A study from the perspective of the education center's character. *JOTSE J. Technol. Sci. Educ.* **2020**, *10*, 47–59. [CrossRef]
15. Nowak, B.M. The development of digital competence of students of teacher training studies-Polish cases. *Int. J. High Educ.* **2019**, *8*, 262–266. [CrossRef]
16. Amhag, L.; Hellström, L.; Stigmar, M. Teacher Educators' Use of Digital Tools and Needs for Digital Competence in Higher Education. *J. Digit. Learn. Teach. Educ.* **2019**, *35*, 203–220. [CrossRef]
17. Del-Moral-Pérez, M.E.; Villalustre-Martínez, L.; Neira-Piñeiro, M.D.R. Teachers' perception about the contribution of collaborative creation of digital storytelling to the communicative and digital competence in primary education schoolchildren. *Comput. Assist. Lang. Learn.* **2019**, *32*, 342–365. [CrossRef]
18. López, J.; Pozo, S.; Fuentes, A.; Domínguez, N. The Level of Digital Competence in Education Professionals: The Case of Spanish Physical Education Teachers. *Zona Próxima* **2020**, *33*, 146–165.
19. Vázquez-Cano, E.; Marín, V.; Maldonado, G.A.; García-Garzón, E. The digital competence of social sciences college students from a gender perspective. *Prisma Soc.* **2017**, *19*, 347–367.
20. Manso-Perea, C.; Cuevas-Cerveró, A.; González-Cervantes, S. Competencias informacionales en los estudios de grado en enfermería: El caso Español. *Rev. Esp. Doc. Cient.* **2019**, *42*, e229. [CrossRef]
21. Waltz, M.J.; Moberly, H.K.; Carrigan, E.E. Identifying information literacy skills and behaviors in the curricular com-petencies of health professions. *J. Med. Libr. Assoc. JMLA* **2020**, *108*, 463. [PubMed]
22. Baranda, J.S.; Díaz, E.R.; González, M.L. Las competencias informacionales: Una necesidad de la formación permanente. *Rev. Cienc. Pedagóg. Innov.* **2017**, *5*, 84–90.
23. Gallardo, I.L.; Lau, J. La alfabetización informacional en docentes de educación básica. *Rev. Transform. Educ.* **2016**, *2*, 190–211.
24. George, S.; Rowland, J. Demonstrating the impact of your teaching: Benefits of Higher Education Academy Fellowship for librarians. *Health Inf. Libr. J.* **2019**, *36*, 288–293. [CrossRef]

5. Grandal, O.V.; Reyes, S.Á.R. Propuesta de programa para la formación de competencias informacionales en estudiantes de pregrado de Estomatología. *Rev. Cuba. Estomatol.* **2017**, *54*, 1–13.
6. Ball, C. WikiLiteracy: Enhancing students' digital literacy with Wikipedia. *J. Inf. Lit.* **2019**, *13*, 253–271.
7. Reche Urbano, E.; Martín Fernández, M.A.; González López, I. Autopercepción de la adquisición de las competencias informacional y comunicativa para la elaboración de trabajos académicos en la universidad. *Perf. Educ.* **2019**, *41*, 131–146. [CrossRef]
8. Al-Qallaf, C.L. Information Literacy Skills of Graduate Students: A Case of the Master's of Information Studies Program in Kuwait. *J. Inf. Knowl. Manag.* **2020**, *19*, 2050011. [CrossRef]
9. Sanches, T. Citar e referenciar: Uma estratégia formativa para o uso ético da informação e prevenção do plágio em meio académico. *Perspect. Ciênc. Inf.* **2019**, *24*, 59–72. [CrossRef]
10. Baji, F.; Bigdeli, Z.; Parsa, A.; Haeusler, C.C. Developing information literacy skills of the 6th grade students using the Big 6 model. *Malays. J. Libr. Inf. Sci.* **2018**, *23*, 1–15. [CrossRef]
11. Hernández, C.; Vall, A.; Boter, C. Formación, la clave para mejorar las competencias informacionales en e-salud del alumnado de bachillerato. *Gac. Sanit.* **2018**, *32*, 48–53. [CrossRef]
12. Kultawanich, K.; Koraneekij, P.; Na-Songkhla, J. Development and Validation of the Information Literacy Assessment in Connectivism Learning Environment for Undergraduate Students. *Procedia—Soc. Behav. Sci.* **2015**, *174*, 1386–1390. [CrossRef]
13. Chanchinmawia, F.; Kumar, M. Assessment of Information Literacy Skills among Research Scholars of Mizoram Univer-sity: A Study. *Int. J. Libr. Inf. Stud.* **2018**, *8*, 387–399.
14. Santharooban, S.; Premadasa, P.G. Development of an information literacy model for problem based learning. *Ann. Libr. Inf. Stud. (ALIS)* **2015**, *62*, 138–144.
15. Rashidov, A.S. Development of creative and working with information competences of students in mathematics. *Eur. J. Res. Reflect. Educ. Sci.* **2020**, *8*, 10–15.
16. Pinto, M. Design of the IL-HUMASS survey on information literacy in higher education: A self-assessment approach. *J. Inf. Sci.* **2010**, *36*, 86–103. [CrossRef]
17. Kurbanoglu, S.; Akkoyunlu, B.; Umay, A. Developing the Information Literacy Self-Efficacy Scale. *J. Doc.* **2006**, *62*, 730–743. [CrossRef]
18. Egaña, M.J.U.; Araya, S.C.B.; Núñez, M.L.G.; Camus, M.P.M. Métodos óptimos para realizar validez de contenido. *Educ. Méd. Super.* **2014**, *28*, 547–558.
19. Wieserma, L.D. Conceptualization and development of the sources of enjoyment in youth sport questionnaire. *Meas. Phys. Educ. Exerc. Sci.* **2001**, *5*, 153–157.
20. Hernández, R.; Fernández, C.; Baptista, P. *Metodología de la Investigación*; McGraw-Hill: New York, NY, USA, 2014.
21. Haladyna, T.M.; Rodríguez, M.C. *Developing and Validating Test Items*; Routledge: London, UK, 2013.
22. Muñiz, J.; Fonseca-Pedrero, E. Diez pasos para la construcción de un test. *Psicothema* **2019**, *31*, 7–16.
23. Navarro, C.; Casero, A. Análisis de las diferencias de género en la elección de estudios universitarios. *Estud. Sobre Educ.* **2012**, *22*, 115–132.
24. Pérez, V.D. *Procedimientos de Muestreo y Preparación de la Muestra*; Síntesis: Madrid, Spain, 2016.
25. Tomarken, A.J.; Waller, N.G. Structural equation modeling: Strengths, limitations, and misconceptions. *Annu. Rev. Clin. Psychol.* **2005**, *1*, 31–65. [CrossRef]
26. Wilson, M. *Constructing Measures: An Item Response Modelling Approach*; Lawrence Erlbaum Associates: Mahwah, NJ, USA, 2005.
27. Lane, S.; Raymond, M.R.; Haladyna, T.M.; Downing, S.M. Test development process. In *Handbook of Test Development*; Routledge: London, UK, 2015; pp. 19–34.
28. Asparouhov, T.; Muthén, B. Weighted least squares estimation with missing data. *Mplus Tech. Append.* **2010**, *2010*, 1–10.
29. Ruiz, M.A.; Pardo, A.; San Martín, R. Modelos de ecuaciones estructurales. *Pap. Psicól.* **2010**, *31*, 34–45.

education sciences

MDPI

Article

Exploring the BME Attainment Gap in a Russell Group University: A Mixed Methods Case-Study

Aunam Quyoum [1], Stephanie Powell [2] and Tom Clark [3,*]

1   School of Urban Studies, University of Glasgow, Glasgow G11 6EW, UK
2   Department of Psychology, University of Sheffield, Sheffield S10 2TL, UK
3   Department of Sociological Studies, University of Sheffield, Sheffield S10 2TN, UK
*   Correspondence: t.clark@sheffield.ac.uk

Abstract: Presenting the results from a mixed methods case-study, this paper draws together insights from the fields of 'BME attainment' and 'student transition' to explore how differential levels of degree attainment might be experienced within the context of a higher tariff university in England. Across a five-year period (2010/11–2014/2015) it compares the levels of degree attainment between UK-domiciled White and Black and Minority Ethnic (BME) students in relation to prior attainment, qualification type, and socioeconomic group (POLAR 3). A range of qualitative data then outlines a series of dynamic factors that can, when compounded, serve to constrain BME students' capability to negotiate their way through very particular university landscapes. These include: academic expectation and preparedness; the pedagogic terrain; pastoral engagement and sense of belonging; finance; and, the lived experience of diversity and 'othering'. The paper argues that attainment gaps should not be viewed in terms of an individual deficit that needs to be 'fixed' or 'filled'. Instead, greater attention needs to be directed toward enhancing the capacity of higher tariff universities to respond positively to the needs of a changing demographic.

Keywords: student transition; differential attainment; ethnicity; higher education

Citation: Quyoum, A.; Powell, S.; Clark, T. Exploring the BME Attainment Gap in a Russell Group University: A Mixed Methods Case-Study. *Educ. Sci.* **2022**, *12*, 860. https://doi.org/10.3390/educsci12120860

Academic Editors: Diana Dias, James Albright and Billy Wong

Received: 20 June 2022
Accepted: 22 November 2022
Published: 25 November 2022

Publisher's Note: MDPI stays neutral with regard to jurisdictional claims in published maps and institutional affiliations.

1. Introduction

Research in the UK Higher Education (HE) sector has consistently demonstrated an attainment gap between home-domiciled Black Minority Ethnic (BME) students and their White counterparts. In the context of the UK, BME primarily refers to students labelled as Black, Mixed, Asian, Chinese, who are identified as 'home'—that is, UK domiciled students. While the term BME cannot be considered cohesive with rates of attainment and retention varying within the category [1], the attainment gap between BME students and White students is persistent over time and still exists when factors such as entry qualifications and socioeconomic status are considered [2–5]. However, whilst some research has explored how applicants from under-represented groups are less likely than their peers to be offered places into more highly selective, higher tariff 'Russell Group' universities [4–6], there has been comparatively little exploration of how this might be translated into the experiences of BME students who do enter such institutions—particularly in the post-2012 context of a three-fold increase in tuition fees [7]. Drawing on the results of a mixed methods case-study of a UK Russell Group University (NRGU), this paper explores how students identified as 'BME' have performed over a five-year period in a Russell Group Institution, and how BME students understand and experience their transition into, and through, the university.

2. Context

Research across the UK HE sector has repeatedly pointed to the existence of a BME Attainment Gap [1,8–11]. This attainment gap is generally taken to be the difference between the proportion of UK-domiciled White students who gain higher degrees—1:1

or 2:1s—and the proportion of UK-domiciled BME students who are awarded the same degrees. Whilst there is variation between those groups that fall under the BME label the evidence continues to suggest that a significantly smaller proportion of BME students receive these degree classifications compared to their White counterparts [1,3]. The Equality Challenge Unit, for instance, demonstrated that whilst there has been a gradual increase in the overall number of students receiving 1:1/2:1s, there remains a consistent gap between BME and White students. In 2013/14, this gap was 15.2% points nationally, with the largest discrepancy occurring between Black and White students—a gap of 26.1% points [12].

Such gaps can have far reaching consequences. A number of studies have explored disparities in the graduate employment and highlighted that BME graduates are more likely to experience lower rates of progression into highly skilled employment or further study [13,14].

If the existence and consequence of the BME attainment gap are well established, the reasons why it occurs are much less secure. However, the research-base does have two key foci: factors that influence attainment before entering HE; and, factors that influence attainment during study. In respect to the former, a number of interrelated factors have been highlighted as being important, these include: schooling, in terms of both prior attainment and type of institution [15]; cultural differences in participation [16]; institution and subject choice [6]; socio-economic background [17]; and, familial influence [18]. In respect to the latter, however, preparedness [9], curriculum design and styles of learning and teaching in HE [19], unconscious bias [20,21], institutional culture [22,23], and the lack of awareness of BME-related issues [24] have all been highlighted as significant.

While the more qualitatively driven evidence suggests that the experiences of BME students in HEIs are both nuanced and variable [25], the thrust of more measurement-focused research has generally highlighted that such gaps exist even when other demographic and institutional data have been considered [1]. This includes entry qualification, socio-economic group, type of course (FT/PT), discipline, gender, and whether the HEI is research intensive or not [1,26,27]. For instance, Richardson reports evidence to suggest that when controlling for entry qualification only around half of the disparity in attainment is attributable to prior achievement [8,10]. Similarly, whilst characteristics such as entry qualification and socio-economic group can, in themselves, be shown to also have both independent influence over attainment, there is evidence to demonstrate that these factors do not fully account for the BME attainment gap [11].

Elsewhere, more critical accounts of institutional policy and practice have sought to highlight how notions of 'whiteness' are embedded within HEIs [18]. These, often deeply implicit, institutional cultures and discourses can serve to constrain both BME engagement and attainment. Several commentators have highlighted how the process of 'othering' locates both the gap and the solution within BME groups themselves. This process both individualises and stigmatises the student(s) in question [28,29]. Indeed, there is a well-established literature that has examined how the discursive practices associated with the institutional 'habitus' of HEIs works to exclude both working-class and BME groups—particularly in the context of Russell Group institutions. Whilst there is variation both within and between university landscapes, the net result is that these groups find it much more difficult than their white middle class peers to engage with, and develop, the social and cultural capital necessary to perform in such terrains [30–33].

As an adjunct to the literature on the BME attainment gap, there is also a growing interest in the field of 'student transition' within the context of HE. Broadly speaking, this refers to students' capability to navigate change. Whilst this field is still considered to be both 'under conceptualised' and 'under-theorised' [34], initial uses of the term primarily saw transition in terms of a relatively linear process of induction and/or development over time. Some formulations of the term have, however, understood transition as a process of 'becoming'. For instance, Gale and Parker highlight how transitions are dialectically structured through the administrative apparatus of institutions and the reflexive experiences of both staff and students [35]. Moving away from an understanding of transition that constructs progress as a linear and temporal movement from 'there to here', they argue student transitions in HE are more than a process of change over time. They are: often non-linear, and sometimes unresolved; both horizontal and vertical in that they have multiple dimensions that intersect and go beyond the first year experience; reflexively experienced, hence they are open to both interpretation and change; and, far from universal. As a result, discourses that might normalise or unify experience by mapping points of transition across the student life cycle, or simply identifying 'deficits' or 'stress points' in experience are problematic. This is because these approaches have a marked tendency to construct the need for enhancement within the individual. Instead, and much like Stevenson [29], Gale and Parker argue for an emphasis on how individuals make sense of the changes they experience within HEIs and through the course of their degree. This necessitates examining how those experiences are shaped by the institution in question.

The key thread that ties both the BME attainment and transition literature together is the need to build research base that has an emphasis on student engagement across a range of institutional types and programmes. To this end, little specific attention has currently been given within the literature to the BME attainment gap and the transitions that BME students make within 'Russell Group' universities specifically. The Russell Group is a term that refers to an association of twenty-four universities based in the UK that are typically non-collegiate and civic in origin. They are widely perceived to have a research-intensive focus and are selective, attracting some of the highest achieving students in the country. However, while recent research has demonstrated that applicants from traditionally underrepresented groups are less likely to be offered places than their peers [4,5,36], there has been comparatively little exploration of how this might be translated into the experiences of BME students who *do* enter such institutions.

To this end, this paper is directed toward first examining the nature of the BME attainment gap in such an institution, and secondly, how BME groups transition into, and through the university. Using a 'northern Russell Group University' (NRGU) as a case-study, and drawing on primary and secondary data within the context of a mixed-methods research design, it describes the levels of attainment of White and BME students in relation to a range of characteristics across a five-year period, before reconciling that data with a qualitative account of how BME students understand their experience of transitioning into and through the University.

3. Methodology

Using an embedded mixed-methods research strategy [37], this project sought to explore how and why differential attainment exists and persists within the context of a UK-based 'northern Russell Group University' (NRGU). Findings are drawn from secondary quantitative data in the form of the NRGU's student record, and primary qualitative data Together, the data offers a comprehensive overview of the attainment gap, as well as illuminating how it is experienced by BME students at university.

The quantitative element of the study was based on the student record of all full-time UK-domiciled undergraduate students who completed their studies between 2010/11 and 2014/15. Data was extracted from the University's student database and refined by removing: duplicate records; degree outcomes associated with intercalated programmes, students who received non-honours degrees (for example, diplomas); students who were awarded a degree by aegrotat; and, students whose registration status did not indicate successful completion of studies. Unfortunately, the student record does not contain any self-reported data such as family income or parental capacity for financial support.

Independent variables were created to reflect national data—in particular the Equality Challenge Unit analyses [11]. This included generalised ethnicity categories, simplified prior attainment grade banding based on A-Level equivalences, and simplified prior attainment types. Given the vast majority of students were under 21, it was not possible to determine any interaction between BME status/attainment and age. The categories of analysis are summarised in Table 1.

Table 1. Categories of Analysis.

Ethnicity	Prior Attainment	Prior Attainment Type	SEG (POLAR3)
White	AAA* and above	A-Level	Quintile 1
Black	AAA	BTEC	Quintile 2
Asian	AAB	Access	Quintile 3
Chinese	ABB	Combined A-Level and Other Qualifications	Quintile 4
Mixed	BBB	International Baccalaureate	Quintile 5
Other	BBC or Below	Other	
Unknown/Undeclared	Other		

The dependent measurement of 'degree attainment' also followed the standard procedure adopted by the ECU. This involved collapsing 1:1 and 2:1 degree classifications into a single category, and 2:2, 3:1 and Pass into another. Any attainment gap can thus be calculated as the difference between BME groups with respect to the proportion of 1:1/2:1 and other awards. Any differences can then be cross-referenced with respect to the independent variables described above. Descriptive analyses of the resultant data are presented in Section 4.

Running alongside this analysis, the qualitative strand of the study aimed to identify and understand the specific institutional context of NRGU and place this alongside how students experience their transition(s) through university. Adopting a case-study approach, the qualitative element of the project focused on 'Faculty A' because they had proportionally more BME students, and an attainment gap had already been identified within earlier institutional research. Given the emerging importance of BME recruitment, retention, and attainment, it was felt that such a case-study—where the gap has been broadly recognised, and an initial response made—would offer something of a 'typical-case' for investigation that could be instructive for those who were beginning to approach the issue elsewhere [38]. Beyond the case level, the study employed a sampling strategy of maximum variation at unit level. This approach sees participants selected based on a range of pre-identified characters to maximise the diversity of respondents.

Semi-structured interviews (n = 18) were conducted with BME students both past and present. Interviewees were selected with respect to socio-economic background (POLAR 3) and parental education. Although interviewees came from a range of BME backgrounds, we do not distinguish within the BME category. Not only would this reduce some categories to some very small numbers, it would also challenge the anonymity of participants. Similarly, we did not analyse the data to discern any possible intersecting factors such as gender, age, etc. Given that the numbers of BME students were so low we chose to keep the 'empirical primacy' of race intact as much as possible [39]. All interviews were audio recorded and transcribed. In addition, ethnographic data based on observations of learning and teaching and conversations with key stakeholders across individual departments based in the Faculty A were also collected. Triangulating and contextualising emergent findings, informal discussions with existing students took place during the ethnographic element, as did further conversations with graduates and academic and support staff across the Faculty over a six-month period. Using a thematic approach initial themes were identified and coded within the data, with emerging relationships between the themes mapped [40]. Both elements of the research received separate ethics approval from the University's Student Services Ethics Committee.

4. Results

4.1. Quantitative Results

Taken between 2011 and 2015, the institutional data consisted of a total of 17,384 stu dent records. Most of the full-time, UK-domiciled students who graduated from the university between these years were White (90.4%), with BME students collectively making up 9.6% of the population (1812 students). This is roughly half the size of the national pro portion of BME students enrolled in UG programmes, but not untypical of Russell Group institutions [1,4,5]. Descriptive analyses of the data similarly reveal that there has been a persistent attainment gap between White and BME groups at NRGU across this time frame with BME groups under-performing against White counterparts. White students received an average of 85.8% higher degrees across the time frame, compared to 72.988.7–73.9% of BME students. The average gap across the institution in the five-year period was 12.8% Figure 1 provides a breakdown of the trend.

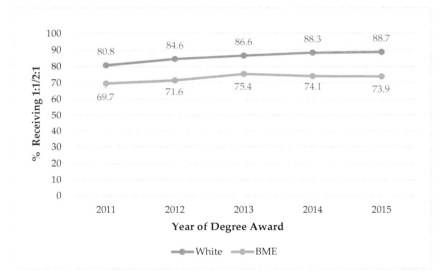

Figure 1. BME Attainment Gap at NRGU between 2011 and 2015.

While the gap was 3.7% points higher in 2015 than it was in 2011, attainment is considerably higher than the national average with respect to both groups. Indeed, the gap itself was also lower than the national average, which was 18.4% points in 2011, and 15.2% points in 2013/14 [11].

Further, while Table 2 demonstrates a clear and consistent attainment gap for all BME students when compared against White students, there is also variation within the BME category.

The smallest attainment gap existed between Mixed students and White students (5% overall), with the difference between White and Chinese students demonstrating the most variance across time. The largest and most consistent attainment gap was be tween White and Black students (22.2% overall), a finding which is reflective of previous nationalresearch [11].

Table 2. Proportion of 1:1/2:1 degrees and above by ethnicity.

Year of Award	Ethnicity						
	White	Black	Asian	Chinese	Mixed	Other	Unknown/ Undeclared
2011	80.8%	61.2%	66.3%	64.7%	78.9%	72.7%	77.3%
2012	84.6%	60.8%	71.6%	76%	77.3%	66.7%	75%
2013	86.6%	62.9%	74.8%	62.5%	81.6%	100%	93.9%
2014	88.3%	63.8%	73.2%	66.7%	81.7%	73.3%	93.1%
2015	88.7%	68.4%	66.3%	75%	84%	78.6%	81.3%
Overall	85.8%	63.6%	70.6%	68.6%	80.8%	77.2%	83.5%

Figure 2 similarly demonstrates that the attainment gap between White and BME students is persistent across the level of entry qualification.

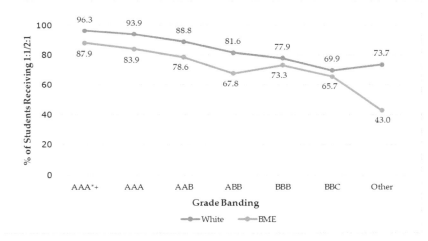

Figure 2. Attainment by BME status and level of entry qualification.

Generally, as the level of entry qualification decreases, the proportion of students receiving 1:1/2:1s also decreased. However, there is a relatively consistent gap between White and BME students. While the 30.7%-point gap between White and BME students who entered with 'other' level of qualifications is striking, this does reflect national trends [11].

Figure 3 also demonstrates that the attainment gap does appear to be persistent across type of entry qualification.

Although some of the disparities in Figure 3 appear to be large, it is important to note that just over 95% of students entered NRGU with A-Levels (16,539 students). In comparison, 1.1% (196 students) entered with Access to HE qualifications, and 1% entered with BTEC qualifications (168 students). The 'other' category was an assemblage of national qualification, foundation programmes, and diplomas, with most in low single figures. It is likely that very specific circumstances account for the differences here, rather than BME status more generally (for example, transnational students). Indeed, a relatively small number of students are represented by qualifications other than A-Levels, which is likely to account for the large variations observed.

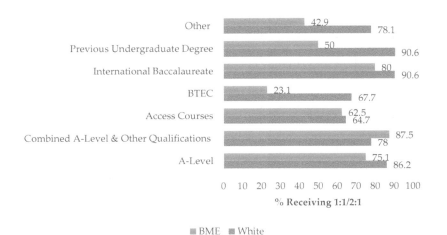

Figure 3. Attainment by BME Status and Entry Attainment Type.

The attainment gap was similarly persistent with respect to socio-economic status, as Figure 4 demonstrates.

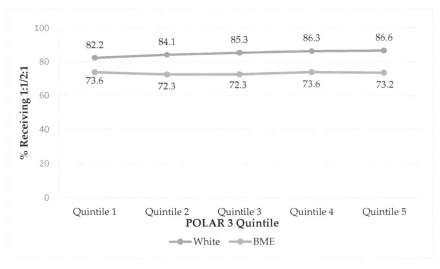

Figure 4. Overall 1:1/2:1 Attainment by BME Status and POLAR 3 Quintiles.

While there remains some discussion about the validity of the measure [12], the participation of local areas classification (POLAR) is based on the proportion of young people who participate in higher education and how this varies by geographical area POLAR classifies local areas into five groups—or quintiles—based on the proportion of young people who enter higher education aged 18 or 19 years old. Quintile 1 shows the lowest rate of participation while Quintile 5 shows the highest rate of participation [3]. The data demonstrates that the proportion of 1:1/2:1s gradually increases with each POLAR 3 quintile for White students. This means that those students who enter NRGU from the most advantaged areas are also more likely to leave with a higher degree—if the student self classifies as 'White'. For BME students however, attainment remains relatively stable, with slight decreases in Q2, Q3 and again at Q5.

4.2. Qualitative Results

Having established that an attainment gap exists at NRGU, and does not appear to be accounted for by a variety of intersecting factors, the qualitative element of the study sought to explore how BME students experienced their transition into, and through their chosen degree programme. The following discussion outlines the key themes that emerged during data analysis. A number of key points of transition are highlighted which include: academic preparedness; navigating the pedagogical terrain; pastoral engagement and sense of belonging; finance; and the lived experience of 'diversity'. Each is dealt with in turn.

4.2.1. Academic Expectations and Preparedness: Moving into, through and beyond Higher Education

While questions of academic expectation and preparedness are usually directed toward those entering university, the relationship between expectation and experience—and the resonance between the two—was the key defining feature of the qualitative data see [40]. Indeed, interviewees stressed that their transitions into, through, and in some cases beyond HE were replete with the attempt to reconcile their expectations of their degree programme with their lived experience of academic standards and institutional practices associated with the university. All students, for example, stressed a lack of prior appreciation for the 'work ethic' required in undertaking successful degree level study. One student highlighted that:

' . . . [subject] is a very tough course and I kind of just resumed the level of work that I would have been doing at A-level. I did okay in my A-levels but in my first year I didn't do so well, but after that experience I sort of reflected and realised that I had to pick up my work ethic, so then it [academic progress] improved gradually . . . ' (5th year student)

Some students were also unsure of the level of independent research required to support their learning, whilst others were less familiar with more baseline tasks such as finding and reviewing appropriate academic journals. Issues of time-management, and information processing in the form of 'email overload' from central and departmental communications were similarly described as challenging.

However, explanations that located the reason for differences in expectation and experience in individual terms were shaped by structural factors.

' . . . in the first year everyone said it was really easy and it's the same as A-Level. People were saying there's not really a big jump, but when I did my first year it was completely different to what people said; so that was a big change from my expectation. And the second year was a big jump from the first year as well: there were more exams and assignments and it was much harder as well. You had to remember everything you learnt from the first year to be able to know the stuff in second year . . . ' (3rd year student)

Indeed, the key dimension by which the relationship between expectation and experience was articulated revolved around students' ability to negotiate programmes of study. For instance, many pointed out that initial their A-Level experiences were predicated on 'moving-on' once an exam was completed. The nature of a degree programme, on the other hand, was much more nuanced as it was both modular and incremental, but often lacked adequate narration at either level. The different levels of the programme were often reported to be mismatched, with students not given sufficient articulation of both aims and structure for each year of study, and the types of knowledge that were required to be taken forward and built upon in subsequent years.

Differences in expectation and experience with respect to the substantive content of the course were also highlighted as a concern. Many interviewees had assumed that the courses would be, to one degree or another, 'applied'; but frequently they found themselves having to contend with theory-heavy, research-based study:

> 'The course has been very theoretical and not very applied. So I've done [subject] as I want to learn about [topic], but you haven't mentioned [topic] for like the past five months! ... I think that sort of transferrable knowledge, showing how it is applied is very important because otherwise, you start to lose interest.' (2nd year student)

This left some students struggling to keep themselves motivated and engaged as they had specifically applied to courses that had appeared to be more 'practical'.

More generally, many interviewees felt that assumptions had also been made by staff about the academic context that they had transitioned from, with expectations not being made explicit from the outset:

> 'I think there were communication gaps in terms of expectation management to say 'hey, you are in a different setting from where you were before and this isn't the way we do things here ... " (Graduate from 2013)

It is also of note that some students explained that it was only when they were 'up to-date' with their workloads that they could really take advantage and benefit from the wider academic support available across the University. However, many students felt as if they were either 'playing catch-up' or left struggling to put all the pieces of the programme together themselves.

4.2.2. Learning and Teaching: Navigating the Pedagogical Terrain

Elsewhere, all interviewees within the sample also described their experiences of teaching as 'patchy' or 'inconsistent'. Collectively, they identified a range of issues that modified the course of their transition through their degree programme. These included a lack of diversity in both the methods and style of teaching; an over-reliance on talking over PowerPoint slides; a general lack of opportunities for meaningful interaction; poor visualisation; and, in the form of abstract research, a lack of applicability. Although some students expressed concerns around the ability to note-take effectively because the pace of some lecturing was 'too quick', others also felt there were issues around general communication in lectures. This included linguistic competence of the lecturers, audibility and meaningful opportunities for the consolidation and practical application of ideas. Many interviewees also made the perceptive point that there was an obvious discrepancy between how they were advised to deliver presentations and how they experienced them as an audience.

The issue of feedback was also highlighted as a particular point of contention:

> ' ... I haven't received any feedback on my course so far [6 months] so I'm not sure how I'm progressing ... it's actually been one of the few downfalls of [NRGU].' (1st year student)

Both the lack of individualised or formative feedback and lengthy turnaround times did not facilitate an ability to reflect on assessments or sense check their academic performance. Whilst feedback for exams was often described as perfunctory—and frequently non-existent—coursework-based feedback was often reported to be little more than generic. This meant comments were rarely descriptive enough to be taken forward towards future assignments, thereby limiting opportunities for reflection and progression.

Similarly, interviewees suggested that existing feedback loops between staff and students appeared to be something of a departmental 'formality'. One interviewee commented on the general distance between students and academics:

> 'It's not that we're being shy or something, even now we're making a lot more of an effort, but it's hard to get academics to really support you ... the lack of support is very tough because, especially in first year, because through A-levels you have a teacher who is really trying to help you get into university and get the

right grades ... whereas in university there's absolutely no connection between academics and the students; it's very, very distant. Even if there's a departmental event, academics are separate and there's never an overlap—which I find really weird.' (5th year student)

By contrast, lecturers who were cited as being 'engaging' and 'good' were those who had solicited ongoing feedback and had been responsive to students, by implementing direct changes:

' ... we had one lecturer this year, he was really good ... the students gave him some feedback saying that we didn't really see the benefit in a certain type of assignment so he completely changed the module and responded to the feedback immediately which was really good.' (5th year student)

Other students who had undertaken a year in industry also sought to emphasise the transformative impact that it had in terms of academic and personal progression—mainly in terms of an increased confidence in negotiating the pedagogical terrain by experiencing a workplace culture.

' ... before I did that year out [in industry] I was quite shy, quite timid. Whereas, doing that year out you get a lot more confidence; so at the time in third year I probably would never have gone and approached another lecturer unless it was desperate times. Whereas, now I'd quite happily email and say, "Hi, I need help with this ... "' (5th year student)

However, other interviewees who were not achieving their initial aspirations clearly felt more disheartened and/or disappointed with their current academic progress. Such students often felt isolated, having to rely on their own skills to negotiate any difficulties faced:

'In first year I barely sort of passed, second year I just about got a 2:1, very closely, third year it's getting better. So it's been a gradual improvement but I would say that it's largely been through self-reflection and my own appreciation' (5th year student)

Again, this was often experienced as an imbalance between expectation and experience and led to one describing themselves as 'lazy', despite spending an average of 25 h per week in part-time work to sustain a living. Another had resigned themselves to the belief that pushing for a first-class degree would compromise their mental health and general wellbeing, despite entering NRUB with high qualifications.

4.2.3. Pastoral Engagement and Sense of Belonging

This nexus of enabling and constraining factors within the environments of learning and teaching continued with respect to their wider experiences of university networks. Indeed, students achieving 1:1/2.1s typically had a broader network of peer relationships across the University. This was facilitated particularly through their involvement in societies and departmental or social sports teams—suggesting a sense of social belonging bears a positive relationship towards academic progression. In fact, all students felt there was great importance in establishing good peer relationships for both course progression and general wellbeing.

However, some also commented on the difficulties in developing or maintaining relationships with different course peers over time, with others highlighting the dominance of alcohol as the defining feature of social events and societies. The negative social stigma attached to working 'hard' in the first year—which 'doesn't even count'—was also perceived to be a problem:

'In first year there's a stigma if you do work, if that makes sense? So if you do work they're like, "Why are you doing work? It's first year!" Then you don't really appreciate tutorial sessions. And then the further through uni you go, you stick with that mind-set almost.' (3rd year student)

Some students also commented on unhelpful assumptions made by non-BME students about aspects of their identity, which frequently appeared to be ignorant and insensitive. This included being conflated with, or mistaken for, international students; the use of inappropriate/offensive language or behaviour; and, stereotyping:

'It's ridiculous ... I mean some students will say "coloured" and when you're like, "you can't say that," they just make it into a joke and make out that the issue is with you and you're being overly sensitive.' (1st year student)

Interviewees described these assumptions as being difficult to challenge. This was largely because they appeared to stem from a lack of exposure to cultural and ethnic diversity, with non-BME students often maintaining that the choice of language made by their white peers was somehow unproblematic when challenged. Indeed, many interviewees suggested that prior assumptions regarding home students from BME backgrounds meant they were perceived to come from poorer neighbourhoods, were international students, had issues around language, and, had generally poorer schooling—none of which is reflective of the actual diversity of BME students at NRGU.

Of course, there are systems in place to support students through their academic and pastoral life whilst at university. However, the reliance on a personal tutoring system that was largely seen to be ineffective meant that interviewees felt that they were, again, left to their own devices:

' ... there's definitely a divide there between what a tutor should do and what a tutor actually does do. And whether it's because the tutor doesn't know what they're supposed to do? I don't know ... ' (2nd year student)

Whilst some felt 'lucky enough' to find an engaging tutor, the lack of clarity in the personal tutor role and a general lack of opportunities for connection meant that many students regarded the system as not particularly helpful, leading to lower motivation and confidence to engage with NRGU and a poorer sense of belonging.

4.2.4. Finance: Information, Employment, and Money-Related Stress

'I know I'm missing out on some things but I just can't afford to go on this trip ... or can't afford to buy this kit to play sports.' (1st year student)

A key modifier in the transition of BME students through NRGU coalesced around the issue of finance. Three topics of concern emerged: timely access to financial information, the necessity for part-time work to sustain a living; and, finance-related stress. In response, a number of students also indicated the positive impact of a financial bursary scheme for eligible widening participation students.

In the first instance, some students highlighted that they experienced difficulties in completing Student Finance England (SFE) forms—which facilitates access to loans and grant funds. This was particularly the case where household circumstances were seen as more 'complex' or 'non-traditional,' for example, due to ongoing divorce settlements. This led to some students receiving neither the finance they may have been entitled to, nor the financial support offered by the University:

'My student finance isn't sorted out properly because they [Student Finance England] need more evidence ... I don't have the evidence so it doesn't cover my rent, so I have to work a lot ... I've just given up now on getting it sorted ... I'm contracted 16 h, but I do roughly maybe 25 to 30 h a week ... and because they don't have enough information, neither does the University so I end up missing out in two places.' (2nd year student)

In many cases, interviewees constructed issues of student finance as being distinct from the University, and therefore did not seek direct help. Financial concerns were articulated as an internalised struggle, with many considering 'cash-flow' to be a private issue that was simply part and parcel of working towards better prospects for themselves and also their families.

' ... I just want to do well, just for myself really, because my parents are always like having money struggles and stuff so it'd be nice to get a good degree and get a job so it's less pressure for them ... ' (2nd year student)

This heightened sense of individual responsibility with respect to financial information had two related outcomes in both the 'here-and-now' and the 'future', particularly for those students from lower income backgrounds. Firstly, whilst interviewees fully understood the negative implications of working over the University recommended 16 h per week, they could envisage little alternative. Acquiring income was essential to daily living—and many were regularly working over 20 h per week, in addition to studying full-time.

' ... the loan doesn't really cover rent ... I had quite a bit last year with the grant but due to some sort of change etc., now it doesn't even cover rent.' (2nd year student)

These concerns were to have a further impact. The stress that stemmed from financial concerns appeared to have a significant impact on the academic progression of students, greatly reducing the ability of students in managing their time effectively. One quarter of students participating in the interviews were experiencing challenging financial situations. Moreover, those students working more than 16 h a week—the recommended limit during term time—had not approached any staff in Professional Services regarding finance, nor departmental staff, but some had been warned by the latter that they were at risk of academic failure. Unsurprisingly, this caused much worry.

However, such stress was negated if the interviewee had received additional monies from elsewhere, either through a family contribution or a bursary/fee waiver from the University. If they had, they felt more able to participate in various aspects of university life in addition to covering essential living costs:

'Having that bursary ... it's just ensuring that I've got something steady ... .' (1st year student)

Students in receipt of the bursary appeared to experience less day-to-day anxiety around financial concerns compared to those who did not receive any financial support. Indeed, students, who also received 'top-up' money from their families every week or month, were also noticeably more confident in articulating their student experiences and were positive about their university journey ahead. Those who were in receipt of a bursary or fee waiver from the university similarly highlighted how the additional income helped them negotiate the financial landscape of university expenses. 'Middle-income' students, as dictated by SFE income boundaries, on the other hand, appeared to experience general anxieties around finance due to the inherent assumption that families both can and will contribute to university study costs—this was not always the case. Equally, those who saw a reduction in the amount of money after the annual SFE reassessment also experienced difficulties in trying to adjust to the shortfall of incoming money, without relying on parental contributions.

4.2.5. The Lived Experience of 'Diversity'

The relationship between expectation and experience was again imbued within interviewees' experience of diversity, with previous educational environments seen as being considerably more diverse than the sociocultural environment at NRGU. Indeed, beyond the surface of an international student body, NRGU was perceived to be a white, middle-class university.

That said, all of the BME students interviewed maintained they would not be happy in being 'singled out' based on their ethnicity. They were conscious of non-BME students or organisations having negative perceptions that might serve to homogenise minority ethnicities and that this could lead to tokenistic attitudes and propagate ignorant practices:

'I didn't want to put down any more details than I needed to. You don't need to know that information [ethnicity] so I wouldn't give it because I don't feel it's important ... I've not experienced any direct racism, but from what I've been told of what goes on ... I'm just pre-empting that from happening, basically.' (1st year student)

Students who were vocal about racist experiences also talked about the lack of challenge that occurs in educational environments. In their experiences, incidents of racism were often downplayed, as opposed to having the potential to play out across different areas and through a variety of attitudes and perceptions. Diversity might be nominally recognised within such environments, but it was often not understood by others in their interactions with participants. Interviewees indicated that many people were ignorant about the nature and effects of racism, particularly when challenged with the reality of the consequences of that ignorance.

Elsewhere, interviewees also felt that the lack of exposure to BME role models at a younger age could potentially manifest in BME students thinking they were incapable of progressing towards university, or that HE study was fundamentally not for 'people like them':

' ... I do think it's actually quite important for young kids to be able to see oh, there is someone like me, doing [subject] and therefore "I can do [subject] ... "' (5th year student)

Having worked towards getting into university, interviewees identified positive role models as those people who were 'down-to-earth' individuals with industry experience had good communication skills and student engagement/rapport—regardless of BME status:

'I don't think it's important to have 'diverse' role models, you just need people who know their stuff, that are competent, approachable and respectful ... somebody with industry experience would be more of a role model to me ... ' (1st year student)

Role models were thought to be particularly important where social factors in the form of a lack of professional exposure at home, an absence of meaningful relationships with teaching staff, and social pressures from peers, could constrain their development.

5. Conclusions

This paper presents the results from a case-study of a Russell Group University with respect to the BME attainment gap. Using a mixed-methods research strategy, it reveals the presence of a BME attainment gap at NRGU. It also shows that when considering level and type of prior attainment, and socio-economic background, the differences between the proportion of White and BME students receiving 1:1/2:1s remains persistent. The qualitative data suggests a series of factors that act as key modifiers in the transition experiences of BME students and attempts to sketch the complex interplay of social, structural and institutional factors that can disproportionately impact on those experiences. Significant themes within these transitions include: academic preparedness; the pedagogical terrain; pastoral engagement; access to finance; and, the lived experience of diversity.

There are, of course, several limitations to the study. The first is to acknowledge the diversity of BME experience. Whilst using the five-fold BME classification system can help reveal general trends, there will be much variation within each BME category. Homogenizing a diverse group of student voices and experiences, based on an umbrella identity of 'BME', is highly problematic [41,42]. Neither should we attempt to look for the general in the particular: BME students can, and frequently do, receive the very highest marks at NRGU. While the study design in this instance was limited by the relatively low number of BME students, further research may seek to capture some of this difference by taking more intersectional approaches where it is possible. Secondly, the case-study design means that attempts to generalize to other contexts may be problematic. However, the aim of study was to ensure that a range of meanings and experiences were explored. Indeed, the case-study approach adopted here is intensive rather than exhaustive. That said, and whilst the results are necessarily descriptive of the sample—and the quantitative component is, perhaps, not as recent as we might wish—moderate generalizations can be made and there is reason to suspect that many of the findings would resonate and transfer across faculties and other similar universities [1,21,36]. We also recognize that issues relating to class and socio-economic circumstance are likely to feature heavily in the experiences of some BME groups. However, the nature of our sample—where there were few BME students generally, and even less who would identify as 'low income'—prevented us from being able to offer any conclusive insight regarding this intersection. Evidently, the findings do highlight issues of finance and how low incomes can easily become difficult to negotiate. However, there is more to class than finance alone and further empirical investigation of such intersections will help to elucidate the relationship between class, ethnicity, and alienation in HEIs [43].

Despite these limitations, the present study does offer a revealing insight into the nature of the BME attainment gap and how it is experienced within a particular Russell Group institution. A recent review of developments in relation to BME students' participation in UK HEIs has once again drawn attention to the fact almost all of England's higher tariff providers continue to report large attainment gaps associated with ethnicity [1]. These gaps are also reflected in graduate outcomes, with BME students recording consistently lower rates of highly skilled employment or graduate study [8,13]. Therefore, it remains imperative to understand those micro and micro processes that continue to alienate students, and BME students in particular, from HEIs [1]. Indeed, as suggested by Mann, this process of alienation goes further than a pedological concern with surface and deep learning, and/or simplistic statements of equality and diversity [44]. Instead, it is the whole ecosystem through which students experience HEIs that contribute to feelings of estrangement. To these ends, models of student transition that emphasize the multi-dimensional nature of student needs, experiences, and capabilities appear more suitable in developing supportive environments for students.

What is particularly striking about some of the results reported here is that some of what our interviewees commented upon does not only apply to BME students. Experiences of academic preparedness are related to structural misalignments between further education qualifications and degree-level curricula. Ineffective models of learning and teaching that are designed to be efficient rather than effective are similarly beyond the influence students, although those who less isolated are probably better equipped to negotiate such efficiencies. Similarly, the financial requirements of study necessarily require additions from elsewhere. While this will always be more forcefully felt by those with the least economic power, all student budgets need augmentation [43]. The impersonal nature of pastoral care is also felt by all student groups, although again, this is likely to be more difficult to navigate for those with less experience of bureaucratic structures.

None of this is to deny that BME students experience HEIs in ways that are different to their white counterparts. However, in contexts that can be experienced as 'sink or swim', further experiences of racism and notable constraints in diversity can only compound feelings of alienation yet further. Indeed, in line with Gale and Parker [35] the evidence presented here suggests that all student transitions need to be seen as a process of ongoing interactions between institutional structures and individual experience. To this end, the paper demonstrates that the attainment gap should not be viewed in terms of an individual deficit that needs to be 'fixed' or 'filled'. It supports those, such as Crozier et al. [28] and Stevenson [29], who are critical of interventions based around notions of 'student resilience' that serve to both stigmatize and emphasize the role of the individual. Instead, greater attention needs to be placed upon universities and how they can enhance their capacity for equality at organizational, departmental, and inter-personal levels so they are less likely to facilitate exclusory practices [23]. Of course, how this might be achieved is the key question. While there is little reason to suspect that talking to those on the receiving end of such pressures should provide the solution, much of the literature already suggests that the answer is unlikely to lie within those methods that seek to 'uplift' aspects of their identity [18]. Instead, more effective methods for inclusion will be predicated on sustaining accessible, relevant, and engaging HEIs. Evidently, issues of (in)equality relating to BME students need to be consistently recognised, particularly where they feature issues of racism and surface-level claims of diversity. However, while the intersecting social characteristics of BME students make them particularly vulnerable to the tacit exclusory practices of HEIs, all students are likely to benefit from genuinely more responsive HE environments.

Author Contributions: Conceptualization, A.Q., S.P. and T.C.; Formal analysis, A.Q. and S.P.; Data curation, A.Q.; Writing – original draft, A.Q., S.P. and T.C.; Writing – review & editing, A.Q. and T.C.; Supervision, T.C. All authors have read and agreed to the published version of the manuscript.

Funding: This research received no external funding.

Institutional Review Board Statement: The study was conducted in accordance with the Declaration of Helsinki, and approved by the Ethics Committee of The University of Sheffield (date of approval: February 2016).

Informed Consent Statement: Informed consent was obtained from all subjects involved in the study

Data Availability Statement: Not applicable.

Conflicts of Interest: The authors declare no conflict of interest.

References

1. Arday, J.; Branchu, C.; Boliver, V. What do we know about Black and minority ethnic (BME) participation in UK higher education? *Soc. Policy Soc.* **2022**, *21*, 12–25. [CrossRef]
2. Boliver, V.; Powell, M. *Fair Admission to UK Universities: Improving Policy and Practice*; Nuffield Foundation: London, UK, 2021.
3. Office for Students (OfS). *Topic Briefing: Black and Minority Ethnic (BME) Students*; Office for Students: London, UK. Available online: https://www.officeforstudents.org.uk/media/145556db-8183-40b8-b7af741bf2b55d79/topic-briefing_bme-students.pdf (accessed on 20 March 2019).
4. Boliver, V. Ethnic inequalities in admission to highly selective universities. In *Dismantling Race in Higher Education: Racism, Whiteness and Decolonising the Academy*; Arday, J., Mirza, H.S., Eds.; Palgrave MacMillan: London, UK, 2018; pp. 67–85.
5. Reay, D. Race and elite universities in the UK. In *Dismantling Race in Higher Education: Racism, Whiteness and Decolonising the Academy*; Arday, J., Mirza, H.S., Eds.; Palgrave MacMillan: London, UK, 2018; pp. 47–66.
6. Boliver, V. How fair is access to more prestigious UK Universities? *Br. J. Sociol.* **2013**, *64*, 344–364. [CrossRef] [PubMed]
7. Clark, T.; Hordosy, R.; Vickers, D. We will never escape these debts: Undergraduate experiences of indebtedness, income-contingent loans, and the tuition fees rises. *J. Furth. High. Educ.* **2017**, *43*, 708–721. [CrossRef]
8. Richardson, J.T.E. Understanding the under-attainment of ethnic minority students in UK higher education: The known knowns and the known unknowns. In *Dismantling Race in Higher Education: Racism, Whiteness and Decolonising the Academy*; Arday, J., Mirza, H.S., Eds.; Palgrave MacMillan: London, UK, 2018; pp. 87–102.
9. Stevenson, J. *Black and Minority Ethnic Student Degree Retention and Attainment*; Higher Education Academy: York, UK, 2012.
10. Richardson, J.T.E. The under-attainment of ethnic minority students in UK higher education: What we know and what we don't know. *J. Furth. High. Educ.* **2015**, *39*, 278–291. [CrossRef]
11. Equality Challenge Unit (ECU). *Equality in Higher Education: Statistical Report*; ECU: London, UK, 2016.
12. Boliver, V.; Gorard, S.; Siddiqui, N. Who counts as socioeconomically disadvantaged for the purposes of widening access to higher education? *Br. J. Sociol. Educ.* **2022**, *43*, 349–374. [CrossRef]
13. Lessard-Phillips, L.; Swain, D.; Pampaka, M.; Nwabuzo, O. *When Education Isn't Enough*; The Runnymede Trust: London, UK, 2014.
14. Zwysen, W.; Longhi, S. Employment and earning differences in the early career of ethnic minority British graduates: The importance of university career, parental background and area characteristics. *J. Ethn. Migr. Stud.* **2018**, *44*, 154–172. [CrossRef]
15. Stamou, E.; Edwards, A.; Daniels, H.; Ferguson, L. Young people at-risk of drop-out from education: Recognising and responding to their needs. In *Report for the Oxford Centre for Sociocultural and Activity Theory Research*; Department of Education: London, UK, 2014.
16. Bagguley, P.; Hussain, Y. *The Role of Higher Education in Providing Opportunities for South Asian Women*; Joseph Rowntree Foundation: York, UK, 2007.
17. Reay, D.; David, M.; Ball, S. *Degrees of Choice: Social Class, Race, and Gender in Higher Education*; Trentham Books Ltd.: London, UK, 2005.
18. Modood, T. Capitals, ethnic identity, and educational qualifications. In *Social Inclusion and Higher Education*; Basit, T., Tomlinson, S., Eds.; Policy Press: Bristol, UK, 2012.
19. Bale, I.; Broadhead, S.; Case, K.; Hussain, M.; Woolley, D. Exploring the black, Asian and ethnic minority (BAME) student experience using a Community of Inquiry approach. *Widen. Particip. Lifelong Learn.* **2020**, *22*, 112–131. [CrossRef]

10. Mahmud, A.; Gagnon, J. Racial disparities in student outcomes in British higher education: Examining Mindsets and bias. *Teach. High. Educ.* **2020**, *25*, 1–16. [CrossRef]

11. Smith, S.V. Exploring the BME student attainment gap: What Did It Tell Us? Actions to Address Home Black and Minority Ethnic (BME) Undergraduate Students' Degree Attainment. *J. Perspect. Appl. Acad. Pract.* **2017**, *5*, 48–57. [CrossRef]

12. Peterson, C.; Ramsay, D. Reducing the gap! Reciprocal mentoring between Black, Asian and minority ethnic (BAME) students and senior leaders at the University of Gloucestershire. *Perspect. Policy Pract. High. Educ.* **2021**, *25*, 34–39. [CrossRef]

13. McDuff, N.; Tatam, J.; Beacock, O.; Ross, F. Closing the attainment gap for students from black and minority ethnic backgrounds through institutional change. *Widening Particip. Lifelong Learn.* **2018**, *20*, 79–101. [CrossRef]

14. Caplan, P.J.; Ford, J.C. The voices of diversity: What students of diverse races/ethnicities and both sexes both tell us about the college experiences and their perceptions about their institutions' progress toward diversity. *APORIA* **2014**, *6*, 30–69. [CrossRef]

15. Singh, G. *Black and Minority Ethnic Students' Participation in Higher Education: Improving Success and Retention and Success: A Synthesis of Research Evidence*; Higher Education Academy: York, UK, 2011.

16. Naylor, R.A.; Smith, J. Determinants of Educational Success in Higher Education. In *International Handbook on the Economics of Education*; Johnes, G., Johnes, J., Eds.; Edward Elgar: Cheltenham, UK, 2004; pp. 415–461.

17. Berry, J.; Loke, G. *Improving the Degree Attainment of Black and Minority Ethnic Students*; Equality Challenge Unit/Higher Education Academy: London, UK, 2011.

18. Crozier, G.; Burke, P.J.; Archer, L. Peer relations in higher education: Raced, classed and gendered constructions and Othering. *Whiteness Educ.* **2016**, *1*, 39–53. [CrossRef]

19. Stevenson, J.; O'Mahony, J.; Khan, O.; Ghaffar, F.; Stiell, B. Understanding and overcoming the challenges of targeting students from under-represented and disadvantaged ethnic backgrounds. *Rep. Off. Stud.* **2019**. Available online: https://www.officeforstudents.org.uk/media/d21cb263-526d-401c-bc74-299c748e9ecd/ethnicity-targeting-research-report.pdf (accessed on 5 May 2020).

20. Crozier, G.; Reay, D.; Clayton, J.; Colliander, L.; Grinstead, J. Different strokes for different folks: Diverse students in diverse institutions—Experiences of higher education. *Res. Pap. Educ.* **2008**, *23*, 167–177. [CrossRef]

21. Reay, D.; Crozier, G.; Clayton, J. Fitting in 'or' standing out: Working-class students in UK higher education. *Br. Educ. Res. J.* **2009**, *32*, 1–19. [CrossRef]

22. Crozier, G.; Reay, D.; Clayton, J. The socio-cultural and learning experiences of working class students in higher education. In *Improving Learning by Widening Participation*; David, M., Ed.; Routledge: London, UK, 2010.

23. Reay, D. *Miseducation*; Policy Press: Bristol, UK, 2017.

24. Briggs, A.J.R.; Clark, J.; Hall, I. Building bridges: Understanding student transition into university. *Qual. High. Educ.* **2012**, *18*, 3–21. [CrossRef]

25. Gale, T.; Parker, S. Navigating change: A typology of student transition in higher education. *Stud. High. Educ.* **2014**, *39*, 734–753. [CrossRef]

26. Boliver, V.; Banerjee, P.; Gorard, S.; Powell, M. Reconceptualising fair access to highly academically selective universities. *High. Educ.* **2021**, *84*, 85–100. [CrossRef]

27. Creswell, R. *Research Design: Qualitative, Quantitative and Mixed Methods Approaches*, 3rd ed.; Sage: London, UK, 2014.

28. Patton, M.Q. *Qualitative Research & Evaluation Methods*, 3rd ed.; Sage: Thousand Oaks, CA, USA, 2002.

29. Gillborn, D. Intersectionality, critical race theory, and the primacy of racism: Race, class, gender, and disability in education. *Qual. Inq.* **2015**, *21*, 277–287. [CrossRef]

30. Braun, V.; Clarke, V. Using thematic analysis in psychology. *Qual. Res. Psychol.* **2006**, *3*, 77–101. [CrossRef]

31. Jenkins, R. *Rethinking Ethnicity*; SAGE Publications Ltd.: London, UK, 2008. [CrossRef]

32. Williams, M. Interpretivism and Generalization. *Sociology* **2000**, *34*, 209–224. [CrossRef]

33. Hordosy, R.; Clark, T. Student Budgets and widening participation: Comparative experiences of finance in low and high income graduates at a northern red brick university. *Soc. Policy Adm.* **2019**, *53*, 761–775. [CrossRef]

34. Mann, S. Alternative Perspectives on the Student Experience: Alienation and engagement. *Stud. High. Educ.* **2001**, *26*, 7–19. [CrossRef]

Article

A Process Evaluation of a Learning Community Program: Implemented as Designed?

Tonya Scott Lanphier [1],* and Robert M. Carini [2]

[1] Division of Mathematics and Sciences, Southcentral Kentucky Community & Technical College, Bowling Green, KY 42101, USA
[2] Department of Sociology, University of Louisville, Louisville, KY 40292, USA; bob.carini@louisville.edu
* Correspondence: tonya.lanphier@kctcs.edu

Abstract: Learning communities can be useful to counter some of the challenges encountered by first-semester students as they transition to college. This 2-year process evaluation examines the launch of a campus-wide learning community initiative for developmental reading students at a community college in the USA. Students, instructors, and administrators were interviewed about the implementation of the program, and program-related materials were reviewed. Findings suggested ways to enhance the effectiveness of learning communities of the linked-course variety through program implementation that is more faithful to key design aspects. Suggestions include (1) implement team-teaching across linked courses; (2) carry out an integrated curriculum across courses; (3) provide in-depth and continued instructor training as well as specialized resources; (4) expand support services available to students and require them to use at least some; and (5) create tools/methods for instructors and administrators to regularly assess processual aspects rather than just program outcomes.

Keywords: learning community; community college; developmental reading; student persistence; first-year students; transition

Citation: Lanphier, T.S.; Carini, R.M. A Process Evaluation of a Learning Community Program: Implemented as Designed? *Educ. Sci.* **2022**, *12*, 60. https://doi.org/10.3390/educsci12010060

Academic Editor: Diana Dias

Received: 1 December 2021
Accepted: 13 January 2022
Published: 17 January 2022

Publisher's Note: MDPI stays neutral with regard to jurisdictional claims in published maps and institutional affiliations.

1. Introduction

Learning communities can be useful to counter some of the challenges encountered by first-semester students as they transition to college life [1,2]. For the purposes of this study, we consider a learning community to be "A curricular model that links two or more classes together for a cohort of students" [3]. Often labeled a "high-impact" practice [4,5], learning communities can impact how students experience college and forge meaningful experiences via people, places, and/or programs, and are thus important levers for student success in college [6–8]. Specifically, learning communities may help students transition more effectively from high school by increasing recognition and access to important on-campus resources and study skills, as well as enhancing social integration of students on campus [9]. Social integration leads to greater student persistence [7,8,10,11], and Nancy Shapiro and Jodi Levine [12] also report that learning community students enjoy " . . . higher levels of involvement with peers and the campus, and express greater overall satisfaction with the college experience". A higher level of collegiate satisfaction operates as another pathway to student persistence [13]. Further, effective learning communities can both demonstrate to students that expectations are quite different in college than high school and help students to cultivate adaptive habits and new goals in a supportive social environment [14]. While benefits of learning communities have been routinely touted over the past two decades, research shows that they are not always associated with beneficial effects—or uniform effect sizes—at different colleges [4,15] or for different groups of students [16]. Some argue that sometimes disparate outcomes reported for learning communities may be due, in considerable part, to their varying degrees of successful implementation [4,17].

Further, surprisingly few studies provide practical suggestions—gleaned from data as well as theory—on how to implement learning communities for student success; even carefully planned learning communities will experience difficulties if implemented in clumsy, inappropriate, or less than thorough ways. To better understand how implementation of a learning community program can shape its success, our study provides evidence from a 2-year process evaluation that may help would-be program designers, administrators, and instructors to implement more effective learning communities during students' first semester of college, a critical juncture in both their transition to—and ultimate trajectory within—college.

Current Study

This study examines a learning community program newly implemented in 2015 for developmental reading students at a two-year public college in the USA. The college chose to implement learning communities because, in prior years, less than 20 percent of students in developmental reading earned six or more college-level credits, and this percentage was lower than those for students in other developmental courses such as math and English [18]. Accordingly, short-term goals of the program included increasing retention in the developmental reading course (RDG), improving reading skills, developing study strategies, boosting academic self-confidence, enhancing attitudes about reading, and heightening a sense of community. An intermediate goal was to increase student persistence in college-level courses beyond students' first semester (including introductory English, which followed in the second semester).

The learning communities were designed to be of the linked-course type; students were concurrently enrolled in RDG and a first-semester experiences course (FSE) that introduced students to general study skills and strategies; goal setting; how to cope with competing demands of school, work, and/or family; as well as support offices and resources available on campus and beyond. Learning communities were implemented for first-semester, developmental reading students at the college during spring and fall 2015, thus there were two cohorts of learning community students under study. The duration of each learning community was for a single semester, which is typical for most learning communities [3], and class sizes were capped at 24. Each learning community was taught by two instructors (one for RDG and another for FSE), and these same instructors volunteered to teach both cohorts studied. Instructors had previously taught their respective courses in semesters prior to the introduction of the program. Students could enroll in the program if they scored between 38 and 42 on the Computer-adapted Placement Assessment and Support Services (COMPASS) placement exam for reading level; they could only enroll in six credit hours for that semester (RDG and FSE). If there was an open seat in one of the two concurrent learning communities and the student met the COMPASS exam criterion, advisors encouraged the student to register during their first-semester orientation, although students were not required to join a learning community.

This study does not aim to evaluate the effectiveness of the learning communities on student outcomes per se (however, see [19] for a qualitative analysis of students' perceived outcomes from the program). Rather this study centers on a process evaluation that gauges the degree to which learning communities were implemented as designed, and if not, what implications might have arisen for program stakeholders, including students. Process evaluations can distinguish between interventions that were fundamentally faulty and interventions that were merely poorly implemented [20] and thus may shed light on how to ultimately improve both the operational and effectiveness aspects of learning communities. For this study, interviews were conducted with students, instructors, and administrators (both program and institutional) during spring and fall 2016, and a content review was conducted of program-related documents, both publicly available and internal to the college. Based on empirical data collected from these various sources, we share various lessons learned by stakeholders and also analyze qualitative data for key themes regarding both positive and negative aspects of the implementation processes. Finally, we offer suggestions toward more effective strategies for the design, implementation, and assessment of learning communities; policymakers, stakeholders, and researchers alike may find use in our conclusions.

2. Materials and Methods

In order to collect rich processual information about the learning community program's design and implementation, in-depth and semi-structured interviews were relied upon for data collection. In total, 13 one-on-one interviews were conducted in person and on campus near the end of both the spring and fall 2016 semesters; seven students, two instructors, and four learning community program or institutional administrators were interviewed. By interviewing various types of stakeholders, we sought to capture their viewpoints on various aspects of implementation, and to triangulate information when appropriate. In general, there was a high degree of concordance across the student, instructor, and administrator interviews on the vast majority of issues discussed. The mean interview length was 43 min with a standard deviation of 16 min, and interviews were audio-recorded and transcribed for analysis.

Interview invitations were sent to college email addresses of 20 randomly selected students from those who took part in a learning community during 2015 and were still enrolled at the college in 2016. Students were thus two or three semesters removed from learning community involvement when they were interviewed for the study. As an incentive to be interviewed, students were offered a $20 Visa card. While both women and men students were invited for interviews, only women responded to the request. Students were asked about (1) their reading and study habits, (2) the degree to which they had achieved their goals at the college, (3) their learning and grades, and (4) whether/how the learning community contributed to their collegiate experiences. Students were also asked about enrollment in the program, their likes and/or dislikes, their experiences, and if their ideas or person was changed because of the learning community.

All program administrators and instructors associated with the program participated in this study. Administrators were asked about why learning communities were initiated, perceptions of the learning communities on campus; design and operation of the program strengths, weaknesses, and surprises regarding the program; and modifications to the program throughout the two years it had been implemented. Administrators, particularly those in broader institutional roles, were also asked about the extent to which they were connected to the program. Instructors were asked similar questions but were also queried about their teaching practices and interactions with students and administrators.

For the content review, internal and publicly available materials were collected during spring and summer 2016. Materials consisted of three types: documents relating to an action plan (16 total) from 2015, training documents for learning community instructors (20 total), and course syllabi (three). Internal materials were provided by program administrators and instructors, and all internal materials were requested in an attempt to reduce selection bias. Publicly available materials included training documents from other colleges or organizations that were used by the instructors and/or administrators in this program.

Based on a pilot study from fall 2014 [21], these sensitizing concepts guided the interviews as well as their analysis: program goals for developmental reading, program design, "high impact practices", perceptions of the program by stakeholders, administrator involvement, program training and resources, team teaching, integration of linked course content, student support, and assessment of implementation processes. A sensitizing concept " . . . gives the user a general sense of reference and guidance in approaching empirical instances . . . directions along which to look" [22]. Line-by-line coding was used, with responses categorized by question. Memoing was carried out throughout the analysis to make sense of the nascent codes and potential linkages between them. Thematic analysis was used for both the interview data and the content review; thematic analysis was used to both describe and interpret data. Themes were identified using the constant comparison method [23]. This method "involves searching for similarities and differences by making systematic comparisons across units of data" [24].

3. Results

3.1. Program Design and Implementation

Based on instructor and administrator interviews, as well as the content review of materials, there were numerous identifiable components within the program's design. During the process evaluation, however, five design components took on particular importance with respect to how they were actually carried out within the learning communities: (1) team teaching across linked RDG and FSE courses; (2) integration of learning themes, other content, and assignments between linked courses; (3) comprehensive and continued training for instructors, as well as access to specialized resources; and (4) introduction of students to support offices, services, and related resources available on campus that have been consistently linked to student success.

Instructors reported a fair amount of collaborative communication regarding their linked courses. However, team teaching wherein instructors were concurrently present in the classroom was not commonly practiced. Team teaching reportedly occurred only a few times throughout the first semester the learning communities were introduced. As one teacher put it, "We would do some team teaching within the classroom. We would both be in the class together at certain periods throughout the semester, and we called these workshops. And we would do three workshops a semester". The fact that instructors received credit for teaching only one of the courses—not both—appeared to serve as a disincentive toward team teaching since "true" team teaching was seen as requiring considerably more time than for a single course. Thus, the actual implementation of team teaching appeared to fall short of what the program designers intended.

Although the learning community instructors did not consistently team teach, they wanted to do so more frequently and expressed positive views about its effectiveness, both for students' learning and their own professional development. As a teacher opined:

"From a personal growth standpoint, that is another really big strength of the program is that ... I learned so much about teaching and different strategies and how to relate to students. And just having that connection with [my team teacher] and that resource to be able to go to [my team teacher] all the time, it was just invaluable to me". Students also enjoyed instances of team teaching when it occurred. One student stated, "They [instructors] worked together so ... we were working on kind of the same thing at like the same time ... it made it easier". Another expounded on this notion, "Every so often we would have a day where both teachers were in there at the same time, and we would like bring in together what we were learning in both classes ... Those days were actually my favorite days".

Second, the program's design specified strategic integration of content and assignments across linked courses; this goal of course integration was to be supported with comprehensive training for instructors who volunteered for the program. Instructors reported little formal training on learning communities prior to and during their first semester in the program, i.e., training primarily consisted of attending a professional conference. Yet their level of training appeared to have increased during later semesters. Due to their increased amount of training and expanded experiences with learning communities over the semesters, both instructors and administrators grew to feel confident about instructors' knowledge of—and ability to carry out—learning communities. For instance, as an instructor stated:

> They [administrators] were great about sending us to conferences to learn a whole lot more because locally we didn't really know. We knew the research and we knew what we were trying to do with the learning communities, but as far as implementing everything that we needed to do—administration knew that we needed to go somewhere else to kind of learn a little bit more about best practices and what other colleges were doing. So [my fellow linked course instructor] and I

have attended a . . . learning communities conference for the last couple of years, and that has been very, very helpful. Learning about different course pairings and different things to do in the classroom.

Due to the cumulative effects of training and day-to-day experiences with the program learning community instructors increased the level of integration between RDG and FSE over subsequent semesters. As one administrator recounted "The first semester . . . they had a few overlapping assignments. But as each semester progressed, they have kind of been folding in more and more commonalities". Students also liked when they detected topical linkages across the linked courses. For instance, one student noted: "It was just kind of cool how they brought everything together and . . . made it one whole class of two subjects". Students in this study were able to identify several other content areas that were covered in both courses. RDG was a course that could feature virtually any topic, and instructors appeared to take advantage of this to build topical linkages between RDG and FSE. For instance, another student recalled learning about music during RDG "[RDG instructor would] . . . get on YouTube and we'd listen to music because we were in a music—the chapter in our book—for like 3 weeks of music. Jazz and hip hop, how hip hop got here". Other topics that appeared in both courses were personal finance, community service, diversity, culture, politics, history, math, English, and health. As the student put it: "We did everything . . . in [FSE]. There was one girl that always had trouble with her history and she would ask [FSE instructor]. So we would have like a 30 min history lesson". Students also mentioned that studying strategies and goal setting—important components to FSE—were treated in assignments required for RDG.

A common feature of learning communities is for instructors to incorporate prominent and recurring learning themes to foster integration and deeper learning within paired courses. In the present study, learning themes were present across both linked courses for the duration of the semester. Instructors used two primary themes in their courses: (1) healthful living inspired via a book common to RDG and FSE, and (2) motivational materials/lessons that highlighted how visualization of a goal and dedicated work toward it can result in its attainment. Some learning themes were pre-planned during the design stage of the program, especially those that originated from the book-in-common. As an instructor recalled:

We really decided that [book] was going to be one of the main themes in our learning communities. That our students were—both classes—our students were going to read those books and we were going to use the themes within those books to kind of merge the content as far as reading strategies and then also the goal setting, and the themes, whatever it is, in that book for that semester.

Rather than being designed a priori, the theme of motivation emerged more spontaneously during the learning communities.

The importance of learning themes surrounding the book-in-common and motivation were echoed in interviews with students. For instance, students in one learning community initiated a campus health fair because the book-in-common focused on healthful living. One instructor described how the learning community students organized and held the health fair for the college after reading the book. Another student mentioned career-themed writing assignments as an example of an important theme; students' careers goals were a major thematic focus of the learning communities:

We had to do career-themed papers, which helped me a whole lot discover if I was truly interested in the career I was going for. Which I'm still kind of iffy on it but . . . I like being able to write the paper about it that helped me get in touch more with the career I was wanting to do.

One instructor also suggested that successful attainment of career goals was likely a theme in her classes: "The teachers that we had . . . they just were all about being successful . . . So maybe success was it [a theme]". One student seemed to share a similar perspective about motivation: "A theme . . . study. Do your work on time. Be punctual. It's just like having a job". Although only a few students explicitly used the word "success" when asked about a theme across their courses, students often mentioned their instructors being "all about success". In addition, the chosen book every semester centered around an inspiring story of a person overcoming difficulties to attain their goals. Thus, the overarching goals of the learning community were designed around the notion of helping academically underprepared students to persist and succeed, and it appeared that students sensed this purpose and its related learning theme.

3.2. Administrator Involvement and Support

Successful implementation of a learning community often hinges on the degree of involvement and/or support provided by administrators, student advisors, and other key staff on campus. Accordingly, we sought to understand the amount and nature of administrator involvement and support with the program. Interviews revealed that all administrators felt connected to the program, but the degree to which the administrators were involved varied by their roles. One administrator offered:

> Very much [connected to the program] . . . I may not be in the classroom day in and day out with the students and faculty. But from the very beginning of this thing, from the research standpoint to really the decision-making standpoint to making sure that people across the college—faculty and staff—knew what this thing was.

Administrators expressed that they valued and supported the learning community program. "We will support our faculty. They are not just out there on an island by themselves trying to enforce something that is a good practice," voiced an administrator. In turn, learning community instructors felt that the program was supported by the administration. Both instructors mentioned that administrators were eager to fund their professional developmental for teaching in the learning communities. They described moral support as well as material support:

> They [administrators] were super, super excited and supportive of us doing the health fair . . . They actually came in to visit the booths and ask our students questions . . . We have a learning community conference that we go to [regularly], so they're always eager to sign for us to go . . . other changes we can make to boost the communities . . . See what else other schools are doing. They are very supportive as far as professional development. If we do any kind of activity, they always make sure that they are there to support the students . . . they really jump in 100 percent.

Learning community instructors reported satisfaction with the level of involvement from administrators. They described administrators as being primarily facilitative and supportive rather than directly managing or assessing them. Indeed, one instructor appreciated the freedom to teach their course within the learning communities in the manner that instructors deemed appropriate:

> They are involved just the perfect amount. [*Laughter.*] They have given us direction, and they have given us resources . . . asking us what we need for those learning communities. I know they are looking at the data and want to see the effectiveness of it. And they're looking at, of course, our evaluations. But they really give us freedom within those classes, and I think that is really important.

Administrative support and enthusiasm for learning communities was also evident by the fact that all administrators were in favor of expanding learning community opportunities for students at the college, e.g., for other paired developmental courses, paired courses for college-ready students, and to train other instructors in methods that were seen to be widely beneficial for student engagement. One administrator suggested "For me, learning communities being improved would mean—not necessarily improve in the way our current faculty teach in learning communities—but exposing more faculty to it". Another noted the many possible subjects amenable to learning communities: "The learning community concept could be expanded to other areas ... the faculty have discussed—are there other opportunities for learning communities? ... I mean there could be all kinds of different pairings out there".

3.3. Training Materials

Training materials primarily consisted of exemplars or "good practices" for learning communities. These materials were juxtaposed with how learning communities were actually implemented at the college. Training documents consisted of materials that instructors received from two conferences on learning communities during fall 2014 and fall 2015. Many presentations at a conference on learning communities focused on best practices for learning communities, conveying what has worked at their institutions. Most of the learning communities discussed were of the linked-course variety and a substantial number focused on academically underprepared students. Linking two or three courses was most common, although there were a few cases where four classes were linked; in the current study, instructors believed that adding a third linked course would enhance the program. Finally, a majority of these presentations were to inform instructors on how to integrate content areas between linked courses. While learning community instructors in the present study enhanced their level of integration between RDG and FSE as the program evolved, the courses were never commingled under a single unifying curriculum.

As an example of a specific conference paper, Huot and Palm [25] reported that Georgia State University implemented a learning community program that began in the summer and ended the following spring. This learning community consisted of three courses: New Student Orientation, English 101, and a Social Science. The program, called "Success Academy", had four major components: Summer Bridge Program, Mentorship, Academic Support, and Personal & Professional Development. Students were required to engage in student services (a feature that learning community instructors in the present study wished was a component of their program). Further, students had to attend meetings with a peer mentor and met three times per semester with their academic coaches and academic advisers. If students did not meet GPA requirements during the summer, they were involved in an academy recovery plan. This plan required meetings with instructors, attending workshops, identifying barriers (academic and personal) to their success in college, planning how to remove these barriers, and calling students to reflect on their goals for college. Some key features of this program, such as mandating student services and meetings with peer mentors, instructors, and advisers, may have dramatic effects on student performance and persistence. Note that all these elements included increasing involvement for students, which is consistent with Astin's [26] student involvement theory. Additionally, through involvement, students experience academic and social integration according to Tinto's [27] student departure theory. Involvement is important for students in gaining Bourdieu's [28] forms of cultural and social capital that are prevalent in the institution. Instructors in the present study believed that students should be required to go to tutoring, counseling, etc. In some cases, services were available (such as tutoring), but many students did not attend because it was not required under the program. Additionally a counselor was unavailable for learning community students at the time of this study.

Another study was presented by Baham and Finley [29] that highlighted what they believed to be "best practices" of learning communities: " ... fostering partnerships with student services, including advising, media, marketing, institutional research, and administration". In addition, Gebauer [30] identified student engagement, academic affairs and enrollment management as pivotal to the success of learning communities. As such buy-in for learning communities is important and the effectiveness of learning communities is contingent on multiple services provided by the college. In the current study, advising and administrative support proved to be program strengths. However, other student services and marketing for the program were limited and thus constituted areas of weakness.

for the program. In-depth interviews with instructors revealed that students were largely unaware of the program if they did not directly participate.

4. Discussion

This process evaluation identified several important design components that were not fully implemented in practice, or not implemented as the designers intended. At most postsecondary institutions, more attention is likely devoted to the design and assessment of outcomes for learning communities than for the specifics of their implementation. Yet how the design is enacted should be of great concern since implementation mediates learning and other program outcomes. To increase the probability that the design is readily implementable, we concur with Fosnacht and Graham [4] that instructors and those from teaching and learning centers should be consulted or actually brought onto the design team. Those most deeply involved with learning communities on a regular basis also may offer insights as to the specificity of design goals, and how these may be operationalized to ultimately measure success, whether it be with respect to implementation or student outcomes. Bringing in learning community instructors early in the program would also permit them a "big picture" vantagepoint, as well as a better understanding of exactly how their teaching efforts may contribute to program effects.

In this study, there was mention of outcomes assessment by instructors and administrators, but little monitoring of processual aspects was discussed, e.g., team teaching and integration of content across linked courses. While instructors and administrators appeared knowledgeable about the intended design, it would seem prudent for the parties to revisit the original design aspects on a regular basis to ensure alignment of implementation questions and nuances as they arise, i.e., to assess consistency across implementation and design. Alternately, when decisions are necessitated concerning processes not expressly laid out in the design, at least these extemporaneous "mini-design" decisions could be documented as discretionary, and rationales noted. To our knowledge, this sort of process assessment was not conducted in a formal and routinized fashion for this program. A regular assessment schedule with respect to processes—as well as specialized tools and/or procedures—would likely prove useful for guiding implementation. Instructors might chafe at this form of compliance given that they reportedly enjoyed considerable freedom from oversight of administrators, yet they might ultimately appreciate the structure and feedback inherent in the process, especially if instructors took the lead in carrying out assessment themselves. Through more intensive program monitoring, program strengths and weakness could be noted, and adaptations could be made in response to changes in demand from students as well as the college. It should be noted that the learning community coordinator's reported duties included professional development; updating progress to the college; marketing the program; budgeting; forming and facilitating the related college committee; as well as design, implementation, and assessment—in addition to responsibilities for other college reform initiatives. As evident from this list of responsibilities, this position may approach a full-time workload, and thus having a full-time coordinator or two co-coordinators may be warranted, especially if additional assessment of implementation processes were to be included.

Initial instructor training with respect to the learning communities in this study appeared to stem mainly from attending conference sessions on learning communities and studying associated conference papers from a single conference. Ongoing mentorship or additional resources to assist with unfolding questions or problems that arose during the first semester were not reported by instructors or administers. Yet instructors felt more confident and equipped as they gained more training—primarily through attending a yearly conference—and experience over subsequent semesters. More thorough and varied training, especially for instructors new to the program, would likely enhance the effectiveness of the learning communities at their inception. Further, it became apparent from the interviews that there was interest at the college with respect to implementing additional learning communities, such as in history and English. Given the high interest level, the formation of an informal professional learning community might result in more pooled training resources for the instructors. Such a professional learning community might result in increased "word of mouth" for the student learning communities on campus and could diminish pressure on instructors to quickly become de facto local experts on learning communities.

Team teaching, where both instructors teach together for the duration of both classes occurred only a few times throughout each semester. Ideally, learning communities should be team taught during a majority of classes or more for the entire semester: "The daily practice of team teaching creates an environment of continuous learning for everyone and for acculturating new members of the community" [31]. However, team teaching in this form may be impractical due to both instructors' time and college budgetary constraints. When instructors did team teach, students described these days as their "favorite days". On these days, the methodologies of learning communities were in full effect with a variety of active learning opportunities that allowed for frequent instructor-instructor interaction, student-student interaction, and student-faculty interaction. As such, a full implementation of team teaching into the learning communities would likely enhance the effectiveness of the program, including potentially facilitating more integration of course content, primarily via common themes. Even though there was increased integration of content as the program evolved, there was not anything approaching a comprehensive curriculum between the two courses, which represented a missed opportunity in these learning communities.

Last, as evident from the literature, many learning communities require students to partake in a variety of student services [9,32]. For the program at this college, student services were voluntary, but mandating students to attend weekly or bi-weekly meetings with their instructors, tutors, and advisers could be particularly beneficial for academically underprepared students. In fact, findings from this study revealed the importance of student services. In-depth interviews with learning community students revealed that they primarily learned about student services from inside the program. These services included a learning center, where tutors were available in various subjects, and a writing center. Increasing students' confidence to seek help, and the subsequent involvement with student services, instructors, and peers, are key steps in helping academically underprepared students to succeed in college [9,19]. The present study suggests that more intensive models of learning communities, equipped with tutors, counselors, and other student support services, may be needed for optimal learning communities, especially with respect to developmental education.

As an implication for the future, our study points to the need for more widespread use of process evaluations when others are considering future learning community programs. Locally conducted process evaluations would permit stakeholders to detect potential problems or areas for improvement "on the fly" before program outcomes have crystalized. Further, process evaluations could pinpoint variables or processes idiosyncratic to each institution that may serve as powerful mediators of program success, e.g., student or instructor characteristics, institutional culture(s) and resources, relations with the external community, and so forth.

Like all studies, this one has its limitations. First, the process evaluation examined a program implemented for academically underprepared students in reading at a two-year public college. While our findings may or may not be generalizable to other groups of students, other types of institutions, or even other two-year colleges, there is little reason to believe apriori that they would *not* apply to many other learning communities elsewhere. Second, while all instructors and administrators in the program participated in the study, student attrition occurred over the two-year study. For instance, students who participated in a learning community but dropped out of the college were not available to be interviewed and it is possible that those who left might have provided different perspectives than those who remained. Further, there was the potential for nonrespondent bias in terms of those who declined to be interviewed. Third, data for this study were collected over 2015 and 2016. Since then, the COVID-19 pandemic has ushered in more widespread use of—and innovation in—remote and hybrid learning opportunities. Concomitantly, there has been increased interest in online-based learning communities, e.g., in terms of how they can foster a sense of community when conditions occur that constrain physical proximity, or can reduce digital inequality for those students living in rural areas [16]. That said, our primary findings and conclusions appear quite relevant in the contemporary educational landscape. In fact, the challenges to learning communities that we identified on the campus, such as more comprehensive instructor training, fully realized team teaching, and providing student support services may prove even more challenging remotely than in person, particularly given the technological and coordination demands that must be surmounted.

5. Conclusions

More careful implementation of learning communities may result in greater program success for students. Based on this process evaluation of a linked-course learning community for developmental reading students, we offer the following suggestions for implementation (1) define specific goals that are, in fact, easily implementable; (2) fully implement team-teaching across linked courses; (2) implement an integrative curriculum; (3) provide in-depth and ongoing instructor training, along with specialized resources; (4) expand support services available to students and require them to use at least some as part of the learning community experience; and (5) create tools/methods for instructors and administrators to assess processual aspects rather than just program outcomes.

Author Contributions: Conceptualization, T.S.L. and R.M.C.; methodology, T.S.L. and R.M.C.; software, T.S.L. and R.M.C.; validation, T.S.L. and R.M.C.; formal analysis, T.S.L.; investigation, T.S.L. and R.M.C.; resources, T.S.L.; data curation, T.S.L.; writing—original draft preparation, T.S.L. and R.M.C.; writing—review and editing, T.S.L. and R.M.C.; visualization, T.S.L. and R.M.C.; supervision, T.S.L. and R.M.C.; project administration, T.S.L. and R.M.C. All authors have read and agreed to the published version of the manuscript.

Funding: Funding was neither received in support of this research nor to cover article processing charges.

Institutional Review Board Statement: The study was approved by the Institutional Review Board at the University of Louisville, KY, USA.

Informed Consent Statement: Informed consent was obtained from all subjects involved in the study.

Data Availability Statement: Data are covered by a confidentiality agreement and thus are not available.

Conflicts of Interest: The authors declare no conflict of interest.

References and Note

1. Kern, B.; Kingsbury, T. Curricular Learning Communities and Retention. *J. Scholarsh. Teach. Learn.* **2019**, *19*, 41–52. [CrossRef]
2. VanOra, J.P. The Impact of Learning Communities on the Experiences of Developmental Students in Community College: A Qualitative Study. *Learn. Communities Res. Pract.* **2019**, *7*, 2.
3. Cerna, O.; Richburg-Hayes, L.; Sansone, C.; Schneider, E.; Visher, M.G.; Ware, M.; Washington, H. *The Learning Communities Demonstration: Rationale, Sites, and Research Design*; National Center for Postsecondary Research: Washington, DC, USA, 2008.
4. Fosnacht, K.; Graham, P. Is a HIP Always a HIP? The Case of Learning Communities. *J. Stud. Aff. Res. Pract.* **2021**, *59*, 59–72. [CrossRef]
5. Kuh, G.D. *High-Impact Educational Practices: What They Are, Who Has Access to Them, and Why They Matter*; Association of American Colleges & Universities: Washington, DC, USA, 2008.
6. Ewert, S. Fewer Diplomas for Men: The Influence of College Experiences on the Gender Gap in College Graduation. *J. High. Educ.* **2012**, *83*, 824–850. [CrossRef]
7. Kuh, G.D.; Kinzie, J.; Schuh, J.H.; Whitt, E.J. *Student Success in College: Creating Conditions That Matter*; Jossey-Bass: San Francisco, CA, USA, 2010.
8. Pascarella, E.T.; Terenzini, P.T. *How College Affects Students: A Third Decade of Research*; Jossey-Bass: San Francisco, CA, USA, 2005; Volume 2.

9.   Baier, S.T.; Gonzales, S.M.; Sawilowsky, S.S. Classroom Learning Communities' Impact on Students in Developmental Courses. *J. Dev. Educ.* **2019**, *42*, 2–8.

10.   Braxton, J.M. (Ed.) *The Role of the College Classroom in College Student Persistence: New Directions for Teaching and Learning*; Number 115; Jossey-Bass: San Francisco, CA, USA, 2008.

11.   Sax, L. *The Gender Gap in College: Maximizing the Development Potential of Women and Men*; Jossey-Bass: Hoboken, NJ, USA, 2008.

12.   Shapiro, N.S.; Levine, J.H. *Creating Learning Communities: A Practical Guide to Winning Support, Organizing for Change, and Implementing Programs*; Jossey-Bass: San Francisco, CA, USA, 1999.

13.   Schreiner, L.A.; Nelson, D.D. The Contribution of Student Satisfaction to Persistence. *J. Coll. Stud. Retent. Res. Theory Pract.* **2013**, *15*, 73–111. [CrossRef]

14.   Goodlad, K.; Cheng, S.; Sears, J.; Diaz, M.; Satyanarayana, A.; Freniske, P. Our Stories': First-year Learning Communities Students' Reflections on the Transition to College. *Learn. Communities Res. Pract.* **2019**, *7*, 5.

15.   Weiss, M.J.; Visher, M.G.; Weissman, E.; Wathington, H. The Impact of Learning Communities for Students in Developmental Education: A Synthesis of Findings from Randomized Trials in Six Community Colleges. *Educ. Eval. Policy* **2015**, *37*, 520–541 [CrossRef]

16.   Welser, H.T.; Khan, M.L.; Dickard, M. Digital Remediation: Social Support and Online Learning Communities Can Help Offset Rural Digital Inequality. *Inf. Commun. Soc.* **2019**, *22*, 717–723. [CrossRef]

17.   Weiss, M.J.; Visher, M.G.; Wathington, H. *Learning Communities for Students in Developmental Reading: An Impact Study at Hillsborough Community College*; National Center for Postsecondary Research: New York, NY, USA, 2010.

18.   Internal College Report. 2013. Details withheld to mask the identity of the college.

19.   Lanphier, T.S.; Carini, R.M. Insights from a Learning Community Program for Developmental Reading Students: Developing a Conceptual Model. *Community Coll. Enterp.* **2021**, *27*, 22–37.

20.   Oakley, A.; Strange, V.; Bonell, C.; Allen, E.; Stephenson, J. RIPPLE Study Team. Process Evaluation in Randomized Controlled Trials of Complex Interventions. *BMJ* **2006**, *332*, 413–416. [CrossRef] [PubMed]

21.   Lanphier, T.S. Evaluation of a Learning Community Program for Developmental Reading Students at a Two-Year College Doctoral's Dissertation, University of Louisville, Louisville, KY, USA, 2019. Available online: https://ir.library.louisville.edu/etd/3181/ (accessed on 1 December 2021).

22.   Blumer, H. What is Wrong with Social Theory? *Am. Sociol. Rev.* **1954**, *18*, 3–10. [CrossRef]

23.   Glaser, B.G.; Strauss, A.L. *The Discovery of Grounded Theory: Strategies for Qualitative Research*; Aldine: New York, NY, USA, 1967.

24.   Ryan, G.W.; Bernard, H.R. Techniques to Identify Themes. *Field Methods* **2003**, *15*, 85–109. [CrossRef]

25.   Huot, N.; Palm, J. Year-long LC: Rethinking the Summer Bridge. In Proceedings of the Annual Meeting of the National Learning Communities Conference, Bay City, MI, USA, 7 November 2014.

26.   Astin, A.W. Student Involvement: A Developmental Theory for Higher Education. *J. Coll. Stud. Dev.* **1999**, *40*, 518–529.

27.   Tinto, V. *Leaving College: Rethinking the Causes and Cures of Attrition*, 2nd ed.; University of Chicago: Chicago, IL, USA, 1993.

28.   Bourdieu, P. The Forms of Capital. In *Handbook of Theory and Research for the Sociology of Education*; Richardson, J.G., Ed.; Greenwood Press: New York, NY, USA, 1986; pp. 241–258.

29.   Baham, M.; Finley, D. Jumping on the Bandwagon: Encouraging Collaboration through Student Engagement, Success, and Retention. In Proceedings of the Annual Meeting of the National Learning Communities Conference, Kansas City, MO, USA, 13 November 2015.

30.   Gebauer, R. We're All in: Creating a Collaborative Culture of Learning Communities on Campus. In Proceedings of the Annual Meeting of the National Learning Communities Conference, Kansas City, MO, USA, 13 November 2015.

31.   Smith, B.L.; MacGregor, J. Learning Communities and the Quest for Quality. *Qual. Assur. Educ.* **2009**, *17*, 118–139. [CrossRef]

32.   Gonzales, S.M.; Brammer, E.C.; Sawilowsky, S. Belonging in the academy: Building a 'casa away from casa' for Latino/a undergraduate students. *J. Hisp. High. Educ.* **2015**, *14*, 223–239. [CrossRef]

Article

Measuring a University's Image: Is Reputation an Influential Factor?

Belén Gutiérrez-Villar [1,*], **Purificación Alcaide-Pulido** [2] and **Mariano Carbonero-Ruz** [3]

[1] Departamento de Gestión Empresarial, Universidad Loyola Andalucía, Escritor Castilla Aguayo 4, 14014 Córdoba, Spain
[2] Departamento de Comunicación y Educación, Universidad Loyola Andalucía, Escritor Castilla Aguayo 4, 14014 Córdoba, Spain; palcaide@uloyola.es
[3] Departamento de Métodos Cuantitativos, Universidad Loyola Andalucía, Escritor Castilla Aguayo 4, 14014 Córdoba, Spain; mcarbonero@uloyola.es
* Correspondence: belengut@uloyola.es

Abstract: Today, the higher education sector can be considered a market and, within it, private university education is a common marketable service in the literature on higher education management. Research on the analysis of the variables that generate the university image has been the subject of numerous investigations. Although there is no generally accepted definition, most authors approach the measurement of image through multi-factor scales, with variables relating to functional and psychological elements. This research aims to contribute to study of the most determinant variables in measuring a product's image, assessing especially the effect of the reputation construct. This was done through measuring the image of the "private university" product as perceived by citizens of Andalusia, based on a standardized model with three dimensions—functional and affective aspects and reputation. After adapting and validating the questionnaire, a two-phase procedure is performed with double validation through exploratory and confirmatory factor analysis. The results show an adapted scale valid for measuring the image of a generic product; with presentation and discussion of a series of advantages of incorporating reputation and measuring image through models with three dimensions. This article goes deeper into the possible influence of reputation as a determinant factor in measuring image, an assumption arising from some models for measuring image, something that so far has not been sufficiently contrasted.

Keywords: image measurement; reputation; private university; confirmatory factor analysis

Citation: Gutiérrez-Villar, B.; Alcaide-Pulido, P.; Carbonero-Ruz, M. Measuring a University's Image: Is Reputation an Influential Factor? *Educ. Sci.* **2022**, *12*, 19. https://doi.org/10.3390/educsci12010019

Academic Editor: Han Reichgelt

Received: 11 November 2021
Accepted: 21 December 2021
Published: 30 December 2021

Publisher's Note: MDPI stays neutral with regard to jurisdictional claims in published maps and institutional affiliations.

1. Introduction

The implementation of marketing to university is an area that is growing in importance as competition between universities increases. Thus, the irruption of marketing philosophy in higher education institution (HEI) is understood as a competitive strength where globalization of HEIs has played a part [1,2]; and has pushed the universities to develop new marketing strategies to increase brand engagement [3]. According to this marketing philosophy, the study of two intangible assets in higher education, image and reputation, have received increasing academic research in recent years [4–8].

There is considerable consensus on the benefits of a good university image, such as a source of differentiation from other competitive institutions [9], or to improve the relations with stakeholders [10]; Mainly, a good image can contribute to the achievement of new students [11–13].

However, the analysis of image in perceptual meaning becomes an ambiguous concept [14,15]. This may be due to related but different concepts revolving around the idea of image, these being: corporate image, brand image, product image, brand personality, positioning, identity, and reputation, which are sometimes used erroneously as synonyms [16–18]. Certainly, reputation, and its differentiation from image, is a subject that has given rise to various stances, without there being consensus as to the relation of dependence between these two concepts [19].

Nevertheless, there is considerable agreement on the premise that image can be measured, but it is hard to measure [20]. Various authors support the idea that the image of a product, brand or company are subjective phenomena that can be measured by compiling the opinions of individuals or groups of individuals, with no need for them to be consumers [17,21–23]. However, there is no generally accepted model to measure image, with the methodologies proposed, and the variables used in published models being disparate [15].

Following on from the above, this study aims to contribute more evidence to the discussion on perceptual measurement of university image with a twin objective: from the theoretical bases and results of empirical work published, it was decided to submit to examination the brand image measurement scale proposed by Martínez et al. [24] formed of three dimensions—functional image, affective image and reputation, to confirm its validity when the object measured is a product unconnected to a specific brand; and secondly, the study seeks to confirm the significance of reputation as an independent and necessary construct to measure image.

The brand measurement scale was chosen due to its versatility since it considers a set of items adaptable to each specific context –as the authors themselves point out; because it is conceived as universalizable and has been used successfully to measure brand image in different sectors of activity with the model being validated in subsequent studies [25–27]

In this way, the main research question is to know what are the factors that shape the image of a private university in the minds of people in general, regardless of their level of studies or other sociodemographic characteristics. In addition, given the importance of the reputation construct in the university context, this study aims to determine whether reputation is one of the influential factors in the measurement of the image of a private university, when no specific institution or brand is mentioned.

The Spanish university system has 83 universities, of which 50 are public and 33 are private. Although private universities account for 40% of Spanish universities, according to official statistics from 2018 onwards, they only account for around 14% of university students. In Andalusia, there is only one private university to date. The decision to focus the study on private education is considered pertinent, as this topic is widely debated in society, with all individuals finding it easy to give their appreciation and opinion.

2. Literature Review and Hypothesis

2.1. Concept of Image and Levels of Measurement

Academic interest in the concept of image dates to the 1950s, and authors at that time were suggesting that human behavior depends more on image than on objective reality itself [28,29]. Transposed to the world of products and brands, since the mid-20th century, many authors have proposed definitions of image which highlight the perceptual component leading individuals to form a mental image of the object (product, brand company, sector or even person) through a set of sentiments, ideas and attitudes, rather than a sum of physical attributes and characteristics.

The review of the literature on the concept of image reveals many commonalities in the definitions that emphasize the cognitive or mental process through which individuals create an image. Many authors describe aspects such as ideas, sentiments, attitudes mental constructs, perceptions, beliefs, expectations, impressions, or stereotypes as essential determinants [4,15,19,30].

This research is based on the definition of image proposed by Currás [17] (p. 29) who sees it as: "the sum, result, or accumulation of beliefs, attitudes, experiences, sentiments, impressions or information that a subject—consumers, stakeholders, individuals in general—has of an object".

In addition, a more detailed study of the degree of generality or specificity of the object of the image allows what is usually known as levels of image measurement. In this case, the few authors who have addressed this topic open the field of study, with it being possible—and interesting—to analyze individuals' mental image of objects other than brands. Although the number of levels forming these studies does not coincide, there is unanimity regarding the existence of a product image, understood as what individuals perceive about a product or service in general, beyond brands or companies [28]. In consequence, there are different objects/levels that can be of interest for the measurement of image—a sector, a generic product, a company, or brands [21]. This paper focuses on the measurement of a generic service, the private university, without alluding to a specific university brand.

2.2. Reputation and Image

As happens with image, reputation has been studied in different areas related to business [31], such as strategy, communication, marketing, sociology and even finance. But unlike image, many of the studies published on reputation do not give a definition, taking this for granted [32].

However, this study takes as a reference the definition proposed by Fombrun et al. [33] (p. 87), where reputation is: "collective representation of a company's past behavior and its consequences, which shows the company's capacity to deliver valuable results to multiple stakeholders". Also, as with image, reputation can be applied to different objects, such as products or services [19,34].

Another important consideration arrived at after reviewing studies is the existence of difficulties in establishing differences between the concepts of image and reputation [35,36]. So, a minority of work considers them similar [31,32]; but the majority argue that they are interrelated concepts:

1. some studies consider reputation as the result of combining the different images of a company [37,38];
2. and others consider it as the global assessment and influential element in measuring the image of products or brands [12,20,23,24,39–42]. This study is based on the second group.

Following the review above, the first hypothesis is formulated:

Hypothesis 1 (H1). *Reputation is a significant factor in measuring a product's image.*

2.3. Measurement Scales for University Image

There is great consensus in research based on university image as a multivariate concept generated in different subjects [10,12,20,30,39,43,44]. Also generalized is the thesis covering inter-related cognitive and emotional aspects [39]. The cognitive (knowledge about the object) and affective (motivations, sentiments and benefits) dimensions are complementary, allowing better measurement and understanding of image [23].

There is no consensus on how to measure image and how many factors are necessary, which has led to multiple measurement scales. In this context, there are two methodologies [24]: (1) ad-hoc scales that can capture image but cannot be generalized; and (2) standardized scales which, although allowing generalization, are not globally recognized.

Therefore, three multi-dimensional scales including reputation as a factor have been reviewed. Two ad-hoc scales designed to measure university image—those of Beerly et al. [39] and Sung & Yang [4]—and a standardized scale proposed by Martínez et al. [24], which was used for vehicles and would be applicable to all types of products.

The first of the above-mentioned models establishes six dimensions to measure the university's brand image: the university's orientation and training, reputation, massification, accessibility, age and affective dimension. This scale was reduced to four dimensions in the works published later [23,45], where the dimensions associated with cognitive aspects emerge as significant: reputation and emotional aspects.

The second model [4] finds three factors significant: personality of the university, external prestige, and reputation; with the university's external prestige being the factor with the most weight in the image.

To explore other possibilities for study, this research opted to use the standardized scale [24], which has not previously been applied to measure university image. According to the authors, brand image would be formed of three constructs: functional image, covering aspects related to attributes or benefits linked to the brand; affective image, including the personality of the brand; and reputation, formed of the global perception of the brand over time. In the original proposal, a scale of 9 items was used, three for each construct (see Table 1).

Table 1. Studies carried out with the image measurement standardised scale of Martinez et al.

Items Proposed in Each of the Three Dimensions	Significance in Studies			
	Martínez et al. (2004) [24]	Martínez et al. (2005) [25]	Martínez et al. (2007) [26]	Buil et al. (2008) [27]
FUNCTIONAL IMAGE				
F1 The products are high quality.	Signif.	Signif.	Signif.	Signif.
F2 The products present characteristics that other brands do not have.	——	Signif.	Signif.	——
F3 The products have better characteristics than the competition.	——	——	——	Signif.
F4 Consuming this brand is very unlikely to cause problems or unforeseen events.	——	Not Signif.	——	——
F5 The competition's products are usually cheaper.	——	Signif.	——	Not Signif.
F6 The models are cheap in relation to other brands.	Signif.	——	——	——
F7 I like the design of the models.	Signif.	——	——	——
AFFECTIVE IMAGE				
A1 It is a brand that arouses positive feelings.	——	Signif.	Signif.	Signif.
A2 This brand conveys a personality that differentiates it from rival brands.	——	Signif.	Signif.	Signif.
A3 Buying this brand says something about the class of person you are.	——	Not Signif.	——	——
A4 I have an image of the type of people that buy this brand.	Signif.	Not Signif.	——	——
A5 It is a brand that does not disappoint its customers.	——	Signif.	Signif.	Signif.
A6 The brand conveys values that differentiate it from other brands in the sector.	Signif.	——	——	——
A7 The brand strives to innovate in new models, services and/or technology.	Signif.	——	——	——
REPUTATION				
R1 It is one of the best brands in the sector.	——	Signif.	Signif.	Signif.
R2 It is a brand that is committed to society.	——			
R3 It is a much consolidated brand in the market.	——	Signif.	——	——
R4 The brand is highly regarded.	Signif.			
R5 The brand is a professional in its category.	Signif.	Signif.	Signif.	Signif.
R6 You can trust this brand.	Signif.			

It should be noted that the standardized scale has been applied to different brands in various sectors, such as: cars [24], dairy products, sports footwear, and electronics [25]; generic brandless products [26] –a tube of toothpaste and a box of chocolates–; and goods of frequent consumption, lasting consumer goods and services [27].

In all these studies the scale was validated, resulting in explaining the three constructs (functional, affective, and reputation), although as the authors themselves state, the 9 items originally proposed to assess brands in the car sector should be adapted if applied to brands in other sectors, and can be extended or substituted with others, as long as respecting the three-dimensional structure.

Following the review above, it was decided to propose a three-factor model, leading to the formulation of the last hypothesis:

Hypothesis 2 (H2). *The most correct formulation to measure the image of the generic product "private university" is obtained by applying a standardized multi-factor scale with three dimensions: functional image, affective image, and reputation.*

3. Materials and Methods

3.1. Sample

The type of sampling used was intentional. However, since the questionnaire has been implemented in a previously existing consumer panel, we believe that the stability and maturity implied by its past will have transferred to the sample, strengthening its representativeness. So, the questionnaire launching method was online through a consolidated consumer panel, managed by a marketing research company with a consistence control in registered persons. The initial sample consisted of 778 questionnaires. This number was the maximum we could afford with the limited budget we had available for primary data collection. Before proceeding with the estimation and validation of the model, the sample was filtered, eliminating the atypical observations, which resulted in a total of 27 questionnaires being eliminated.

It is not the objective of this work to study differences based on sex or age. Nevertheless, the panel leaders were asked to include men and women of different ages in the sample, so that the sample would not be composed only of young individuals, a priori more familiar with the subject matter of this study.

The questionnaire was validly completed by 751 Andalusians. The sample was 461 men (61.4%) and 290 women (38.6%) between 18 and 65 years old. The distribution by age bracket was equal in the 4 age brackets chosen: 150 persons aged 18 to 25 (20%); 150 persons aged 26 to 35 (20%); 150 persons aged 46 to 55 (20%) and 151 persons aged 56 to 65 (20.1%).

3.2. Instrument

As stated above, there is no agreement in the significance of all the items used in the research published [24–27]. This implied elaboration of a questionnaire including and adapting all the significant items in the studies reviewed previously, as compiled in Table 2, only adding one item in this study for reputation.

Table 2. Brand image measurement scale adapted to the "private university".

Functional Image (F)	Affective Image (A)	Reputation (R)
f1. Education and training in the private university are of high quality.	a1. The private university arouses positive sentiments.	r1. The private university is the best option.
f2. The private university's premises are of high quality.	a2. The private university conveys a personality that differentiates it from the state university.	r2. The private university is committed to society.
f3. The research produced in a private universities is of high quality.	a3. Enrolling in a private university says something about the class of person you are.	r3. The private university is much consolidated in the market.
f4. Private universities present characteristics that state ones do not have.	a4. The private university does not disappoint its customers.	r4. The private university occupies very high positions in university rankings.
f5. The private university gives high value in relation to the price that must be paid for it.	a5. The private university has a differentiated ideological component.	

The addition of item r4, relating reputation to the position in rankings was not tested previously in this scale of image but was considered appropriate in the light of recent research [46,47], which establishes its relevance and links these concepts in the university domain.

As for the formulation of the questions, each one is presented as a statement, and respondents are asked to show their level of agreement or disagreement on a 7-point Likert scale (1 = complete disagreement, 7 = complete agreement).

3.3. Data Collection and Analysis Procedure

To test the hypotheses proposed, the factor analysis method was applied with data arising from a survey made of Andalusian adults. Not having a generally accepted model to measure the image of the private university, but a generic brand this could be likened to, led us to divide analysis of the issue into four phases, as presented in Figure 1. Phase 1 involves adapting the items of the standardized image measurement model and carrying out the corresponding pre-test. In Phase 2, the validity and significance of the items initially proposed are explored. In Phase 3, the standardized model is confirmed in its version with the three original dimensions. In Phase 4, the validity of the result obtained is contrasted. The difference between the third and fourth phases is that while in the third we admit the possibility of improving the initial estimation by modifying the model, in the fourth there is only validation of the result of the first. This strategy of validation meant dividing the sample.

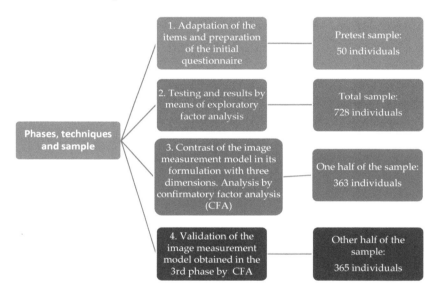

Figure 1. Phases, procedures applied, and sample used.

4. Results

4.1. Phase 1. Pretest of the Questionnaire

As already mentioned, 50 valid questionnaires were used in a pre-test. Validity and reliability were checked through analysis of the Cronbach alpha coefficient (α). A reliability value of around 0.70 is considered acceptable [48]. The figure obtained here was $\alpha = 0.819$, implying validation of the initial questionnaire.

4.2. Phase 2. Initial Validation through EFA

In exploratory factor analysis, examination of the data is a necessary preliminary step, to allow better prediction and more accurate evaluation of the dimensional nature. Otherwise, atypical cases, extreme answers, can unduly influence the result of a multivariate analysis [49]. Measuring the *Mahalanobis distance* to the centroid of the distribution indicated the presence of 22 outliers, which we decided to eliminate [50], leaving a final sample formed of 728 observations.

Although various procedures are available in statistical programs (such as SPSS), in practice two methods are most used an exploratory factor analysis (EFA): Principal Axes and Principal Components. The Principal Axes method only contemplates the variance the variables have in common or co-variance, excluding specific variance and that which can be attributed to measurement. In this case, Principal Components was chosen, since the aim of this analysis, more than a prediction, is the detection of latent dimensions (here, the three blocks forming the questionnaire, functional image, affective image, and reputation) [49].

The results suggest that three factors should be chosen, as from the fourth factor onwards the associated eigenvalues are far below 1. Besides, the percentage of explained variance with the three factors chosen reaches 69.935%, a high percentage, which indicates acceptance of the three factors.

The next step is to contrast the coincidence of their significance. One way to approach factor content is rotation, which consists of their re-organization, reducing as much as possible the variance of each item shared by different factors, at the expense of a simultaneous reduction in the explained variance. After rotating the model, the explained variance is 61.431%.

The factor loadings after rotation show that the 5 items relating to functional image form one factor and that the 4 relating to reputation form another. However, in the case of affective image, two of its items are not significant: variable a3. "Enrolling in the private university says something about the class of person you are", and variable a5. "The private university has a differentiated ideological component". With these results, affective image will be studied from now on with 3 items, due to eliminating the variables about the association between the type of person and the private nature of the university, and about the ideological component.

4.3. Division of the Sample

This study proposes a previous procedure to CFA of dividing the sample, which is common in some areas of quantitative research. This assumes validation of a scale principally through a procedure of dividing the total sample (728 questionnaires) in two homogeneous sub-samples: one for training (confirmation of the scale, corresponding to Phase 3) and the other for validation (ratification of the results, corresponding to Phase 4). The reason for this strategy is that it would not be advisable to use the same observations for construction and validation, as if to evaluate the model we use the same observations as to construct it, we would probably obtain a good result, due to the fact of the parameters of the model being estimated with the same sample as for subsequent validation.

Among the few methods available for division of the sample, the one developed by [51] was chosen. This is an extension of the Wilcoxon-Mann-Whitney test of equality of means without requirements of normality. The contrast is applied to successive divisions of the sample in two sub-sets, obtained randomly, with the similarity being evaluated through a statistic of known approximate distribution (specifically chi-squared) until the sub-samples obtained are statistically homogeneous for the chosen level of significance (5% in this case). Applying this procedure to the initial sample results in two sub-samples of 363 and 365 respectively, whose associated p-value calculated is 0.948, very close to one, which leads us to accept the division with strong guarantees of their similarity. As explained previously, the first sub-sample will be used to confirm the model (Phase 3) and the second to validate it (Phase 4).

4.4. Phases 3 and 4. Estimation and Validation of the Model through CFA

Both the existing literature on the factors measuring image and the previous results indicate it may not be completely clear that there is an affective factor independent of reputation and functional elements. Setting out from the result obtained from EFA, the third phase deals with confirming this, even improving it, through slight modifications to its structure. In the fourth phase, the resulting model is put to test to check its statistic validity.

4.5. Phase 3. Estimation of the Model

To estimate and validate the CFA models we used *EQS 6.1* software, choosing the maximum likelihood (ML) method to estimate the parameters, aiming to find the estimates that make the occurrence of the sample obtained most probable, maximizing its likelihood [52]. In addition, this is a very robust estimation method that can be applied when there is no condition of univariate and multivariate normality of the data (as in this case) without serious losses of the theoretical properties of the estimates obtained [49]. The most important aspect of the results obtained is evaluation of the model's goodness of fit. In each case, we obtained some of the usual indices in this type of analysis, namely the comparative fit index (CFI), the normed fit index (NFI), the non-normed fit index (NNFI), and the root mean square error of approximation (RMSEA).

The CFI is a measure that compares the fit obtained for the estimated model with what would be obtained on the assumption of no relation between the variables used. Its values range between 0 (no adjustment of the model to the data) and 1 (perfect adjustment of the model), with 0.9 being the appropriate threshold value [53]. The NFI and NNFI are similar measures, which situate the estimated model on a scale between the extremes of the nil model and perfect fit, differing in the fact of considering or not the models' degrees of freedom. Both have values between 0 and 1, considering the models with the highest values in these indices as the most adjusted. Finally, RMSEA, as a measure of the magnitude of the errors committed, should be interpreted in the opposite direction, with the most suitable models being those where this indicator has a lower value. A common reference is that its value should not be above 0.06 [53].

Carrying out the confirmatory procedure with the first sub-sample (363) and calculating the adjustment indicators of the model to measure private university image with the three factors (functional, affective and reputational) and the items determined in the exploratory Phase 2, confirmation of the model did not turn out, as expected, to be completely satisfactory (CFI = 0.919, NNFI = 0.895, NFI = 0.905 and RMSEA = 0.119). However, analysis of the *Lagrange multipliers* indicated it was possible to improve the model by modifying its structure slightly.

Those modifications consisted of allowing the functional factor (F) to share one indicator (r3, opinion about consolidation in the market) with reputation (R) and another with the affective factor (f5, quality-price relation). Finally, everything seemed to indicate that variable f4 (private universities present characteristics that state ones do not have) could be linked to the three factors. We consider this possibility is equivalent to stating that the variable is not appropriate to identify the elements defining university image, since it should be associated with all three and is not really a characteristic of any. Therefore, we decided to eliminate it from the model.

The indicators for the model recalculated with these corrections (CFI = 0.965, NNFI = 0.950, NFI = 0.952 and RMSEA = 0.086), much more accurate than the initial ones, together with the results' coherence with theory, led us to consider it definitive, as shown in Figure 2.

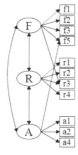

Figure 2. CFA results of the first sub-sample.

4.6. Phase 4. Validation of the Model

The model estimated and modified in Phase 3 was subject to evaluation using the second sub-sample (365 questionnaires) with no option for change. It is a question of determining whether the goodness-of-fit achieved in the previous phase was inherent to the model, or if this had been adapted exclusively to the sample with which it had been obtained (overtraining). In both cases, as detailed below, the result was satisfactory.

The expectations for the 4th phase, on the assumption of the model's validity, are of stability, in that the model proposed, without new modifications, should be acceptable. Moreover, if the structure detected during the first phase is correct, not only the global fit measurements but also the factor loadings should be similar in both estimates.

Tables 3 and 4 present, respectively, the goodness-of-fit indicators and the values estimated for the model's parameters in both phases.

Table 3. Global measurements.

	Phase 3	Phase 4
CFI	0.965	0.963
NNFI	0.950	0.947
NFI	0.952	0.951
RMSEA	0.086	0.088

Table 4. Estimated parameters.

Factor	Variable	Phase 3	Phase 4
	f1	0.865 **	0.883 **
	f2	0.776 **	0.777 **
F	f3	0.816 **	0.838 **
	f5	0.286 **	0.479 **
	r3	0.176 **	0.358 **
	r1	0.852 **	0.854 **
R	r2	0.892 **	0.903 **
	r3	0.835 **	0.827 **
	r4	0.754 **	0.537 **
	f5	0.53 **	0.341 **
A	a1	0.82 **	0.785 **
	a2	0.755 **	0.769 **
	a4	0.772 **	0.732 **
Cov(F,R)		0.631	0.708
Cov(F,A)		0.766	0.822
Cov(R,A)		0.901	0.926

** Parameter statistically significant at 1%.

Both Tables 3 and 4 reveal that, although the structure was estimated from a set of values and partly adapted to them, the degree of reliability obtained is not the result of that adaptation, as the indicators are confirmed to be practically identical with the different samples. Therefore, the results obtained in Phase 3 with the functional, reputational and affective factors, partially modified with regard to the model by Martinez et al. (2004) [24], are not the result of the sample used for the estimate.

5. Discussion and Conclusions

5.1. Discussion

Image and reputation are key assets with which institutions can differentiate their products from those of their rivals, and so it would be useful for managers to have appropriate measuring techniques for use in distinct contexts.

When reviewing the specifics about image and reputation, it is clear that, being concepts generally used in empirical work in management areas, a consensus has not been reached regarding their definitions. Although one stream argues that the concepts are similar, most of the studies reviewed focus on their divergence, defending the need to distinguish between image and reputation. Even within this stance of divergence, it is worth going deeper into the relation between both constructs.

Following the theoretical review, despite nuances, the definition of the image proposed [17] seems best to us, as it can be generalized to any product and any stakeholder. Therefore, image would be defined as the sum of an individual's beliefs, attitudes, experiences, sentiments, or information regarding an object. In relation to reputation, it is more difficult to find work going deeper into its definition, and the definitions reviewed are less homogeneous than in the case of image. Even so, there is a predominance of authors who consider reputation as the assessment or global attitude of a company or brand's behavior and some consider that other objects, such as goods or services, have a reputation [19].

We also found that when designing instruments to measure image, there is a certain gap between what is established theoretically as a possible target of image measurement (product, brand, company, country, etc.) and the empirical contributions published, which are usually greatly focused on similar subjects of study, with brand image being measured most frequently. It was very difficult to find work analyzing a generic product, with no brand, as is proposed here. In our view, this level of analysis would be extremely valuable for subsequent decision-making affecting brand image, or even guiding the first stages in launching a new product.

This study used an adaptation of the brand image measurement scale proposed by Martinez et al. (2004) [24], applied to citizens' perception of the private university. In this model, perceptions of a brand are grouped around three basic dimensions. Firstly, individual's value functional attributes, such as quality and perception of the price. In addition, affective attributes, which are linked to elements of a symbolic and emotional character. Finally, reputation is included. This model was chosen for three reasons:

1. the universality of the measurement scale proposed;
2. its validation through other work in different sectors;
3. considering reputation as a necessary factor in measuring image.

Exploratory factor analysis led to the conclusion that it is possible to measure the image of a product in individuals' minds, without referring to any brand, and that this is a multi-dimensional construct, with cognitive and emotional components. Therefore, the first hypothesis of this study is accepted.

The first hypothesis, seeking to contribute more empirical evidence about the relation between image and reputation, is also accepted, since through confirmatory factor analysis, reputation is found to be a significant factor at the time of measuring a brandless product's image.

The second and final hypothesis of this study—the best formulation to measure the image of the "private university" product is obtained by applying a standardized multi factor scale with three dimensions: functional image, affective image, and reputation—is also accepted.

Concerning the overall results, there are similarities in relation to the results of the study by Martínez et al. [25], since both models have similar goodness-of-fit indicators which corroborates the general validity of their theoretical proposal.

Nevertheless, it is worth making some changes about the initial model. In the first place, it is proposed to eliminate from the scale one of the variables included in the block of functional aspects—private universities present characteristics that state ones do not have -

a result that coincides with the last study published by its original authors [27]. Secondly, a change is proposed so that the price variable loads not only on the functional factor but also on the affective factor, which is logical since perception of the price involves both affective and functional elements.

Furthermore, it is proposed to incorporate an additional variable to measure the reputation of a university, i.e., the position in university rankings, something of great relevance in the sphere of higher education. The analyses confirm that the position in rankings is a significant variable in measuring university image, also being connected to the functional factor as well as the reputational one, although with much greater weight in the latter.

5.2. Conclusions

The relevance of the product category concept is explicit in the positioning concepts of image measurement, but very little research has been done on it. In the analysis of an organization's image, it is assumed that potential customer's group products hierarchically into different levels of specificity. For example, if an adult individual were to consider which path to follow in his or her studies, the possible products would initially be grouped into product categories (i.e., university versus vocational training), into product types (i.e., private university versus public university) and finally, by brand. However, most published empirical studies are concerned with measuring the brand image of a particular university.

A standardized multi-factor scale with three dimensions- functional image, affective image, and reputation- has proved valid for measuring the image of the private university, in general, without referring to any brand.

The results obtained suggest the existence of a differentiated image of private universities compared to public universities, which, to a certain extent, justifies their coexistence with state universities. This work offers some keys to private universities in terms of management and differentiation: if they work on functional aspects, it is convenient to allocate resources to improve the quality of education and research, without neglecting the price charged to students; if they focus attention on the management of emotional aspects, they must find a clearly differentiated brand personality compared to public universities and, finally, if they seek to activate their reputation, they must improve their positions in international rankings, among other aspects.

However, the results of this research, given the type of sampling employed, should be confirmed by other studies that extend the sample to a broader scope. It would also be of great interest to compare the results between two or more different countries.

In this line, and for future lines of research, it would be of interest to contrast whether there are significant differences in the measurement of the image of private universities according to the profile of the respondent.

In the same line of research, it would be very interesting to incorporate image as a second-order construct, which would allow evaluating the weight of each of the three factors (functional, affective, and reputational) in its construction, in particular, that of reputation.

Finally, mention must be made of the methodological contribution as regards the management of the sample, both in its sub-division in two parts used to estimate and then validate the model (a not common practice in this type of study, although theoretically very recommendable) and the supervised way in which this sub-division was carried out to ensure the statistical homogeneity of both fractions.

Author Contributions: Conceptualization, B.G.-V. and P.A.-P.; Formal analysis, M.C.-R.; Methodology, M.C.-R.; Writing—original draft, B.G.-V., P.A.-P. All authors have read and agreed to the published version of the manuscript.

Funding: This research received no external funding.

Institutional Review Board Statement: Ethical review and approval were waived for this study, due to a market research company external to Loyola Andalucía University being used. This company "IDDEALIA Consulting" has the ISO 26362:2009 certification that guarantees the ethical aspects in this type of opinion panel services.

Informed Consent Statement: Informed consent was obtained from all subjects involved in the study.

Conflicts of Interest: The authors declare no conflict of interest.

References

1. Liu, Y.; Green, A.; Pensiero, N. Expansion of Higher Education and Inequality of Opportunities: A Cross-National Analysis. *J. High. Educ. Policy Manag.* **2016**, *38*, 242–263. [CrossRef]
2. Khoshtaria, T.; Datuashvili, D.; Matin, A. The Impact of Brand Equity Dimensions on University Reputation: An Empirical Study of Georgian Higher Education. *J. Mark. High. Educ.* **2020**, *30*, 239–255. [CrossRef]
3. Farhat, K.; Mokhtar, S.S.M.; Salleh, S.B.M. Role of Brand Experience and Brand Affect in Creating Brand Engagement: A Case of Higher Education Institutions (HEIs). *J. Mark. High. Educ.* **2021**, *31*, 107–135. [CrossRef]
4. Sung, M.; Yang, S.-U. Toward the Model of University Image: The Influence of Brand Personality, External Prestige, and Reputation. *J. Public Relat. Res.* **2008**, *20*, 357–376. [CrossRef]
5. Çetin, R. Planning and Implementing Institutional Image and Promoting Academic Programs in Higher Education. *J. Mark. High. Educ.* **2004**, *13*, 57–75. [CrossRef]
6. Lafuente Ruiz de Sabando, A.; Forcada Sainz, F.J.; Zorrilla Calvo, M.P. The University Image: A Model of Overall Image and Stakeholder Perspectives. *Imagen Univ. Modelo Imagen Glob. Perspect. Grupos Interés* **2018**, *19*, 63–86. [CrossRef]
7. Del-Castillo-Feito, C.; Blanco-González, A.; González-Vázquez, E. The Relationship between Image and Reputation in the Spanish Public University. *Eur. Res. Manag. Bus. Econ.* **2019**, *25*, 87–92. [CrossRef]
8. Irfan, A.; Sulaiman, Z.; Qureshi, M.I. Student's Perceived University Image Is an Antecedent of University Reputation. *Int. J. Psychosoc. Rehabil.* **2020**, *24*, 650–663. [CrossRef]
9. Iqbal, M.J.; Rasli, A.B.M.; Ibn-e-Hassan Rasli, A.B.M. University Branding: A Myth or a Reality. *Pak. J. Commer. Soc. Sci. PJCSS* **2012**, *6*, 168–184.
10. Nguyen, N.; Leblanc, G. Corporate Image and Corporate Reputation in Customers' Retention Decisions in Services. *J. Retail. Consum. Serv.* **2001**, *8*, 227–236. [CrossRef]
11. Walsh, C.; Moorhouse, J.; Dunnett, A.; Barry, C. University Choice: Which Attributes Matter When You Are Paying the Full Price? *Int. J. Consum. Stud.* **2015**, *39*, 670–681. [CrossRef]
12. Aghaz, A.; Hashemi, A.; Sharifi Atashgah, M.S. Factors Contributing to University Image: The Postgraduate Students' Points of View. *J. Mark. High. Educ.* **2015**, *25*, 104–126. [CrossRef]
13. Massoud, H.K.; Ayoubi, R.M. Do Flexible Admission Systems Affect Student Enrollment? Evidence from UK Universities. *J. Mark. High. Educ.* **2019**, *29*, 84–101. [CrossRef]
14. Pérez, A.; Bosque, I.R. del. Identidad, imagen y reputación de la empresa: Integración de propuestas teóricas para una gestión exitosa. *Cuad. Gest.* **2014**, *14*, 97–126. [CrossRef]
15. Stern, B.; Zinkhan, G.M.; Jaju, A. Marketing Images: Construct Definition, Measurement Issues, and Theory Development. *Mark. Theory* **2001**, *1*, 201–224. [CrossRef]
16. Balmer, J.M.T. Corporate Identity, Corporate Branding and Corporate Marketing—Seeing through the Fog. *Eur. J. Mark.* **2001**, *35*, 248–291. [CrossRef]
17. Curras Perez, R. Identidad e imagen corporativas: Revisión conceptual e interrelación. *Teoría Praxis* **2010**, *7*, 9–34. [CrossRef]
18. Lee, J.L.; James, J.D.; Kim, Y.K. A Reconceptualization of Brand Image. *Int. J. Bus. Adm.* **2014**, *5*, 1–11. [CrossRef]
19. Martínez, I.; Olmedo, I. Revisión teórica de la reputación en el entorno empresarial. *Cuad. Econ. Dir. Empresa* **2010**, *13*, 59–77. [CrossRef]
20. Kazoleas, D.; Kim, Y.; Anne Moffitt, M. Institutional Image: A Case Study. *Corp. Commun. Int. J.* **2001**, *6*, 205–216. [CrossRef]
21. Barich, H.; Kotler, P. A Framework for Marketing Image Management. *MITSloan* **1991**, *32*, 94–104.
22. Keller, K.L. Conceptualizing, Measuring, and Managing Customer-Based Brand Equity. *J. Mark.* **1993**, *57*, 1–22. [CrossRef]
23. Cervera, A.; Schlesinger, W.; Mesta, M.Á.; Sánchez, R. Medición de la imagen de la universidad y sus efectos sobre la identificación y lealtad del egresado: Una aproximación desde el modelo de beerli y díaz (2003). *Rev. Esp. Investig. Mark. ESIC* **2012**, *16*, 7–29. [CrossRef]
24. Martínez, E.M.; Montaner, T.M.; Pina, J.M.P. Propuesta de una metodología. Medición de la imagen de marca. Un estudio exploratorio. *ESIC Mark.* **2004**, *35*, 199–216.
25. Martínez, E.; Gutiérrez, T.M.; Pérez, J.M.P. Propuesta de medición de la imagen de marca: Un análisis aplicado a las extensiones de marca. *RAE Rev. Astur. Econ.* **2005**, *33*, 89–112.
26. Matínez, E.M.; Montaner, T.M.; Pina, J.M.P. Estrategia de promoción e imagen de marca: Influencia del tipo de promoción, de la notoriedad de la marca y de la congruencia de beneficios. *Rev. Esp. Investig. Mark.* **2007**, *11*, 27–52.
27. Buil, I.B.; Martínez, E.M.; Pina, J.M.P. Un modelo de evaluación de las extensiones de marca de productos y de servicios. *Rev. Eur. Dir. Econ. Empresa* **2008**, *17*, 167–186.

8. Gardner, B.B.; Levy, S.J. The Product and the Brand. *Harv. Bus. Rev.* **1955**, *33*, 33–39.
9. Martineau, P. Sharper Focus for the Corporate Image. *Harv. Bus. Rev.* **1958**, *36*, 49–58.
0. Arpan, L.M.; Raney, A.A.; Zivnuska, S. A Cognitive Approach to Understanding University Image. *Corp. Commun. Int. J.* **2003**, *8*, 97–113. [CrossRef]
1. Kennedy, S.H. Nurturing Corporate Images. *Eur. J. Mark.* **1977**, *11*, 119–164. [CrossRef]
2. Williams, R.J.; Barrett, J.D. Corporate Philanthropy, Criminal Activity, and Firm Reputation: Is There a Link? *J. Bus. Ethics* **2000**, *26*, 341–350. [CrossRef]
3. Fombrun, C.J.; Gardberg, N.A.; Barnett, M.L. *Opportunity Platforms and Safety Nets: Corporate Citizenship and Reputational Risk*; SSRN Scholarly Paper ID 1088404; Social Science Research Network: Rochester, NY, USA, 2008.
4. Iglesias, S.; Calvo, A.; López, V.A. Una aproximación empírica al concepto de reputación. In *Gestión Científica Empresarial: Temas de Investigación Actuales*; Netbiblo: La Coruña, Spain, 2003; pp. 87–104, ISBN 84-9745-051-5.
5. Ruiz, B.; Gutierrez-Broncano, S.; Esteban, Á. Desarrollo de Un Concepto de Reputación Corporativa Adaptado a Las Necesidades de La Gestión Empresarial. *Strategy Manag. Rev.* **2012**, *3*, 9–31.
6. Orozco-Toro, J.A.; Ferré-Pavia, C.C. Los índices de reputación corporativa y su aplicación en las empresas de comunicación. In *Comunicació i Risc: III Congrés Internacional Associació Espanyola d'Investigació de la Comunicació*; Universitat Rovira i Virgili: Tarragona, Spain, 2012; p. 42, ISBN 978-84-615-5678-6.
7. Chun, R. Corporate Reputation: Meaning and Measurement. *Int. J. Manag. Rev.* **2005**, *7*, 91–109. [CrossRef]
8. Ingenhoff, D.; Fuhrer, T. Positioning and Differentiation by Using Brand Personality Attributes: Do Mission and Vision Statements Contribute to Building a Unique Corporate Identity? *Corp. Commun. Int. J.* **2010**, *15*, 83–101. [CrossRef]
9. Beerli Palacio, A.; Díaz Meneses, G.; Pérez Pérez, P.J. The Configuration of the University Image and Its Relationship with the Satisfaction of Students. *J. Educ. Adm.* **2002**, *40*, 486–505. [CrossRef]
0. Flavián, C.; Torres, E.; Guinalíu, M. Corporate Image Measurement: A Further Problem for the Tangibilization of Internet Banking Services. *Int. J. Bank Mark.* **2004**, *22*, 366–384. [CrossRef]
1. Gómez, M. *El Turismo Enológico Desde la Perspectiva de la Oferta*; Editorial Universitaria Ramón Areces: Madrid, Spain, 2011.
2. Almeida, M.G.C.; Coelho, A.M. El impacto de la reputación en el desempeño de la organización en la perspectiva de los miembros de las cooperativas. *ESIC Mark.* **2015**, *46*. [CrossRef]
3. Luque-Martínez, T.; Barrio-García, S. Modelling University Image: The Teaching Staff Viewpoint. *Public Relat. Rev.* **2009**, *35*, 325–327. [CrossRef]
4. Azoury, N.; Daou, L.; Khoury, C.E. University Image and Its Relationship to Student Satisfaction- Case of the Middle Eastern Private Business Schools. *Int. Strateg. Manag. Rev.* **2014**, *2*, 1–8. [CrossRef]
5. Patlán, J.; Martínez, E. Evaluación de La Imagen Organizacional Universitaria En Una Institución de Educación Superior. *Contad. Adm.* **2017**, *62*, 105–122. [CrossRef]
6. Safón, V. Inter-Ranking Reputational Effects: An Analysis of the Academic Ranking of World Universities (ARWU) and the Times Higher Education World University Rankings (THE) Reputational Relationship. *Scientometrics* **2019**, *121*, 897–915. [CrossRef]
7. Luque-Martínez, T.; Faraoni, N.; Doña-Toledo, L. Meta-ranking de universidades. Posicionamiento de las universidades españolas. *Rev. Esp. Doc. Científica* **2018**, *41*, e198. [CrossRef]
8. Nunnally, J.C. An Overview of Psychological Measurement. In *Clinical Diagnosis of Mental Disorders: A Handbook*; Wolman, B.B., Ed.; Springer: Boston, MA, USA, 1978; pp. 97–146. [CrossRef]
9. Hair, J.F.; Black, W.C.; Balbin, B.J.; Tatham, R.L. *Multivariate Data Analysis*, 6th ed.; Pearson Prentice-Hall: Upper Saddle River NJ, USA, 2006; ISBN 0130329290.
0. Dancey, C.P.; Reidy, J. *Statistics without Maths for Psychology*; Pearson Education: London, UK, 2007; ISBN 0273726021.
1. Lung-Yut-Fong, A.; Lévy-Leduc, C.; Cappé, O. Homogeneity and change-point detection tests for multivariate data using rank statistics. *J. Société Fr. Stat.* **2015**, *156*, 133–162.
2. Hoyle, R.H. 16—Confirmatory Factor Analysis. In *Handbook of Applied Multivariate Statistics and Mathematical Modeling*; Tinsley, H.E.A., Brown, S.D., Eds.; Academic Press: San Diego, CA, USA, 2000; pp. 465–497. [CrossRef]
3. Hu, L.; Bentler, P.M. Cutoff Criteria for Fit Indexes in Covariance Structure Analysis: Conventional Criteria versus New Alternatives. *Struct. Equ. Model. Multidiscip. J.* **1999**, *6*, 1–55. [CrossRef]

Article

Highs, Lows and Turning Points in Marginalised Transitions and Experiences of Noncompletion amongst Pushed Dropouts in South African Higher Education

Mukovhe Masutha

Ali Mazrui Centre for Higher Education Studies, University of Johannesburg, Johannesburg 2006, South Africa; mukovhem@uj.ac.za; Tel.: +27-079-1898-717

Abstract: Against a backdrop of dominant deficit, victim-blaming and class/colourblind theories of unequal educational transitions and higher education outcomes, this article analyses thematically in depth narrative interviews with Black working class "dropouts" in South African higher education to explore how this group of former students narrate and make sense of their educational journeys and how their accounts could strengthen efforts to achieve just and equitable experiences and outcomes for students from all walks of life. Their narrative accounts reveal that, (a) in their marginalised educational transitions, despite disrupted and sometimes traumatic formative years (lows), their transformative habitus and community cultural wealth enables them to find highs in nadir moments; (b) their educational pathways are paved with unlikely steppingstones and improvising agents of transformation who overcome the odds of under-resourced schooling experiences; (c) despite policymakers' best intentions, student financial aid moderates but does not ameliorate the perils of being Black and working class in higher education; (d) as pushed dropouts, they are victims of a class and colourblind criminalisation of failure that naturalises injustice in already unjust educational contexts. This study illuminates the transformative and social justice potential in analysing narrative accounts of those who often disappear from higher education without a trace.

Keywords: black working class students; marginalised transitions; pushed dropouts; noncompletion; social justice; South Africa

Citation: Masutha, M. Highs, Lows and Turning Points in Marginalised Transitions and Experiences of Noncompletion amongst Pushed Dropouts in South African Higher Education. *Educ. Sci.* **2022**, *12*, 608. https://doi.org/10.3390/educsci12090608

Academic Editor: Diana Dias

Received: 18 July 2022
Accepted: 22 August 2022
Published: 6 September 2022

Publisher's Note: MDPI stays neutral with regard to jurisdictional claims in published maps and institutional affiliations.

1. Introduction

Transforming and widening participation in higher education (HE) to youth from traditionally marginalised communities remains prominent in HE research and policy agendas, often carrying the promise of more equitable and socially just societies. This article is concerned with experiences of marginalised transitions and high rates of noncompletion amongst financial aid-funded Black working class students in South African HE and related contexts. Despite the proliferation of diversity and inclusion policies and initiatives, the strong global and national level policy commitments have yet to translate to equitable and just educational realities for traditionally marginalised communities [1,2]. Even as working class students gain increased access to HE, social inequality in patterns of access and attainment has been "maximally and effectively maintained" [3]. As race, class and gender-based disparities remain prominent in student transitions, the type of university and field of study accessible, institutional experiences and the odds of successful completion persist in the UK, in the US, in Australia, in Zimbabwe and elsewhere; efforts to better understand the educational journeys and stories of the marginalised remains crucial to the dream of just educational futures [4–7].

The motivation behind this study has been the author's interest in Black working class students (BWS), their experiences of completion and noncompletion in HE and how such experiences are often misunderstood and misrepresented in scholarship and policymaking circles. As a Black working class graduate, the author is intrigued by how dominant forces in these circles, mainly relying on the wisdom of theories with colourblind meritocracy, construct grand narratives that often do not align with this group's lived experiences and instead serve to account and ultimately justify persistent intersectional disparities [8].

As marginalised transitions and experiences of HE continue to facilitate a revolving door of exclusion for the working class [9], dominant narratives and representations that inform teaching, learning and assessment practices remain anchored to flawed notions of HE institutions as progressively transforming, fair, equal opportunity, colourblind and generally well-meaning spaces [10]. Many amongst us remain reluctant to recognise "race as a legitimate object of scrutiny, either in scholarship or policy" and universities' role in reproducing and legitimating racial inequity [1]. In downplaying the exclusionary intersection of race and class in students' educational transitions, advocates of meritocratic theories of the achievement gap, in settler colonial states like South Africa, stand to preserve "a legacy of racial privilege" [8] and serve to "dismiss and mute the realities of people of colour" in educational institutions [10]. As regressive tenets of marketisation, narrow meritocracy, credentialism and related neoliberal conceptions of education and society remain dominant and the welfare university continues to wither [11,12], the task of presenting a counter story and imagining a different and more just university has become urgent. This article heeds this call.

The author joins scholars [13–17] who are continuously challenging the myths of educational institutions as colour and class-blind meritocracies and the extent to which such myths are deployed to explain unequal HE transitions and attainment rates. As Lucido et al. [15] and others point out, the myth of meritocracy in higher education is as a key factor behind the persistent inequality of access and outcomes to higher education. Indeed, 'this myth is often used as a weapon against policies like affirmative action that offer minor admissions advantages to low-income students and racial and ethnic minorities. The deck is stacked in favour of affluent parents who use their privilege and exploit these institutional needs to find their children a way into elite colleges' [15].

Additionally, this article responds to calls for research that examine persisting marginalisation in educational experiences and outcomes from the perspectives and through the voices of the traditionally and presently marginalised [18–20]. The author draws on participants' narrative accounts to illuminate what the deficient framing of this group of students fails to recognise—working class people's community cultural wealth [21]. By community cultural wealth, Yosso [21] is referring to, i.e., "cultural knowledge, skills, abilities and contacts possessed by socially marginalised groups that often go unrecognised and unacknowledged", thereby missing out on what these communities, through their students, bring to the field of university education [22].

The South African HE experience is inextricably linked to the country's history of colonialism and apartheid [23], a history of English and Afrikaans-speaking White minority domination and the subjugation of an African and mainly working class majority that speaks nine indigenous languages. Due to this apartheid and colonial past, South Africa remains sharply segregated by class, gender, racial, linguistic and spatial lines. After 300 years of colonialism and 45 years of apartheid, a policy of legally enforced racial segregation and exploitation, South Africa's 1994 democratic dispensation inherited a fundamentally hierarchical nation resembling two societies in one. Importantly, class and racial domination continue to resemble two sides of the same coin, as the poor and working classes remain almost exclusively Black African, while the middle- and upper-class elite remain the English and Afrikaans-speaking White [6]. The legacy of this segregated and exploitative past continues to reproduce one of the most unequal societies in the world today [23].

Colonial and apartheid's spatial laws concentrated the Black working class majority in peripheral rural homelands from which they can be temporarily drawn into cities and small towns in the form of cheap labour [24]. These rural communities were and remain grossly underdeveloped and overwhelmingly dependent on social welfare and subsistence farming. Alongside opulent cities and towns reside Black migrant workers in overcrowded and under-resourced informal settlements known as townships. They are a legacy of enforced segregation and the resultant inequality of access to education, health, welfare, transport and employment opportunities [23].

Post-apartheid South Africa, the author's research context, established the National Student Financial Aid Scheme (NSFAS), a national loan and grant scheme aimed at powering HE access and success for students from marginalised communities. As a result, two decades since the fall of apartheid, the composition of the university student population in South Africa has changed significantly, with increased access of working class students to HE [25]. Regrettably, the rise in access by financial aid-funded working class students has occurred alongside high dropout and low completion rates amongst this group of students.

Indeed, as a result of the student financial aid budget rising from R400 million in 1999 to over R44 billion by 2022 [26], Black students have gone from constituting less than 25% of university students in the 1980s to exceeding 80% of the university student population in 2018 [27]. Such progress has been derailed by low student retention and completion rates amongst financial aid-funded students [21,28]. Post-apartheid South Africa's first Report of the Ministerial Review of the NSFAS scheme revealed that, between the years 2000 and 2010, '67% of 656,000 financial aid-funded students were no longer in higher education; 72% of this 67% dropped out without completing their studies; and only 28% graduated' [22]. Consequently, despite the government's bold policy targets to achieve equity in HE, by the year 2020, only 5.9% of South Africans between the ages of 25 and 64 had achieved a bachelor's degree from a university (Statistics South Africa Quarterly Labour Force Survey 2010–2020). Moreover, demographically, the South African picture remains firmly unequal, with the HE participation rate amongst African youths at 18% compared to 56% amongst their White counterparts [27].

In their 2018 study on factors affecting the success of first-generation students at a South African university, Kelly-Laubscher et al [28] observed how South Africa's patterns of access, retention and success in higher education persistently reflect the country's class and race-based disparities. They found that:

> ... *even for those participating in higher education, the throughput of African and Coloured students is lower than their White counterparts, with only 20 and 24 per cent of African and coloured students, respectively, graduating within the regulation time for their diplomas/degrees, compared to 44 percent of White students ... It is clear from these statistics that increased participation by these groups has not resulted in a corresponding increase in graduation rates and throughput.* [28]

A cohort study released by the South African Department of Higher Education and Training in 2019 invites researchers to critically examine the challenge of noncompletion amongst Black working class students, with a view to deepen and enrich our understanding of the challenge and ways of responding to it.

> *Transformation imperatives in the system are also challenged by the differential success according to population groups, with African and Coloured students fairing very poorly when compared to their Indian and White counterparts. While all students need to improve their throughput rates in minimum time, support for African and Coloured students to improve their performance is a critical equity issue. All institutions need to invest in data analytics to better understand their student dropout and throughput rates by population group and gender.*

Against this backdrop, the present study responds to the need to gain in-depth insights into the currently understudied marginalised transitions and experiences of noncompletion amongst financial aid-funded Black working class students in South African HE. The article fulfils this task by shining the research spotlight on alternative understandings and explanations of the prevalence of high noncompletion amounts of Black working class students through first person accounts [29]. The author posits that our ongoing pursuit for justice in education and society requires that we move beyond the veneer of diversity and inclusion policies by carefully examining and making explicit the micro-level lived realities of marginalised students—in this case, Black working class students—and the educational contexts in which they are expected to aspire, transition and succeed. This is an important exercise in disrupting unjust and often taken-for-granted practices that continue to exclude those from the margins of society.

In exploring financial aid-funded Black working class students' narratives and accounts of marginalised transitions and experiences of noncompletion at two South African universities with different statuses, this article seeks to contribute to and further develop a growing body of research that foregrounds the voice, counternarratives and lived experiences of the "unheard" in the understanding and theorising of persistent race, class and gender disparities in universities [30]. To this end, the research questions that this article addresses are (a) How do financial aid-funded Black working class students narrate their experiences of marginalised transitions and noncompletion South African universities? How do such narratives deepen our understanding of the challenge of high rates of noncompletion amongst financial aid-funded students in South African higher education (HE)? Within the context of efforts to transform and widen participation in HE to communities in the margins of society, answers to these questions should present opportunities for transformation and further deepen our understanding of the challenge of attrition amongst working class students in higher education. Answers to these questions also enable us to get to know students who disappear without a trace (the so-called dropouts); their life stories and the gaps in our knowledge of their aspirations, transitions and experience of HE.

Why Financial Aid-Funded Black Working Class Students?

'Class matters because it creates unequal possibilities for flourishing and suffering'. [31]

In Miseducation, Reay stresses the importance of reflecting on the history and role of class in education in order to gain an appreciation of "historical processes whereby working class educational failure has become legitimised and institutionalised" [32]. Reflecting on her personal journey and evolving understanding of being working class Reay [33] discourages generalising the working class and reminds us that there are "very many different ways of being working class". The term commonly used in South Africa is "poor and working class students" and it is designated to a category of the student population on the basis of their families' annual household incomes. The concept of working class students in this study is employed to refer to students from South African households earning below a combined annual income of up to R122,000 whose undergraduate studies were funded by NSFAS at a public South African university.

Why examine the marginalised transitions to and experiences of noncompletion amongst financial aid-funded working class students in South Africa? First, there is a deep personal, family and community-wide cost that accompanies high rates of noncompletion amongst students from traditionally excluded communities. The educational transitions and experiences of high noncompletion amongst financial aid-funded students require an ongoing inquiry, as this group is often perceived as more insulated from the perils of being Black and working class in largely untransformed and often violent HE systems [34]. Thirdly, financial aid beneficiaries represent children of the most vulnerable and marginalised households and communities in South Africa. Improving their HE experience is pivotal to redressing the extent to which the South African HE experience reproduces the legacy of colonialism and apartheid.

2. Materials and Methods

2.1. Participants and Procedure

This research is based on data from the author's doctoral study that examined narrative accounts of financial aid-funded Black working class students' experiences of completion and noncompletion in South African HE and how insights from such experiences can help move understandings of (under)achievement rates amongst this group of students beyond the majoritarian narrative. After a combination of purposeful sampling, the maximum variation sampling and snow-balling techniques were employed, and a total of forty-six in-depth narrative interviews with twenty-four financial aid-funded Black working class students and twenty-two academic and support staff were conducted from across faculties at three different status universities. As shows in Table 1, this article reports on a section of the broader study that specifically focused on the narrative accounts of five (5) pushed dropouts (i.e., financial aid-funded Black working class students who got excluded from their studies prior to completion, despite their desires to persist). Linda (25), Wadzi (19) and Naledi (18) are from Merger University, a well-resourced former Whites-only Afrikaans-speaking urban university that merged with a predominately Black Technikon in post-apartheid South Africa. Tali (27) and Martin (26) are from Rural University, an under-resourced, predominantly working class and former Blacks-only university located in Rural Province. Participants are referred to by their pseudonyms throughout this article

Table 1. Participants' demographic profile.

Participant	Gender	Institution	Description
Linda	Male	Merger University	First-generation Black working class university student
Naledi	Female	Merger University	First-generation Black working class university student
Wadzi	Female	Merger University	First-generation Black working class university student
Martin	Male	Rural University	First-generation Black working class university student
Tali	Female	Rural University	Second-generation Black working class university student

2.2. Data Analysis

While being an insider researcher can bring challenges, it did enhance the establishing of a rapport and trust between the author and participants narrating about deeply personal experiences and understandings [35]. Following the Braun and Clarke (2006) guide to doing thematic analysis, the author, as part of their doctoral work, read and reread transcripts multiple times, generated initial codes, collated the data and searched for themes, reviewed themes and defined and named themes.

In this article, narratives of Black working class dropouts who often disappear without a trace are treated as valid, valuable and critical in the theorising of persistent inequality in education [19]. The narrative analysis approach was employed with a view to advance an important body of research in education that foregrounds the voices and lived experiences of those in the margins of society who often go unheard. As such, much of the story of this article is written through illustrative excerpts from participants' narrative accounts.

Crucially, it is through storytelling that our students make sense of their lives whilst providing educational researchers with valuable insight into their journeys to and through educational institutions [2]. Indeed, the narrative approach adopted in this study enabled the author to capture the complexities, multidimensionality and richness of participants educational experiences. Connelly and Clandinin explained the main claim for the use of narrative in educational research [35]:

> *"The main claim for the use of narrative in educational research is that humans are storytelling organisms who, individually and socially, lead storied lives. The study of narrative, therefore, is the study of the ways humans experience the world. This general notion translates into the view that education is the construction and reconstruction of personal and social stories; teachers and learners are storytellers and characters in their own and other's stories"*

The narratives included in this article are not representative of the entire dataset, and the author seeks not to generalise participants' experiences but, rather, to illuminate the key dimensions of their narrative accounts as they relate to noncompletion amongst financial aid-funded Black working class students at two different status universities in South Africa. The author lifted their stories to highlight the many sides of dropouts that are not captured and, in many ways, silenced by dominant conceptions of students who dropout prior to completing their studies in university.

3. Results

Participants narrated a range of positive and negative experiences from their formative years, transitions to HE and their experience of the first year of study at university. Their narrative accounts offer a glimpse into Black working class students' largely understudied transitions to and experiences of noncompletion in South African universities. Common across their narrative accounts was their mostly disrupted formative and sometimes traumatic years (lows/nadir experiences); their HE transitions were mostly paved with unlikely steppingstones and agents of transformation [22] (highs), they experienced turbulent and hard landings on campus during their first year of study (Lows) and turning points that all resulted in unhappy endings to their HE experiences (i.e., noncompletion). From a turbulent transition and hard landing on campus, they were not given an opportunity to recover and persist. They were all dropouts who were pushed out of the university despite their willingness to continue studying. They faced a double-edged sword of academic/financial exclusion. All but one (Tali) dropped out of university in their first year of study. The trauma of being a dropout has not derailed their intention to one day continue with their university studies.

3.1. Lows: Disrupted and often Traumatic Formative Years

Students' communities of origin and family backgrounds (i.e., race, class, gender, language group, family income, geographic location, parents educational and occupational status) are crucial in efforts to deepen our understanding of the patterns of inequality of transitions, experiences and outcomes in HE [30,36,37]. Sociologists of education [29,33,38,39] have shown how, based on their level of education, occupational and social status, elite parents and family backgrounds impart to their children (amongst other privileges) cultural resources such as dominant societal values, language skills, knowledge, attitudes, skills, abilities and dispositions, whose effective transmission leads to successful educational experiences and outcomes. Social reproduction theorists consider the elite intergenerational parent-to-child transfer of family-based endowments and abilities as the primary means through which structured social inequalities are reproduced in educational experiences and outcomes [40].

First, the participants in this study came from South Africa's rural and township communities. These communities have been described as the face of persistent and cyclical poverty, unemployment and general economic stagnation. They are characterised by high levels of unemployment and low HE participation rates, and the vast majority of families remain dependent on subsistence farming, government social security grants for pensioners and children under the age of 18 and proceeds from informal trading activities [34,41]. Research has shown the significance of formative educational milestones as important indicators of lifelong educational achievement and the ability to adapt to uncertain life experiences [42]. All participants in this study experienced disrupted family circumstances and, sometimes, traumatic phases during their formative years, with materially adverse implications on their educational transitions.

Linda, who was excluded from Merger University, was orphaned during his first year of study. Similarly, Tali and Martin, who were both excluded from Rural University, were raised by single mothers who dropped out of high school to work as domestic workers. Naledi's mother toiled as a hawker in an informal settlement, and her father worked as a security guard about 500 kilometres from home. Due to their history as reserves for cheap labour, Naledi's informal settlement community embodies the precarious social, economic, cultural and political past of urban informal settlements that served labour reserves in and around Johannesburg. Wadzi narrated experiences of having to endure traumatic formative years. She was born and raised in a largely degenerated and working class section of the City of Johannesburg. Her parents separated when she was in grade 1, and her mother passed away gruesomely when she was in grade 3. Before her passing, Wadzi's mother worked as a security guard. Her father sold food to manual labourers for a living in order to pay rent and send Wadzi to school.

Implicit in the participants' narrative accounts are experiences of having endured social origins that lack idealised forms of cultural capital operational at HE institutions [25].

Finding Highs in Nadir Moments (Lows)

Whereas disrupted formative years represent lows in participants' journeys to HE, participants' narrative accounts reveal how this group of students still managed to find highs in nadir moments or experiences (lows). Participants' narratives particularly illuminate their possession of crucial community cultural wealth that often goes unnoticed in studies of marginalised communities of colour [21]. Yosso [21] conceptualised marginalised communities of colour as endowed with community cultural wealth: "cultural knowledge, skills, abilities and contacts possessed by socially marginalised groups that often go unrecognised and unacknowledged" (p. 69). She advances that marginalised communities nurture cultural wealth through numerous forms of capital that enables its members to navigate seemingly unbearable conditions. These forms of capitals include, but are not limited to, aspirational, navigational, social, linguistic, familial and resistant capital [21].

With her late mother, Wadzi's father established a small business to sell food to manual labourers in order to pay rent and send her to her school of choice. This was a turning point in her journey to HE. When his mother left the village for the city to work as a domestic worker, Linda was adopted by their neighbour who sought to lend a helping hand. He attributed the experience of being adopted with initially killing his "confidence" and "self-belief" but later forming "some sort of a foundation" for the person he grew up to become.

> *LINDA: Once you know that you don't belong there, no matter how nice you are treated, no matter how good you are treated, there's always the thing that tells you "but I don't belong here", and it kills your confidence . . . So, it was a struggle, but then again, I would say that formed some sort of a foundation, that's what made me who I am today.*

The above excerpt from Linda's interview captures Yosso's notion of the presence in marginalised Black communities of aspirational capital, 'the ability to maintain hopes and dreams for the future, even in the face of real and perceived barriers' [21], which becomes particularly evident in how these communities 'allow themselves and their children to dream of possibilities beyond their present circumstances, often without the objective means to attain those goals' [21]. The presence of aspirational capital was also reflected in Tali and Martin's narrative accounts. Whilst acknowledging her disrupted formative years, Tali immediately shrugs off their significance to her educational journey while projecting firm confidence in her academic ability.

> *TALI: Even in primary school, I'm that person who grew up with my own mother, she was struggling, I could see whatever she was going through, you see . . . but that actually didn't affect me in my education because I was very much clever, if I can say. I was one of the students who was actually clever. Even in my primary school, I never failed. From A to Grade 7 I never failed. I was a good learner, if I can say that.*

With his father absent, and to supplement his mother's income, Martin juggled schooling with part-time work.

> *MARTIN: We had our ups and downs, but it made us stick together as a family. Sometimes you come back home and there is no food, you have to go out and find some food. I took up some part time work so that I can assist my siblings and for them to go to school.*

The negative impact of weakened parental involvement on educational transitions in the educational journeys of all five participants is consistent with the work of Arbouin [18] on Black British students in UK HE. Indeed, consistent with what Arbouin [18] found, the weakened parental involvement was not due to a lack of trying on the part of participants' parents. Despite seeking their children's success, working parents in this study were not in a social, economic or cultural position to facilitate their children's educational success. The parents' desire to disrupt the intergenerational transfer of disadvantage to their children was, however, not in question. By highlighting the presence and operationalising of community cultural wealth in participants' educational journeys, the author seeks neither to downplay nor invalidate Black-working class students' struggles but rather to illuminate, amidst nadir experiences, opportunities for researchers, policymakers and practitioners involved in transforming unequal educational transitions.

3.2. Highs: HE Transitions Paved with Unlikely Steppingstones and Agents of Transformation

The second theme has to do with how this group of underprivileged students transition to HE on the back of unlikely steppingstones [18] and agents of transformation [22]. Despite their lack of HE qualifications, exposure and awareness, participants' mostly single parents found ways to become steppingstones for their children en route to HE. Moreover, in contrast to mainstream narratives of public schooling teachers as generally weak and lacking motivation, in all five cases, participants identified resourceful and improvising role model school teachers who went beyond the call of duty to help them navigate under-resourced schooling experiences. The roles played by these improvising teachers in shoring up students' aspirations and transitions into HE fits the profile of what Mills [22] referred to as "agents of transformation" who are able to "draw upon a variety of cultural capitals" to disrupt the reproductive cycle in working class students' journey to and through higher education. Mills [22] believes that "teachers can act as agents of transformation rather than reproduction . . . through their curriculum, pedagogy and assessment". Mills [22] asserts convincingly that:

> *teachers can either silence students by denying their voice, that is, by refusing to allow them to speak from their own histories, experiences, and social positions, or [they] can enable them to speak by being attentive to how different voices can be constituted within specific pedagogical relations so as to engage their histories and experiences in both an affirmative and critical way.*

Where they encountered difficulties at school, graduates recalled one or two teachers they credit for motivating them, having high expectations of them and, thus, fuelling their HE educational aspirations. Tali proudly remembers being "one of the top students" in secondary school, and this attracting the attention of teachers who saw potential in her. During her final year of high school, cognisant of Tali's potential, her under resourced family background and possible disruptions to her final examination preparations, one particular teacher left nothing to chance:

> *TALI: In Grade 12, one of my teachers stayed with me . . . he wanted to support me because he knew that I'm a serious person but due to my situation, he thought that it might affect me, you see. So he ended up taking me so I stayed with him at his place and then I studied there and did all the things. After that I passed my Grade 12 . . .*

She identified one of her teachers as a role model that enabled early career awareness and HE aspirations.

> *TALI: From primary school I used to say I want to be a doctor. Sometimes I would say, I want to be a teacher. There was this other teacher, she was like a mom to me, I admired her so I ended up saying I wish I was you. She was very much supportive.*

Similarly, despite her school being severely under-resourced, Wadzi "never saw it as a problem". She remembers being "a very smart student" at her school.

> WADZI: *It was a school, but then now that I know how a school should look like, I can recall that the environment was very bad. We'd have a hall and then it's divided by boards . . . you can actually hear what other people are actually also saying. So the environment was very poor, now that I know. But then I never saw a problem. I'm like, it's a school, it's a school.*

Despite his lack of involvement in her schooling, knowing that her father was hustling for her made Wadzi appreciate him the most. She proudly described her strong and positive relationship with her father. *"So my relationship with my dad, it's that relationship, he's my best friend. He's my mum, he's my whatever."* Naledi credited her mother's strict involvement in her schooling and her pursuit for *"independence"* from her parents' curfew propelling both her good grades and her higher education aspirations. The roles played by participants' working class parents in this study offers an alternative lens to the dominant deficit understanding of working class parents and their children's schooling experiences and HE aspirations. The parents' roles as unlikely steppingstones {18} in their children's pathways to HE offers potentially transformative ways of thinking about educational transitions in marginalised communities with low HE participation rates.

Linda's story illuminates the face of improvising and transformative habitus as another understudied steppingstone in Black working class students' transitions to HE According to Mills [22], a 'transformative habitus' is a form of orientation or disposition in marginalised communities nurtured to "recognize possibilities for improvisation" in education. First was the accumulation of cultural capital in the form of computer skills and improving his command of the English language. Having grown up in a community where everybody sounds the same, Linda knew he would struggle with the English language upon arrival on campus. In his village, everybody speaks isiZulu, one of South Africa's eleven languages. Linda recounts how he improvised and improved his command of the English language by watching TV:

> LINDA: *I got to meet my mom's boss, and obviously it was a White person and they're speaking English. I knew nothing. I couldn't speak English at the time and I was bothered by the fact that, as they were talking to me, all I did was laugh because I couldn't understand a thing. And when I got to live with my family, there was a Black and White TV which helped me to learn English. I took it upon myself to say, let me learn this thing, let me have a vocabulary and try to learn this, and it helped.*

Secondly, upon completion of his secondary education, Linda decided to look for a job first, accumulate some economic capital and then pursue his higher education ambitions.

Even though Linda knew no one who had ever been to university and very little about what actually happens at the university, he always wanted to go to university. When asked why, his response points to the perception of HE as a vehicle to break the cycle of poverty in the family. He said *the only reason I worked so hard in school was because I wanted to go to varsity so that obviously the only picture you have in your head is to change your family situation, to change those houses that are made of mud and everything and just, you want a better life. You want a better job. You want to be that guy who changes the situation from home. You want to make your parents proud. And that was the main reason obviously (Linda).*

This phase of Linda's transition represents a disposition to perceive challenging family circumstances and disrupted formative years as both a hindrance and challenge to be taken on. His narratives thus reveal the double role played by challenging social origins and family backgrounds in transitions to HE.

3.3. Turbulent and Hard Landings on Campus

A major challenge (low) in this group of students' transitions into HE was their experiences of turbulent and hard landings on campus from which none of them ever recovered. Tali's transition university matched the experience of a fish out of water [39] and a general sense of isolation. She found everything about the university to be worlds apart from her schooling experience. Apart from her struggle with the university teaching and learning methods being worlds apart from those in high school, as all other participants in this study, Tali's transition was further hindered by financial pressures. Her financial aid funding package only covered tuition fees, and she had to commute from home daily. Consequently, she struggled to afford basics such as toiletries. Being a commuting student also made her feel like an outsider inside the university. Martin's landing on campus was also chaotic. "It was very difficult to register . . . I used to gamble in order to raise money for transport so that I can go and join the registration line with another."

The poor administration and mismanagement of NSFAS resulted in Wadzi's particularly hard landing at Merger University from which she never recovered. Her first semester was the worst. Failure of the NSFAS to pay her fees on time meant she could not measure her academic progress, because the university, as part of their standard practice, withheld the grades of students whose tuition fee was outstanding.

> WADZI: *So first semester when we wrote our exams and then the marks came out and I never saw my marks cause I never paid. So now I'm still waiting for NSFAS. I went to the NSFAS offices, no-one seemed to be willing to explain to me what exactly is going on. They're telling me to come back next week, maybe you'll get your feedback . . .*

Her first year of study went from bad to worse when her father lost his trading licence as a hawker.

Turbulent and hard landings on campus were also related to the hindering effect of a lack of adequate student housing and resultant homelessness. At Rural University, students who live far from campus had to choose between the cost and inconvenience of having to commute daily or illegally squatting (subletting) from those who secured university accommodation. For those who choose to squat, subletting came with its own challenges. Given its informality, those who squat were always at the mercy of the legitimate tenant and at times had to endure abusive conditions. Students told the author about squatting students having to put up with financial extortion and sometimes sexual harassment.

According to Mulrenan et al. [43], student homelessness is a stain on the HE sector's prestigious image in society, so much so that many would rather look away than confront it, and thus, it remains mainly under-researched. It is often accompanied by food insecurity as students struggle with the rising costs of living in and around universities with far-reaching consequences for students. While the student housing crisis is a reality in all South African universities, the picture is worse at historically disadvantaged universities that remain disproportionately under-resourced today.

3.4. Turning Points and Unhappy Endings

3.4.1. Mental Health Challenges

Tali's transition into HE took a sudden turn for the worst when she experienced mental health challenges. She recalled experiencing an imponderable sudden loss of interest in her studies and missing most of her classes. She recounted the trauma of being laughed at by her classmates for failing to qualify for her exams:

> TALI: *It was challenging . . . when people were qualifying and you weren't qualifying to go to write exams. And you know they used to place names on the wall, you see your name is not there, you're not qualified. Everyone could see "she's not qualifying so she's not writing". Even those that I thought were my friends were busy laughing at me.*

Having failed more than 50% of her modules, in her second year of study, Tali's NSFAS funding was discontinued, and she was prevented from registering for her third year of study at Bush University. Tali's experience is consistent with revelations of a recent report that found that 30.6% of students had thoughts of suicide in the past 12 months, 16.6% had made a suicide plan and 2.4% had attempted suicide [44]. Mental health challenges amongst vulnerable students are thus a cause for concern and a rising hindrance to efforts to widen participation in HE.

3.4.2. Let down by Financial Aid

Collectively, participants' narrative accounts show that financial aid moderates, it does not eliminate the challenges of being Black and working class in South African higher education. For this group of students, a mismanaged and poorly administered financial aid scheme was central to their turbulent and hard landings on campus (as shown above) and the tragic and unhappy endings to their HE experiences. Their experiences stand in contrast to the perception that financial aid insulates the educational transitions for marginalised students.

For Linda, Wadzi and Martin, their HE journeys were cut short owing mainly to being mismanaged and poorly administered. Despite his funding constraints, Linda continued attending classes at Merger University under the hope that NSFAS would eventually come through. It did not. At the end of the academic year, Linda's academic records were withheld, and he was denied registration the following academic year due to "outstanding fees". That is how Linda was pushed out of higher education at the end of his first year of study. Similarly, Martin's HE experience was cut short when he was excluded from the university during his first year of study due to an oversubscribed financial aid system. This was a turning point for him. Wadzi attributed high rates of noncompletion amongst working class students to an inefficient, inadequate and poorly administered NSFAS system. She said "the first factor, finance, I think contributes quite a lot . . . I think NSFAS needs to plan their things . . . So I think they need to improve communication . . . So we need more branches of NSFAS because we've got quite a large number of students".

3.5. Pushed, Not Pulled; Failed, Not Finished

As illustrated in the narrative accounts above, participants' experiences of noncompletion in the present study shined a spotlight on a less talked about dimension of the dropout rate of HE, i.e., students who get "pushed" out of the university on academic and financial grounds and against their desire to continue with their studies. This form of academic exclusion, in turn, triggers financial exclusion. A student excluded on the basis of "poor academic performance" loses their financial aid package from NSFAS. In South Africa, this double-edged sword is often referred to as "financial exclusion" and "academic exclusion".

All five "dropouts" in this study were either "academically excluded" because they were "financially excluded", i.e., denied registration because they were dropped by the NSFAS's financial aid programme and have outstanding debt or "financially excluded" because they were "academically excluded", i.e., dropped out of the NSFAS financial aid programme because of their "poor academic record" at the university. All "dropouts" in this study were thus pushed out of their university against their desire to continue with their studies on either of these grounds. All, except Tali at Rural University, were pushed out of the university in their first year of study.

In the end, the author asked each of the students for their future plans in light of their experience of noncompletion in HE. The theme that emerged at this phase of their narratives was that they may have been failed by the HE system but they ewere not finished. Tali explained her future plan to one day return to complete her degree and one day be called "Dr". She acknowledges her failure but insists that this is not the end of her educational journey. She insists on one day earning a degree in order to make her "hero" mother proud.

By the end of the academic year, Martin owed the university a year's worth of tuition fee that he has yet to pay back. He has since been job hunting in order to pay his debt and return to university.

The author asked Linda to look back at his higher education experience and identify what he wishes he'd known about university prior to admission. He wished he knew about the significance of "orientation week" in aiding transition into higher education, he wished he had made friends earlier and he wished he had known about the help offered by university tutors.

> LINDA: I wish I managed to attend the orientation whereby I was going to be able to understand the campus better. But I couldn't be there because I was from far and

obviously, I had to find a place to stay, which I failed to get, and I missed out on the orientation. But I wish I had understood the campus better, I wish I had known most of the things about the campus life and what was expected of me as a student. And I wish I was able to make friends earlier and I wish I had a tutor.

4. Discussion and Conclusions

Against the backdrop of persisting disparities in who gets to go to university, the varied pathways traversed by different groups of students [18], the type of universities and degree programmes that remain inaccessible to some [45] and the stratified HE experiences and odds of completion that remain stacked against Black and working class students in South Africa [25,46] and elsewhere [47–49] and amidst calls for research that deepens and enriches our understanding of student dropout and throughput rates by population group and gender, and that this is done to ensure equal opportunities for success regardless of race, class, gender, language, disability and cultural background [34], this article analyses thematically in-depth narrative interviews with a group of financial aid-funded Black working class students who were excluded from the South African universities prior to completing their studies to explore (a) how this group of former students narrate and make sense of their transitions to and experiences of noncompletion at different status universities in South Africa and (b) how their narratives can deepen and enrich theories of the student achievement gap in HE and efforts to achieve more just and equitable HE experiences and outcomes. A close-up analysis of participants' stories highlights lows (restrictions or hindrances), highs and turning points as encountered in this group's transitions to and experiences of noncompletion in HE. Further research into these phases in student's transitions offer enriched understandings of the challenges marginalised students encounter on their way to and during their first year of study in HE and also shine the spotlight on opportunities for transformation access and participation in HE.

There are four key insights that can be drawn from participants' composite narratives of their transitions to and experiences of noncompletion at the two universities:

First, in their transitions to HE, despite experiences of severely disrupted and often traumatic formative years (lows), participants in this study found highs (inspiration to aspire to HE) in nadir experiences. This way, participants' dispositions matched the Mills's idea of a transformative habitus, a form of orientation that enables marginalised students to "recognize possibilities for improvisation" and approach their studies in ways that transform their conditions and improve their chances of success [22]. Adopting this angle in understanding marginalised students' journeys to HE offers a window of opportunities for researchers, policymakers and practitioners working on socially just and inclusive pedagogies. Participants' narratives affirm the idea of marginalised communities as places that nurtures aspirational and navigational capitals, the ability to aspire and manoeuvre through institutions that were not created with marginalised people in mind [21].

Contrary to deficit theories of working class students, marginalised students that develop a transformative habitus, an embodied form of cultural capital are poised to conduct themselves in a manner that makes things happen in HE as opposed to sitting back and accepting defeat. Indeed, Crozier and Reay [50], Mills [22], and Arbouin [18] have all suggested that, with the help of transformation-oriented teachers and educational institutions with a transformative institutional habitus, working class students carry in them the ability to adapt and thrive.

Secondly, participants' pathways to HE were paved with unlikely steppingstones (in the form of improvising single working class parents) and agents of transformation (in the form of inspirational teachers) who defied the odds of under-resourced rural and township schools to aid participants' HE aspirations and transitions. Mills [22] referred to "agents of transformation" as individuals who "draw upon a variety of cultural capitals" to disrupt the reproductive cycle in working class students' journeys to and through HE. This finding strengthens the case that widening access initiatives would benefit greatly from relating to marginalised students and the communities they come from as epistemic contributors in our theories of unequal transitions to and experiences of HE. This research thus support the call by Mathebula [36], Walker [37], and others for those involved in education research, policy and practice to recognise Black working class youths from marginalised communities as both givers and takes of knowledge or "epistemic contributors" and that doing so constitutes an ethical response to the structural inequalities that limit equitable university access and participation.

Thirdly, the participants' narrative accounts revealed that, despite policymakers' best intentions, financial aid moderates but does not ameliorate the challenges of being Black and working in HE, and when mismanaged, it worsens the working class students' already turbulent transitions into HE and weakens their odds of successfully completing their studies. All participants experienced turbulent and hard landings on campus in their first year of study mainly linked to an inefficient and poorly administered financial aid scheme Their experience is consistent with the findings of a decade old Balintulo Report a South African government commissioned report that drew a direct line between the inadequate funding of tertiary education and lower throughput rates at HEIs [51]. The Balintulo Report [51] further found NSFAS' means testing approach to be flawed, inefficient, costly and vulnerable to abuse.

Consistent with Wadzi, Linda and Martin's stories, in recent years, NSFAS' administrative deficiencies have resulted in the scheme approving funding for more students than it had funding available, and the three participants became victim to this ineptitude. More recently, the Auditor General of South Africa has been probing cases of possible corruption and maladministration within the scheme [52].

Lastly, for all participants in this study, "dropping out" was an imposed institutional decision, not an individual call. All participants were pushed out of the university despite their willingness and determination to persist. This finding shows the limitations in the literature's disproportionate focus on working class students who "choose" to leave HE prior to completion [53] and the implied sense of agency on the part of the student. By foregrounding student noncompletion in HE as an individual student's choice, mainstream narratives are devoid of the power dynamics involved in cases where students are forced out of HE against their will [54]. This form of exclusion is consistent with what Drake [55] referred to as *academic apartheid* and the *criminalisation of failure* under questionable and often flawed meritocratic grounds [15,28] and further exonerate the university's complicity to unequal HE experiences and outcomes. The practice of "pushed dropouts" exemplifies a double standard in framings of marginalised students HE, whereby the success of marginalised students is hailed as evidence of a fair and equal opportunity field of HE, while the failure of the same group of students reduces their individual flaws with punitive consequences (pushed dropout).

While they failed to keep their HE dream going, all participants expressed their intention to return to university to complete their studies at some point. All participants perceived their experience of noncompletion not as individual failures but as failures of the field of HE to serve students from the margins of society. Participants' narrative accounts also support the Allen's [56] call for research in teaching and learning to disrupt narrow conceptions of students that are often out of touch with students' lived experiences and their own personal perceptions of success. Consistent with the call [56], further research is needed to explore the broadening definitions and conceptions of student access and success as one of the initiatives that would serve as a reparative policy that addresses the educational harms that practices such as forced dropouts have inflicted on students from traditionally excluded and currently underserved communities [57].

This is an important exercise given the deep personal, family and community-wide cost of high rates of noncompletion amongst students from traditionally excluded communities The educational transitions and experiences of high noncompletion amongst financial aid-funded Black working class students require ongoing research, as this group is often falsely perceived as more insulated from the perils of being Black and working class in largely untransformed and often violent HE systems [34]. There is a need for research that broadens the boundaries of what constitutes meaningful access beyond the mere presence of traditionally excluded students on campus. In addition to recognizing this group students and their communities as epistemic contributors, future studies need to move from measuring access according to input based key performance indicators (KPIs) (e.g., number of financial aid students enrolled) and move towards output KPIs (e.g., number of financial aid graduating in degrees and institutions that traditionally excluded them).

Funding: This research received no external funding.

Institutional Review Board Statement: The study was conducted in accordance to the guidelines as outlined in the University of Bath's Code of Good Practice in Research Integrity. Ethical approval was granted by the University of Bath's ethic committee as well as the universities under study. The author has already sent certificates of ethics approval to the Editorial Office.

Informed Consent Statement: Informed consent was obtained from all participants involved in the study.

Data Availability Statement: The data that support the findings of this study are available on request from the corresponding author. The data are not publicly available due to privacy or ethical restrictions.

Conflicts of Interest: The author declares no conflict of interest.

References

1. Arday, J.; Mirza, H.S. *Dismantling Race in Higher Education: Racism, Whiteness and Decolonising the Academy*; Springer: Berlin/Heidelberg, Germany, 2018.
2. Meer, N. *The Cruel Optimism of Racial Justice*; Policy Press: Bristol, UK, 2022.
3. Boliver, V. Critically Evaluating the Effectively Maintained Inequality Hypothesis. *J. Educ. Soc. Behav. Sci.* **2016**, *15*, 1–9. [CrossRef]
4. Mills, C.; Gale, T. *Schooling in Disadvantaged Communities: Playing the Game from the Back of the Field*; Dordrecht, Springer Science & Business Media: Berlin, Germany, 2009.
5. O'Shea, S.; Lysaght, P.; Roberts, J.; Harwood, V. Shifting the blame in higher education—Social inclusion and deficit discourses. *High. Educ. Res. Dev.* **2016**, *35*, 322–336. [CrossRef]
6. Chinyoka, A.; Mutambara, E. The challenges of revenue generation in state universities: The case of Zimbabwe. *Cogent Soc. Sci.* **2020**, *6*, 1748477. [CrossRef]
7. Sriprakash, A.; Nally, D.; Myers, K.; Pinto, P.R. Learning with the Past: Racism, Education and Reparative Futures. 2020. Available online: https://www.repository.cam.ac.uk/handle/1810/310691 (accessed on 29 August 2022).
8. Solórzano, D.G.; Yosso, T.J. A critical race counterstory of race, racism, and affirmative action. *Equity Excell. Educ. Univ. Mass. Sch. Educ. J.* **2002**, *35*, 155–168. [CrossRef]
9. Hlatshwayo, M.N.; Fomunyam, K.G. Views from the margins: Theorising the experiences of black working-class students in academic development in a historically white South African university. *J. Transdiscipl. Res. South. Afr.* **2019**, *15*, 11. [CrossRef]
10. Griffin, R.A.; Ward, L.; Phillips, A.R. Still flies in buttermilk: Black male faculty, critical race theory, and composite counterstory-telling. *Int. J. Qual. Stud. Educ. QSE* **2014**, *27*, 1354–1375. [CrossRef]
11. Brown, R.; Carasso, H. *Everything for Sale? The Marketisation of UK Higher Education*, 1st ed.; Routledge: Oxfordshire, UK, 2013.
12. Williams, J.J. The Post-Welfare State University. *Am. Lit. Hist.* **2006**, *18*, 190–216. [CrossRef]
13. Bloodworth, J. *The Myth of Meritocracy: Why Working-Class Kids Still Get Working-Class Jobs (Provocations Series)*; Biteback Publishing: London, UK, 2016.
14. Littler, J. *Against Meritocracy: Culture, Power and Myths of Mobility*; Routledge: Oxfordshire, UK, 2017.
15. Lucido, J.A.; Posselt, J.R.; Polikoff, M. Why Meritocracy Is A Myth in College Admissions. The Conversation (2019). Available online: http://theconversation.com/why-meritocracy-is-a-myth-in-college-admissions-113620 (accessed on 29 August 2022).
16. Simpson, J.L. Blinded by the White: Challenging the Notion of a Color-Blind Meritocracy in the Academy. *South. Commun. J.* **2010**, *75*, 150–159. [CrossRef]
17. Wiseman, A.W.; Davidson, P.M. Institutionalized inequities and the cloak of equality in the South African educational context. *Policy Futures Educ.* **2021**, *19*, 992–1009. [CrossRef]
18. Arbouin, A. Black British Graduates: Untold Stories. In *Trentham Books*; UCL IOE Press: London, UK, 2018; Available online: https://www.ucl-ioe-press.com/ (accessed on 29 August 2022).
19. Osbourne, L.; Barnett, J.; Blackwood, L. Black students' experiences of "acceptable" racism at a UK university. *J. Community Appl. Soc. Psychol.* **2022**, 1–13. [CrossRef]
20. Souto-Manning, M. Critical narrative analysis: The interplay of critical discourse and narrative analyses. *Int. J. Qual. Stud. Educ. QSE* **2014**, *27*, 159–180. [CrossRef]

21. Yosso, T.J. Whose culture has capital? A critical race theory discussion of community cultural wealth. *Race Ethn. Educ.* **2005**, *8*, 69–91. [CrossRef]
22. Mills, C. Reproduction and transformation of inequalities in schooling: The transformative potential of the theoretical constructs of Bourdieu. *Br. J. Sociol. Educ.* **2008**, *29*, 79–89. [CrossRef]
23. Mpofu-Walsh, S. *New Apartheid*; Tafelberg: Cape Town, South Africa, 2021.
24. Bailey, M. The neoliberal city as utopia of exclusion. *Globalizations* **2020**, *17*, 31–44. [CrossRef]
25. Masutha, M.; Naidoo, R. Stories from the margins: Working class graduates' narrative accounts of completion in South African higher educayion. In *Knowledge Beyond Colour Lines: Towards Repurposing Knowledge Generation in South African Higher Education*; Ralarala, M., Hassan, L., Naidoo, R., Eds.; UWC Press: Belville, NC, USA, 2021; pp. 59–77.
26. Cloete, R. Nzimande Announces Increased NSFAS Funding For 2022. *Skills Portal*. Available online: https://www.skillsportal.co.za/content/nzimande-announces-increased-nsfas-funding-2022 (accessed on 29 October 2021).
27. Department of Higher Education and Training. FACT SHEET: The Highest Level of Education Attainment in South Africa. Pretoria. 2021. Available online: https://www.dhet.gov.za/Planning%20Monitoring%20and%20Evaluation%20Coordination/Fact%20Sheet%20on%20the%20Highest%20Level%20of%20Education%20Attainment%20in%20South%20Africa%20-%20March%202021.pdf (accessed on 29 August 2022).
28. Kelly-Laubscher, R.; Paxton, M.; Majombozi, Z.; Mashele, S.S. Factors affecting the success of first generation university students at a South African University. In *Understanding Experiences of First-Generation University Students: Culturally Responsive and Sustaining Methodologies*; Bell, A., Santamaría, L.J., Eds.; Bloomsbury Academic: London, UK, 2018; pp. 97–120.
29. O'Shea, S. Transitions and turning points: Exploring how first-in-family female students story their transition to university and student identity formation. *Int. J. Qual. Stud. Educ. QSE* **2014**, *27*, 135–158. [CrossRef]
30. Cross, M. Steering Epistemic Access in Higher Education in South Africa: Institutional Dilemmas. CLACSO. 2018. Available online: http://biblioteca.clacso.edu.ar/clacso/sur-sur/20180425114100/Web_Steering.pdf (accessed on 29 August 2022).
31. Sayer, R.A. *The Moral Significance of Class*; Cambridge University Press: Cambridge, UK, 2005; p. 247.
32. Reay, D. *Miseducation: Inequality, Education and the Working Classes*; Policy Press: Bristol, UK, 2017.
33. Reay, D. Working class educational transitions to university: The limits of success. *Eur. J. Educ.* **2018**, *53*, 528–540. [CrossRef]
34. Harris, D.; Vigurs, K.; Jones, S. Student loans as symbolic violence. *J. High. Educ. Policy Manag.* **2021**, *43*, 132–146. [CrossRef]
35. Connelly, F.M.; Clandinin, D.J. Stories of Experience and Narrative Inquiry. *Educ. Res.* **1990**, *19*, 2–14. [CrossRef]
36. Mathebula, M. Recognising poor black youth from rural communities in South Africa as epistemic contributors. *Crit. Stud. Teach. Learn.* **2019**, *7*, 64–85. [CrossRef]
37. Walker, M. Failures and possibilities of epistemic justice, with some implications for higher education. *Crit. Stud. Educ.* **2020**, *61*, 263–278. [CrossRef]
38. Gast, M.J. "you're supposed to help me": The perils of mass counseling norms for working-class Black students. *Urban Educ.* **2016**, *56*, 1429–1455. [CrossRef]
39. Reay, D.; Crozier, G.; Clayton, J. "Fitting in" or "standing out": Working-class students in UK higher education. *Br. Educ. Res. J.* **2010**, *36*, 107–124. [CrossRef]
40. Naidoo, R. Fields and institutional strategy: Bourdieu on the relationship between higher education, inequality and society. *Br. J. Sociol. Educ.* **2004**, *25*, 457–471. [CrossRef]
41. Terreblanche, S. *Lost in Transformation*; KMM Review Publishing: Johannesburg, South Africa, 2012.
42. Kern, M.L.; Friedman, H.S. Early educational milestones as predictors of lifelong academic achievement, midlife adjustment, and longevity. *J. Appl. Dev. Psychol.* **2009**, *30*, 419–430. [CrossRef] [PubMed]
43. Mulrenan, P.; Atkins, J.; Cox, S. 'I get up in the night to cry': The impact of homelessness on higher education students in London, UK. *Crit. Soc. Policy* **2017**, *38*, 143–154. [CrossRef]
44. Bantjes, J. South African Universities Need to Know Why Students' Suicide Risk is So High. Available online: http://theconversation.com/south-african-universities-need-to-know-why-students-suicide-risk-is-so-high-129821 (accessed on 8 September 2020).
45. Boliver, V. Why are British ethnic minorities less likely to be offered places at highly selective universities. In *Aiming Higher: Race, Inequality and Diversity in the Academy*; Alexander, C., Arday, J., Eds.; Runnymede Trust: London, UK, 2015; pp. 15–18.
46. Moodley, P.; Singh, R.J. Addressing student dropout rates at South African universities. *Alternation* **2015**, *17*, 91–115. Available online: https://openscholar.dut.ac.za/handle/10321/1648 (accessed on 29 August 2022).
47. Brabner, R. Study Finds Ethnic Minority and Poorer Students More Likely to Drop Out of English Universities. *UPP Foundation*. Available online: https://upp-foundation.org/study-finds-ethnic-minority-poorer-students-likely-drop-english-universities/ (accessed on 19 July 2017).
48. Bulman, M. Black Students 50% More Likely to Drop Out of University, New Figures Reveal. The Independent. Available online: https://www.independent.co.uk/news/uk/home-news/black-students-drop-out-university-figures-a7847731.html (accessed on 19 July 2017).
49. Quinn, J. Drop-Out and Completion in Higher Education in Europe Among Students From Under-Represented Groups. An Independent Report Authored for the European Commission. NESET: European Commission. 2013. Available online: https://www.voced.edu.au/content/ngv:60845 (accessed on 29 August 2022).

60. Crozier, G.; Reay, D. Capital accumulation: Working-class students learning how to learn in HE. *Teach. High. Educ.* **2011**, *16*, 145–155. [CrossRef]
61. Department of Higher Education and Training. Report of the Ministerial Committee on the Review of the National Student Financial Aid Scheme. *Pretoria*. 2010. Available online: https://www.nsfas.org.za/content/downloads/nsfas-report.pdf (accessed on 29 August 2022).
62. Hlati, O. National Students Financial Aid Scheme Audit the 'Worst Ever'. IOL | News That Connects South Africans. Available online: https://www.iol.co.za/capetimes/news/national-students-financial-aid-scheme-audit-the-worst-ever-eeabb55c-3c76-489d-8036-43487e8cc536 (accessed on 11 February 2021).
63. Quinn, J. *From Life Crisis to Lifelong Learning: Rethinking Working-Class "Drop Out" from Higher Education*; Joseph Rowntree Foundation: York, UK, 2005.
64. McKinney, L.; Novak, H.; Hagedorn, L.S.; Luna-Torres, M. Giving Up on a Course: An Analysis of Course Dropping Behaviors Among Community College Students. *Res. High. Educ.* **2018**, *60*, 184–202. [CrossRef]
65. Drake, S.J. *Academic Apartheid*; University of California Press: Berkeley, CA, USA, 2022. [CrossRef]
66. Allen, K. "When does hot become cold": Why we should be disrupting narrow and exclusive discourses of success in higher education. *Int. Stud. Widening Particip.* **2020**, *7*, 8–21. Available online: http://hdl.handle.net/1959.13/1419047 (accessed on 29 August 2022).
67. Wozniak, J.T. *The Mis-Education of the Indebted Student*; Columbia University: New York, NY, USA, 2017; Available online: https://search.proquest.com/openview/f3c5f45297b8a4fe124bd0b0b54149dc/1?pq-origsite=gscholar&cbl=18750 (accessed on 29 August 2022).

MDPI

St. Alban-Anlage 66

4052 Basel

Switzerland

www.mdpi.com

Education Sciences Editorial Office

E-mail: education@mdpi.com

www.mdpi.com/journal/education

Milton Keynes UK
Ingram Content Group UK Ltd.
UKHW052003040324
438900UK00004B/146